The Art of Modern PHP 8

Learn how to write modern, performant, and enterprise-ready code with the latest PHP features and practices

Joseph Edmonds

BIRMINGHAM—MUMBAI

Windsor and Maidenhead

95800000189667

The Art of Modern PHP 8

Associate Group Product Manager: Pavan Ramchandani
Publishing Product Manager: Pavan Ramchandani
Senior Editor: Sofi Rogers
Content Development Editor: Feza Shaikh
Technical Editor: Saurabh Kadave
Copy Editor: Safis Editing
Project Coordinator: Manthan Patel
Proofreader: Safis Editing
Indexer: Subalakshmi Govindhan
Production Designer: Sinhayna Bais

First published: September 2021

Production reference: 1240921

Published by Packt Publishing Ltd.
Livery Place
35 Livery Street
Birmingham
B3 2PB, UK.

978-1-80056-615-6

www.packt.com

To my family, who have always supported me.

– Joseph Edmonds

Foreword

I've known Joseph as a member of the local-to-me PHP community here in Yorkshire, England, for what feels like a very long time. Over the years I taught PHP to him and then to the staff he worked hard to train up – and so I was delighted to hear about this book and to be invited to write a few words to introduce it. I know your author as a thoughtful and technical contributor and someone who works to raise his own game and also to share his skills and knowledge with others.

Taking care to learn and keep learning is such an important thing for anyone working in a technical career, or even as a hobby. The only constant is ... that nothing is constant! We always need to be learning, exploring, and developing ourselves. Perhaps you will consume this book quickly, wolfing down the information as fast as you can. Or maybe your style is more to dip in, to make space for a little more knowledge when you are ready to learn and apply something new. Some of you probably won't read the whole book, looking to graze on the parts that interest you or where you are keen to update your knowledge. All of you are investing in yourself, your future, and taking the care to learn.

In this Internet Age, the wealth of information available is incredible. And sometimes? It's too much to swim through it all and somehow fish out just the nugget we need. Reading a well-structured book means taking a prescribed route through complex information and receiving a curated collection of applicable wisdom. If there's something you want to know more about, then you can dive into the uncharted waters of other resources – and you already have a good idea of what you are looking for and how it fits the bigger picture.

Thinking about keeping up to date is one of the big preoccupations of our technical lives. With PHP, there's a disconnect where the language is perceived by others as being old-fashioned, and yet in recent years, it has changed beyond recognition and continues to grow and evolve. I have yet to see data indicating a meaningful decline in PHP's popularity, and rarely hear negativity from anyone with real recent experience of modern versions of PHP. Joseph has been working with PHP throughout these changes and covers the topics you need to understand to make the best use of PHP 8 and beyond.

As a fellow author, who once passed on her knowledge to other PHP people, I am so proud to be part of this thriving tech community still sharing the knowledge and paying it forward. I hope this book will boost your PHP activities, bringing solid theory to things you already know, as well as shining a light onto things you may not have encountered yet. And one day? Who knows, maybe it will be you that writes the next blog post, article, or even book to help inform and inspire the next generation.

Lorna Mitchell

Developer Advocate, Engineer, Author and Speaker

Contributors

About the author

Joseph Edmonds is a business owner, developer, and author. He is a Zend Certified Engineer, among his other credentials.

He's been a part of the e-commerce, tech, and PHP development worlds since the dawn of the millennium. He witnessed the exploding growth of e-commerce from the early days, helping several companies advance and expand their operations. During this time, he has had the pleasure of seeing PHP grow from a fairly amateur language, punching way above its weight, into a modern and highly performant language for serious enterprise projects.

Responding to a growing demand for highly specialized PHP development services, he launched Edmonds Commerce (https://edmondscommerce.co.uk) in 2007. As an independent agency, Edmonds Commerce provides highly specialist PHP development services to businesses that use open source PHP, and predominantly Magento, as the backbone of their online systems, solving even the most complex and unique PHP development challenges.

As a way to offer a high-level, interrelated service to businesses who want to accelerate their growth, he started an exciting new venture in 2020. LTS (Long Term Support Ltd.) provides expert help in recruitment, training, DevOps and infrastructure, consultancy, and development.

You can see his personal website and contact him via:

https://joseph.edmonds.contact

 Feel free to get in touch!

Many people have helped me get where I am today and I can't thank everyone. Specifically, I would like to thank Zach Stein, who has been a great help as a technical reviewer and has given me lots of useful feedback. I'd also like to thank the people who stepped up to join my small Slack-based focus group and helped me bounce ideas and get some general feedback. My wife, Nolwenn, deserves special thanks for putting up with my late-night writing sessions and generally putting up with me for many years. Ross Mitchell and Daniel Callaghan, who are the lead developers of Edmonds Commerce, deserve a special thank you for working with me for years and bringing many useful ideas and practices that have no doubt made their way into these pages. And finally, my thanks to Sofi, Pavan, and the rest of the team at Packt who managed to accommodate my unorthodox ways and allowed the book to be created as closely to my vision as possible. I even managed to avoid using MS Word :)

About the reviewer

Zach Stein is a developer who has been using PHP for 18 years and has been a professional developer for 15 years, with a focus on enterprise application development. In that time he has been involved in building numerous types of applications, ranging from e-commerce to healthcare, to social networking using a variety of frameworks, such as Laravel, Symfony, Magento, and Zend. Zach has a passion for design patterns and the sometimes-tedious task of refactoring code. In addition to his passion for software, Zach loves building teams and helping other developers hone their craft.

He holds a master of science degree from La Salle University in computer information science.

In his spare time, you can find Zach on the golf course or in the woodshop making furniture.

> *I'd like to thank my wife, Jill, and my three cats, Rory, River, and Lilly, for allowing me to spend the time reading and testing the code in this book. I'd also like to thank Joe, without whom this book would not exist, and I hope readers of The Art of Modern PHP 8 find it at least as informative, if not more so, as I did.*

Table of Contents

3

Advanced OOP Features

Section 2 – PHP Types

4

Scalar, Arrays, and Special Types

5

Object Types, Interfaces, and Unions

6

Parameter, Property, and Return Types

Coercive and strict modes   170

Section 3 – Clean PHP 8 Patterns and Style

7

Design Patterns and Clean Code

8

Model, View, Controller (MVC) Example

9

Dependency Injection Example

Section 4 – PHP 8 Composer Package Management (and PHP 8.1)

10

Composer For Dependencies

11

Creating Your Own Composer Package

Section 5 – Bonus Section - PHP 8.1

12

The Awesomeness That Is 8.1

Other Books You May Enjoy

Index

Preface

I've had the great pleasure of seeing PHP grow; from a somewhat amateur, and often mocked, language that exploded in popularity, punching way above its weight and powering huge swathes of the burgeoning web into a modern and highly performant language that is often used to power large-scale enterprise systems.

With the release of PHP 8, and the upcoming (at the time of writing) release of PHP 8.1, we can really see a bright future for PHP.

You will first read about **object-oriented programming** (**OOP**) in PHP, starting with the basics and then going on to more advanced topics. You will work through modern programming techniques, such as inheritance, contrasting this with composition, and finally looking at more advanced language features. You will learn about the MVC pattern by building your own toy MVC system. In addition to this, you'll explore what a **dependency injection** (**DI**) container does by building a toy DI container. Later chapters will give you an overview of Composer and will explain how to create reusable PHP packages with it. You'll also find techniques to deploy these packages effectively so that other developers can use them.

By the end of this PHP book, you will have gained a rounded understanding of some of the fundamentals of modern PHP and will have the grounding you need to be able to update your code.

Who this book is for

As PHP has such a long history, it also means that there are many developers out there who are still standing with at least one foot in the past and are missing out on the bright and beautiful future of modern PHP. This book is for you, most of all.

The book is for existing PHP developers and CTO-level professionals who are working with PHP technologies, including legacy PHP, in production. The book assumes a reasonable level of knowledge of PHP programming and may require you to hit the PHP documentation to fill in gaps in your knowledge as they come up.

What this book covers

Chapter 1, Object-Oriented PHP, includes a quick overview of what OOP means and how it contrasts with functional and procedural styles. We review some popular OOP PHP projects that you might want to have a look at and then we go over the basics of classes, objects, interfaces, and namespaces.

Chapter 2, Inheritance and Composition, Encapsulation and Visibility, Interfaces and Concretions, following the theme of looking at OOP, explores inheritance in some detail and then contrasts this with a more modern approach of using composition. You are encouraged to download the code in order to get the most out of this chapter.

Chapter 3, Advanced OOP Features, the third and final chapter in *Section 1*, continues looking at OOP, and this time we're looking at the **SPL** (**Standard PHP Library**), exceptions and error handling, and finally meta-programming with reflection and attributes.

Chapter 4, Scalar, Arrays, and Special Types, explains that since PHP 7, types have become a major feature in modern PHP. This chapter looks at the simpler types, including scalars, arrays, and iterables, and then the "nothing" types of null, void, and uninitialized.

Chapter 5, Object Types, Interfaces, and Unions, continues looking at types, but our focus shifts onto looking at exactly how the type system works when dealing with classes and interfaces.

Chapter 6, Parameter, Property, and Return Types, the final chapter in *Section 2*, looks at how types can be enforced strictly and examines their usage as parameter, property, and return types. We conclude by looking at covariance and contravariance and confirm how this works in PHP 8.

Chapter 7, Design Patterns and Clean Code, moves on from learning about the language itself and starts to look at ways we write it. We look at some clean coding practices and then have an overview of design patterns that are tried and tested approaches to common requirements.

Chapter 8, Model, View, Controller (MVC) Example, sees us work through the MVC pattern by building a toy MVC system. You are definitely encouraged to download the code for this chapter.

Chapter 9, Dependency Injection Example, as in *Chapter 8, Model, View, Controller (MVC) Example*, looks to learn by doing, and this time our goal is to understand all about DI. We will create an entire toy DI container to understand how this pattern works.

Chapter 10, Composer for Dependencies, introduces Composer—one of the most important things to happen in the PHP world. We will learn how to use Composer to use third-party packages in our projects.

Chapter 11, Creating Your Own Composer Package, continues with Composer but this time looks at how we can use it to create our own packages, share them with our private projects, and even publish them for the benefit of the PHP community.

Chapter 12, The Awesomeness That Is 8.1, the final chapter of the book, is all about PHP 8.1 and the excellent new features that are included in this new release. It is not an exhaustive list but instead focuses on a selection of features that are most likely to matter to you day to day.

To get the most out of this book

This is a book for PHP developers, and the main thing that you need is a way to write and run PHP code. For editing, modern development practices have very much embraced the IDE as an essential tool. Popular IDEs include PhpStorm and NetBeans. You may choose to use a more lightweight code editor, such as VSCode or Sublime Text, if you prefer.

You will need to be able to run PHP 8 code on the command line, and if you want to run the last chapter, then you will need PHP 8.1 as well. Installing PHP is beyond the scope of this book and is dependent on your specific operating system or virtualization technology.

Practically all code samples in this book (excluding very minor snippets) are included in the public Git repository available on GitHub at `https://github.com/PacktPublishing/The-Art-of-Modern-PHP-8`. You are strongly encouraged to clone or download all this code so that you can load it in your IDE, run it, and generally play around with it.

If you are using the digital version of this book, we advise you to type the code yourself or access the code from the book's GitHub repository (a link is available in the next section). Doing so will help you avoid any potential errors related to the copying and pasting of code.

Download the example code files

You can clone or download the example code files for this book from GitHub at `https://github.com/PacktPublishing/The-Art-of-Modern-PHP-8`. If there's an update to the code, it will be updated in the GitHub repository.

We also have other code bundles from our rich catalog of books and videos available at `https://github.com/PacktPublishing/`. Check them out!

Conventions used

There are a number of text conventions used throughout this book.

`Code in text`: Indicates code words in text, database table names, folder names, filenames, file extensions, pathnames, dummy URLs, user input, and Twitter handles. Here is an example: "The preceding code has shown us the fact that an instance of `ChildClass` passes as an instance of all of its parent items all the way up the inheritance tree."

A block of code is set as follows:

```
{
    "php": ">=7.0.0",
    "egulias/email-validator": "^2.0|^3.1",
    "symfony/polyfill-iconv": "^1.0",
    "symfony/polyfill-mbstring": "^1.0",
    "symfony/polyfill-intl-idn": "^1.10"
}
```

When we wish to draw your attention to a particular part of a code block, the relevant lines or items are set in bold:

```
<?php

declare(strict_types=1);

namespace Book\Part3\Chapter8\ToyMVC\View\Data;

interface TemplateDataInterface
{
}
```

Any command-line input or output is written as follows:

```
cd /my/project/root/directory
composer init
```

Bold: Indicates a new term, an important word, or words that you see onscreen. For instance, words in menus or dialog boxes appear in **bold**. Here is an example: "It's very easy to remove a package from Packagist. Simply click the red **Delete** button."

> Tips or important notes
> Appear like this.

Get in touch

Feedback from our readers is always welcome.

General feedback: If you have questions about any aspect of this book, email us at customercare@packtpub.com and mention the book title in the subject of your message.

Errata: Although we have taken every care to ensure the accuracy of our content, mistakes do happen. If you have found a mistake in this book, we would be grateful if you would report this to us. Please visit www.packtpub.com/support/errata and fill in the form.

Piracy: If you come across any illegal copies of our works in any form on the internet, we would be grateful if you would provide us with the location address or website name. Please contact us at copyright@packt.com with a link to the material.

If you are interested in becoming an author: If there is a topic that you have expertise in and you are interested in either writing or contributing to a book, please visit authors. packtpub.com.

Share Your Thoughts

Once you've read *The Art of Modern PHP 8*, we'd love to hear your thoughts! Scan the QR code below to go straight to the Amazon review page for this book and share your feedback.

https://packt.link/r/1800566158

Your review is important to us and the tech community and will help us make sure we're delivering excellent quality content.

Section 1 –
PHP 8 OOP

Object-Oriented Programming (OOP) is a fundamental feature of modern PHP. In this first section, we are going to go over this in detail, starting with the basics and working our way up to more advanced features.

This section contains the following chapters:

- *Chapter 1, Object-Oriented PHP*
- *Chapter 2, Inheritance and Composition, Encapsulation and Visibility, Interfaces and Concretions*
- *Chapter 3, Advanced OOP Features*

1
Object-Oriented PHP

In this first part of the book, we are going to explore modern object-oriented PHP. While there isn't sufficient space in this book to do a deep dive into this topic, we hope that you will be able to use the contents of the following three chapters as a jumping point for your own further study and experimentation. To be clear, for any PHP language features you see that you don't understand, you are absolutely encouraged to put the book down and go and start reading the PHP docs so that you can gain a fuller understanding of that particular feature. To underline this, you will see frequent links to the official documentation. You are encouraged to follow these links and read into any feature that you are not intimately familiar with.

Some readers may already be very familiar with **object-oriented programming** (**OOP**) in PHP and for those, this first part might be a nice refresher. You never know, you might learn something new! If you are not familiar with modern object-oriented PHP, then there is likely to be a lot to take in. I seriously hope you don't find this overwhelming. All I can say is, it's worth persevering as OOP is fundamental to modern PHP.

This chapter is an introduction to OOP in general and includes a review of some popular object-oriented PHP projects and frameworks that you are encouraged to go and have a look at.

By the end of part 1, especially if you take the time to fill in the gaps by hitting the official docs, you should be fairly up to date with how OOP works in modern PHP.

The following topics will be covered in this chapter:

- What is OOP?
- PHP OOP basics

Before we begin this chapter in depth, you are strongly encouraged to have a thorough read through the official documentation on classes and objects:

PHP: Classes and Objects - Manual

`https://www.php.net/manual/en/language.oop5.php`

In this chapter, we are going to look in general at what we mean by OOP and what it means to you. We'll start by understanding what the phrase OOP actually means and compare it to some other programming styles. I will recommend some PHP projects and packages that you can look at if you want to get your hands dirty with an existing code base. After that, we are going to jump in at the deep end with a look at inheritance, and then also look at using composition instead of inheritance. After that, we'll take a quick look at the Standard PHP Library, have a look at exceptions, and understand how modern PHP projects ensure that they have robust error handling. For the big finale of this chapter, we'll dip our toes in the deep waters of metaprogramming with reflection and attributes. It's a huge amount of content to cover in a comparatively tiny amount of text.

For this chapter, and all the other chapters in the book, you can find all the code samples in the main repo for the book available on GitHub at `https://github.com/PacktPublishing/The-Art-of-Modern-PHP-8`

What is OOP?

If you don't really know what OOP even means, then this section is for you! We're going to take a step back and start right from the beginning to try to understand the meaning of the phrase, then try to understand OOP as compared to other programming styles, and finally, have a quick tour of some modern object-oriented PHP packages and projects.

So, let's get started with looking at what OOP really means.

Understanding the phrase

OOP stands for **object-oriented programming**. It sounds like one of those CS phrases that get bandied about quite a bit without people really understanding what they mean. Let's unpack it, starting from the end…

Programming

Hopefully, you already have a good idea of what we mean by programming. PHP is a programming language and by that we mean simply that it is a set of coding words, symbols, and phrases that you can use to create code that ultimately does something.

There is a lot of inane debate about whether PHP truly is a programming language but let's not go there. We're here to get things done and that is where PHP excels.

Oriented

Oriented means "showing the direction in which something is aimed, directed towards or interested in something." So, we're programming in a way that is directed toward or interested in something. The "something" we are interested in is objects. In OOP, we use classes and objects for everything.

Object

What is an object? Well, in PHP, an object is an "instance" of a "class."

Here is the simplest class in PHP

```php
<?php

class Foo {}
```

Simply enough, it is defined with the word `class` and it has a name and then a body, which is delineated by the curly braces. On its own, this is pretty useless, of course. It gets more interesting as we add code to the body of the class and meta information to the class definition.

To create an object, we use the word `new` and can then optionally assign the result of this call to a variable. We now have an object:

```php
<?php

$foo = new Foo();
```

When we are talking about OOP, what we really mean is that we will compose our program entirely using objects. There must always be some code that resides at the global scope, but in an OOP program, this code is very limited indeed and is simply used to bootstrap and initialize the OOP code.

For example, this is the index.php file that all web requests are directed to when looking for a page in a Symfony project:

public/index.php

Repo: https://git.io/JqJxu

```php
<?php

use App\Kernel;
use Symfony\Component\Dotenv\Dotenv;
use Symfony\Component\ErrorHandler\Debug;
use Symfony\Component\HttpFoundation\Request;

require dirname(__DIR__).'/vendor/autoload.php';

(new Dotenv())->bootEnv(dirname(__DIR__).'/.env');

if ($_SERVER['APP_DEBUG']) {
    umask(0000);

    Debug::enable();
}

if ($trustedProxies = $_SERVER['TRUSTED_PROXIES'] ?? false) {
    Request::setTrustedProxies(explode(',', $trustedProxies),
Request::HEADER_X_FORWARDED_ALL ^ Request::HEADER_X_FORWARDED_HOST);
}

if ($trustedHosts = $_SERVER['TRUSTED_HOSTS'] ?? false) {
    Request::setTrustedHosts([$trustedHosts]);
}

$kernel = new Kernel($_SERVER['APP_ENV'], (bool) $_SERVER['APP_DEBUG']);
$request = Request::createFromGlobals();
```

```php
$response = $kernel->handle($request);
$response->send();
$kernel->terminate($request, $response);
```

As you can see, every single line of code apart from the call to umask is instantiating or calling methods on classes or objects. The file procedurally represents an entire application, and the entire application's code is encapsulated in the classes instantiated in this file, and the classes they are composed of.

OOP alternatives

It might be easier to understand what OOP is if we compare it with other programming styles. Let's explore two other programming styles to help deepen our understanding.

Procedural programming

This is the classic PHP style and is probably the reason why PHP often gets bad press. Procedural code works like a long list of instructions. You start at the top and continue reading till you hit the bottom.

Of course, all code works like this really, but the point is that in procedural code, there is much less use of scoping. A lot of work is done in the global scope, though there will generally be lots of calls to global functions and maybe even a few objects floating around.

The benefit of procedural code is that it is highly optimized for writing. You can write the code like a logical stream of consciousness.

The downsides to procedural code are that it can be quite difficult to reuse chunks of code, there can be a large number of variables in the global scope, which can make debugging things somewhat challenging, and finally, the ability to test distinct parts of the code is somewhat diminished – you can only really test the system as a whole with end-to-end tests.

One procedural project that has stood the test of time and is almost unbelievably popular and successful is WordPress:

GitHub – WordPress/wordpress-develop

https://github.com/WordPress/wordpress-develop

I think it would be fair to say that the exception proves the rule, though – the general trajectory of modern PHP has gone very much toward OOP.

Procedural code can be great for creating smaller scripts of maybe 1-200 lines, but for building full-blown projects it is no longer regarded as a good idea by most PHP developers.

The chunk of code you are about to read is entirely fictional but created from long years of dealing with this kind of code in production. It's big, verbose, and old-fashioned. I'm sure many of you will recognize this kind of file. Those of you that don't, count your blessings!

```php
<?php
# product_admin.php
// bring in an application top file that contains 1000 lines of
bootstrapping and including things
require __DIR__.'/../../application_top.php';
if(isset($_GET['products_id'])){
    // 500 lines of product related stuff
    if(isset($_POST['action'])){
        switch($_POST['action']){
            // 1000 lines of various post actions that might be
happening
        }
    }
}
```

In procedural code, it is normal for each page type to have its own file – this means that public traffic can be loading lots of different PHP files. Your public htdocs folder will generally include a number of PHP files that are publicly accessible and executable, possibly in subfolders as well for different system areas.

Functional programming

Functional programming, as its name implies, predominantly uses functions as the building blocks of code. In functional programming, we try to use "pure functions."

Pure functions are those functions that, when given specific values as inputs, will do the following things:

1.   Always return the same value
2.   Never cause any side effects

Pure functions are fantastic because they are very easy to reason about, very easy to test, and are completely 100% decoupled from any other code or state.

PHP has a powerful functional model and can be a great language for functional styles. I will admit I have never seen a code base in PHP that you would regard as purely written in the functional programming style, but you do often see functional programming styles utilized in OOP and procedural code.

A deep dive into functional programming in PHP is beyond the scope of this book; however, I really encourage you to learn more about functional programming in PHP and hit these docs pages:

- Callables, which are things that can be called as functions, of which there are a few:

  PHP: Callbacks / Callables - Manual

  `https://www.php.net/manual/en/language.types.callable.php`

- Closures, a callable class with parameters and a scope bound to it:

  PHP: Closure - Manual

  `https://www.php.net/manual/en/class.closure.php`

- Anonymous functions, functions that are not defined globally, but are more like values that can be passed and assigned to variables:

  PHP: Anonymous functions - Manual

  `https://www.php.net/manual/en/functions.anonymous.php`

- Arrow functions, which are a shorthand way of creating anonymous functions:

  PHP: Arrow Functions - Manual

  `https://www.php.net/manual/en/functions.arrow.php`

- Finally, the magic __invoke method, which allows you to create callable objects:

  PHP: Magic Methods - Manual

  `https://www.php.net/manual/en/language.oop5.magic.php#object.invoke`

Here is a contrived example of how a functional programming `index.php` file might look:

```php
<?php

declare(strict_types=1);

require __DIR__ .'/../functions.php';

(function(string $responseTxt, array $headers):void{
    array_map(
        fn(string $header):void => header($header),
        $headers
    );
```

```
    echo $responseTxt;
}) (... (function(array $request):array{
    $headers=[];
    $responseTxt='';
    // some code to actually generate the page and headers
    return ['headers'=>$headers, 'responseTxt'=>$responseTxt];
}) ($_REQUEST));
```

While I have never actually seen a proper functional programming-based project in the real world, you can and do see functional programming styles applied to OOP and procedural projects. The benefits of using pure functions and avoiding a shared state are applicable to all forms of programming.

So, now that we have looked at some alternative programming styles, let's move on to ways you can start to learn object-oriented PHP.

Learning object-oriented PHP

The first resource you should hit when learning PHP is the official documentation:

PHP: Classes and Objects - Manual

```
https://www.php.net/manual/en/language.oop5.php
```

This is good, though I do suggest you avoid the comments as many are very old and not relevant at all.

Probably the easiest way to get your head around OOP in PHP is to work on an existing open source project or framework that is written in the OOP style. There are many to choose from, though the quality can vary.

Here is a quick introduction to some popular projects.

Frameworks

The two most popular PHP frameworks are Laravel and Symfony. All modern PHP frameworks that I am aware of adopt the **Model, View, Controller** (**MVC**) structure.

In a nutshell, this means that all requests are directed to a single "front controller," which then handles deciding exactly what the request is asking for and then routing that to the correct Controller. What that means is that there is a single publicly accessible index.php file as the only public PHP file in the htdocs folder.

The Controller's job is to utilize the Model to retrieve any data required and perform any required processing before finally utilizing the View to return a string of text to be rendered as HTML. It's worth reading more on MVC if this is not something you are familiar with.

Symfony

Symfony is one of the oldest PHP frameworks (in active development since 2005) and has matured with the language over time.

It is a great choice for "enterprise" projects that require stability and a clear support lifetime. The general wisdom is that Symfony might be a better choice for long-term projects that are likely to grow in complexity over time.

The way that modern Symfony is constructed is highly modular; it allows you to keep the scale of your application as lean as possible, only bringing in functionality that you need.

Symfony is built upon the concept of "Components," which are actually framework-agnostic decoupled libraries that perform a certain function. This means that the code base as a whole is kept very clean, and you can work in a way that is less about the framework.

To find out more about Symfony, visit:

GitHub - symfony/symfony: The Symfony PHP framework

```
https://github.com/symfony/symfony
```

Laravel

Laravel is by far the most popular PHP framework at the moment. Laravel uses a lot of Symfony components under the hood, which underlines how good the Symfony stuff is. Where Laravel and Symfony differ is primarily in their approach and philosophy.

The general wisdom is that Laravel is easier and faster to work with for more simple projects, but if you are expecting to build the kind of project that might grow very complex over time, then Symfony might be a better choice.

To learn more about Laravel, go to:

GitHub - laravel/laravel: A PHP framework for web artisans

```
https://github.com/laravel/laravel
```

Slim

If you are looking to build something simple, such as a plain API, then you might enjoy working with more of a micro framework such as Slim.

More information on Slim can be found at:

GitHub - slimphp/Slim: Slim is a PHP micro framework that helps you quickly write simple yet powerful web applications and APIs.

```
https://github.com/slimphp/Slim
```

Roll your own!

This is not something that I would recommend for a real production site, but for a personal project, you can't really beat the experience of creating your own bespoke MVC framework.

If you want to avoid reinventing the wheel, you could take the same tack as many successful projects and utilize Symfony components for your basic building blocks, such as HttpKernel.

Find out more here:

GitHub - symfony/http-kernel: The HttpKernel component provides a structured process for converting a Request into a Response.

```
https://github.com/symfony/http-kernel
```

Applications

Learning frameworks is all well and good, but if you need to solve a fairly standard project such as building an online shop or some form of blog or brochure site, then you might be better off choosing a more complete package that already includes all the basic features you need.

I have pulled together a few suggestions for you. These are all generally framework-based and so can give you some good ideas on how to use a framework in a full application.

E-commerce

An area where PHP really shines in terms of theopen source packages available is e-commerce. The main problem facing the modern e-commerce PHP developer is that there is so much choice!

Sylius

Sylius is Symfony-based and has been built using modern practices such as test-driven development (TDD) and behavior-driven development (BDD). It doesn't really claim to be the "all bells and whistles included" platform that perhaps Magento does, but instead it offers itself as a solid platform for a more bespoke e-commerce solution.

Find Sylius here:

GitHub - Sylius/Sylius: Open Source eCommerce Platform on Symfony

```
https://github.com/Sylius/Sylius
```

Magento

Magento is the big daddy in open source PHP e-commerce. Magento is based on quite an old-fashioned framework at its core and is unusual in that it does not use Symfony or Laravel as its framework. Magento 2 uses some interesting strategies such as "aspect-oriented programming" and extensive use of code generation.

Want to know more? Visit:

GitHub - Magento

```
http://github.com/magento/magento2
```

Shopware

The latest version of Shopware is Symfony-based and aims to provide Magento levels of functionality with the development best practice approach of Sylius. It's an interesting proposition and definitely worth a look.

Check Shopware out here:

GitHub - shopware/platform: Shopware 6 is an open source e-commerce platform realised by the ideas and the spirit of its community.

```
https://github.com/shopware/platform
```

CMS

Content management systems (CMSes) are designed to manage generic content-driven sites such as blogs and brochure sites. WordPress alone powers a huge percentage (at least 30%, maybe close to 40%) of sites on the internet, with big names such as `techcrunch.com` and `blog.mozilla.org` proudly running the platform.

Drupal

Drupal has been a very popular CMS in the PHP world for a long time and has gradually morphed from procedural roots into a modern OOP system.

Drupal uses Symfony components such as HttpKernel and routing components along with other more modular components such as Twig and YAML. Drupal 7 had its own components (kernel, router, templating, config management, and so on), and then Drupal 8 was an almost rewrite with more Symfony components and an OOP approach.

It is a large-scale CMS platform suitable for bigger-content projects. It is not a pure Symfony framework project but is a good example of a project that has managed to make itself more object-oriented over time and thereby improved the developer experience significantly.

More on Drupal here:

project / drupal · GitLab

```
https://git.drupalcode.org
```

OctoberCMS

October CMS is a much smaller project than Drupal but worth a look if you prefer something Laravel-based.

Check it out here:

GitHub - octobercms/october: Free, open source, self-hosted CMS platform based on the Laravel PHP Framework.

```
https://github.com/octobercms/october
```

Joomla

Another CMS project with a long history is Joomla. At the time of writing, version 4 is being actively developed. This brings things significantly up to date in comparison to the current version 3.

The main project is here:

GitHub - joomla/joomla-cms at 4.1-dev

```
https://git.io/JZZ5h
```

You can look at some of the various components they have developed here:

Joomla! Framework · GitHub

```
https://git.io/JZZ5j
```

So, this is the end of our *What is OOP?* section. I hope that you now understand what the phrase means and have perhaps even had a chance to peruse some of the code bases suggested so you have an understanding of what object-oriented PHP looks like. Maybe you've even been inspired to kick the tyres on a new project or even have a go at rolling your own. I've heard it said that every PHP developer has an MVC framework in them.

Now it's time to move on to looking at some technical details of object-oriented PHP.

PHP OOP basics

In this section, we are going to cover a very brief overview of the basic OOP features of PHP 8. I am not aiming to be comprehensive here; if this is new to you, then I suggest you visit the official docs, which do a great job of explaining these features in detail:

PHP: Classes and Objects - Manual

`https://www.php.net/manual/en/language.oop5.php`

We will be covering further details throughout the book; however, the following should be enough to whet your appetite and let you know whether your knowledge is up to date. We're going to look briefly at classes, interfaces, and namespaces. This should all be quite familiar to you already and if it is not, then a little extra revision of these topics would be useful so that you can get the most out of later chapters.

Classes

The basic building block of PHP OOP is the class. As briefly mentioned earlier in this chapter, classes are the things that get instantiated in the "objects" that OOP talks about.

A simple class looks like this:

src/Part1/Chapter1/Simple/SimpleClass.php

Repo: `https://git.io/JRw7C`

```php
<?php

declare(strict_types=1);

namespace Book\Part1\Chapter1\Simple;

class SimpleClass
{
    public function __construct(public string $name = 'Simon')
    {
    }
}
```

To create an instance of the class, we use the new keyword, which then gives us an "instance" that we can assign to a variable and generally interact with.

Then, a new instance is created; PHP will check for a method called __construct and if it exists, it will be called. The parameters passed into this method are those that are passed in when calling the class:

src/Part1/Chapter1/simple.php

Repo: https://git.io/JRw7W

```php
<?php

declare(strict_types=1);

namespace Book\Part1\Chapter1;

use Book\Part1\Chapter1\Simple\SimpleClass;

require __DIR__ . '/../../../vendor/autoload.php';

$instance = new SimpleClass();
echo "\n" . $instance->name; // Simon

$instance2 = new SimpleClass('Sally');
echo "\n" . $instance2->name; //Sally
```

Output:

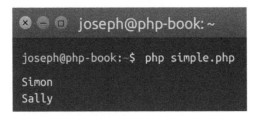

Inside the class, we have a variable called $this, which is available to every method inside the class and refers to the current instance. It provides access to all the methods and properties of that instance:

src/Part1/Chapter1/Simple/SimpleWithGetter.php

Repo: https://git.io/JRw7l

```php
<?php
```

```php
declare(strict_types=1);

namespace Book\Part1\Chapter1\Simple;

class SimpleWithGetter
{
    public function __construct(private string $name = 'Simon')
    {
    }

    public function getName(): string
    {
        return $this->name;
    }
}
```

If the parameters are defined in the constructor with a visibility keyword (`private`, `protected`, or `public`), then the parameter will automatically be defined as a property of the class with that visibility level.

If a visibility level is not specified, then in order to assign the parameter value to the class as a property, we have to do something like this:

src/Part1/Chapter1/Simple/SimpleManualAssignment.php

Repo: `https://git.io/JRw78`

```php
<?php

declare(strict_types=1);

namespace Book\Part1\Chapter1\Simple;

class SimpleManualAssignment
{
    private string $name;

    public function __construct(string $name = 'Simon')
    {
```

```
        // take the constructor param and manually assign to
class property
        $this->name = $name;
    }
}
```

There are three ways that properties can be set in the class:

- In the constructor parameters
- Defining the property in the class body
- Dynamically assigning the property without a definition (don't do this)

Have a look at the following snippet, which demonstrates these three options:

src/Part1/Chapter1/Simple/SimplePropertyAssignment.php

Repo: `https://git.io/JRw74`

```php
<?php

declare(strict_types=1);

namespace Book\Part1\Chapter1\Simple;

class SimplePropertyAssignment
{
    private string $defined = 'defaultValue';

    public function __construct(
        private string $constructorParam = 'constructorValue'
    ) {
        // this is a bad idea, dynamicProperty is untyped and
public
        $this->dynamicProperty = 'dynamicallyAdded';
    }
}
```

When a property is declared dynamically, it can only ever be public, and it cannot be typed. This means that we lose a huge amount of safety and open the door to a whole range of bugs:

src/Part1/Chapter1/simple_properties.php

Repo: `https://git.io/JRw7B`

```php
<?php

declare(strict_types=1);

namespace Book\Part1\Chapter1;

use Book\Part1\Chapter1\Simple\SimplePropertyAssignment;

require __DIR__ . '/../../../vendor/autoload.php';
$instance = new SimplePropertyAssignment();

// dynamic property is public
echo "\n" . $instance->dynamicProperty;

// dynamic property is untyped and can be anything
$instance->dynamicProperty = 123;

echo "\n" . $instance->dynamicProperty;
```

Output:

```
joseph@php-book: ~
joseph@php-book:~$ php simple_properties.php
dynamicallyAdded
123
```

As you hopefully now realise, public properties are generally not something you want, apart from in very particular circumstances. If you ever see dynamically assigned properties, the general expectation is that it is a mistake, and for this reason, most integrated development environments (IDEs) will highlight it as a warning.

Interfaces

Interfaces are pieces of code that never contain any functionality, but what they do define are the… well… interface that classes must provide when they implement the specific interface.

For example:

src/Part1/Chapter1/interface.php

Repo: `https://git.io/JRw7R`

```php
<?php

declare(strict_types=1);

namespace Book\Part1\Chapter1;

interface GetsSomethingInterface
{
    /**
     * This interface defines one method.
     * It must be called "getSomething" and it must return a
string
     */
    public function getSomething(): string;
}

class GetsSomethingClass implements GetsSomethingInterface
{
    public function getSomething(): string
    {
        return 'something';
    }
}

echo "\n" . (new GetsSomethingClass())->getSomething();
```

Output:

```
joseph@php-book: ~

joseph@php-book:~$ php interface.php
something
```

By implementing an interface, the class tells the world that it conforms to a set of strict rules. It must implement the methods in the interface as they are defined. That allows other code to not necessarily care exactly what class it is and confidently call methods as we know they will be there, and we know what types they will return.

Read more about interfaces in the official docs:

PHP: Object Interfaces - Manual

`https://www.php.net/manual/en/language.oop5.interfaces.php`

Namespaces

This is not strictly part of OOP but is highly relevant, so I'm including it here. Namespaces are designed to make naming things a lot, lot simpler. Before we had namespaces, our code needed to worry about the fact that there might be a situation where some other piece of code tries to use the same name as the one you are trying to use for your class, function, or another item. This led to things having very long names, such as `Mage_Catalog_Product_CompareController` – all in an effort to ensure that there is no risk of a name clash, because a name clash is a fatal error.

The advent of namespaces meant that we could now define a clean slate for naming things. We need to define a unique namespace and then within that namespace, we can give things lovely, short, meaningful names with no fear of a name clash:

```php
<?php

namespace My\Library;

class Helper {}

function write(string $value){}
```

There is nothing in PHP itself that defines which namespace any particular file should use; however, modern PHP developers have almost completely adopted something called PSR-4:

PSR-4: Autoloader - PHP-FIG

```
https://www.php-fig.org/psr/psr-4/
```

As you can see if you follow the link, PSR-4 lays out rules around exactly how to use namespaces and how they should correspond to the file/folder structure of your project.

> **What is PSR?**
>
> If you haven't heard of PSR before, it might be worth reading into it a bit. **PSR** stands for **PHP Standards Recommendations**. It is something that was put together and promoted by a group of PHP developers called the **PHP Framework Interop Group – PHP-FIG** for short.
>
> What they have done is tried to put together coding standards and basic interfaces to define general components. The goal is that rather than each framework being its own weird and wonderful isolated pond, there are standard approaches to standard problems. The huge advantage of this is that tooling and libraries are less coupled to frameworks and we can have nice things that were primarily built for one framework or application being useable by the rest of the PHP ecosystem. DI containers are actually a great example of this.

This policy defines a folder structure and naming convention that corresponds a class's namespace. Each \ in the namespace name corresponds to a subdirectory in the folder structure, with a defined prefix applied within a defined base directory.

This example is copied from the PSR-4 page:

FULLY QUALIFIED CLASS NAME	NAMESPACE PREFIX	BASE DIRECTORY	RESULTING FILE PATH
\Acme\Log\Writer\ File_Writer	Acme\Log\ Writer	./acme-log-writer/lib/	./acme-log-writer/lib/ File_Writer.php
\Aura\Web\ Response\Status	Aura\Web	/path/to/aura-web/src/	/path/to/aura-web/src/ Response/Status.php
\Symfony\Core\ Request	Symfony\Core	./vendor/ Symfony/Core/	./vendor/Symfony/Core/ Request.php
\Zend\Acl	Zend	/usr/includes/ Zend/	/usr/includes/Zend/Acl. php

If you have been paying close attention to the code snippets, you may have spotted that the example code for this book also conforms to PSR-4. The root namespace prefix is `Book\` and this corresponds to the `src` directory in the `code` repo. For code that is designed to be shared publicly, this root namespace is like a unique username or brand and is generally standardized for all packages released by the same person or company. We will explore these kinds of packages later in the book.

For any files in the base directory, the namespace is simply the namespace prefix. If the file is in a subfolder, then the namespace is extended to match the subfolder name.

If you look back through the code snippets in this chapter, you can see that as we are in `Part1` and `Chapter1`, the code snippets are being stored in `src/Part1/Chapter1`, and for each code snippet that is in that folder, the namespace is defined as follows:

```
namespace Book\Part1\Chapter1;
```

Any code snippets in a subfolder have the namespace extended to match; for example, the file `/src/Part1/Chapter1/Simple/SimplePropertyAssignment.php` has the namespace defined as follows:

```
namespace Book\Part1\Chapter1\Simple;
```

PSR-4 is a very sane and sensible system to follow, and I highly encourage you to do so.

Read more about namespaces in the official docs:

PHP: Namespaces - Manual

`https://www.php.net/manual/en/language.namespaces.php`

Summary

This brings us to the end of our first chapter. Let's quickly recap what we have covered. First of all, we explored what the term OOP actually means. We looked at some other programming styles and used this to compare with some OOP code to hopefully highlight the differences. We then had a quick look through some popular PHP OOP projects that are worth looking at in more detail if you would like to see some real-world code and maybe get your hands dirty. Finally, we had a very quick overview of some basic OOP features. You should already know these in detail and so we didn't go over them in any depth – if you do not already know them, then you are encouraged to hit the official docs to fill in the gaps. In the next chapter, we are going to look at some more advanced topics in object-oriented PHP related to the ways that we can orchestrate a graph of related objects, either using inheritance or, alternatively, using composition.

2
Inheritance and Composition, Encapsulation and Visibility, Interfaces and Concretions

In this second chapter, we are going to learn as much as we can about the OOP features of PHP when it comes to creating full sets of classes that are related to each other and that work together to provide a specific feature.

First, we are going to learn about encapsulation and the differences between private, protected, and public class properties and methods. Hopefully, you will see the advantage of keeping things as private as possible.

Then we are going to look in detail at the two main ways of creating a graph of related and interdependent classes: classic inheritance and the alternative approach of composition.

As we explore this, I hope that you will also learn some other language features along the way. Anything that you spot that is not immediately clear to you, I really encourage you to go and look it up in the official PHP docs.

This chapter will cover the following main topics:

- Encapsulation and visibility

- Inheritance – the classical parent, child, and "is a" style

- Composition – the modern, flexible "has a" style

As usual, you can find all the code samples for this chapter in the main repo for the book available on GitHub at `https://github.com/PacktPublishing/The-Art-of-Modern-PHP-8`

Encapsulation and visibility

Encapsulation is a foundational feature of OOP in PHP and something you must understand well if you are to successfully grasp OO PHP.

PHP classes "encapsulate data and functionality." The word "encapsulate" simply means "enclose in a capsule." What this means is that the things inside the capsule, in our case the class, are hidden away.

By hiding things away inside our class, we allow ourselves the freedom to change and refactor the internal workings of the class without any fear of issues outside the class – as long as the public methods and properties remain the same. What this means is that the general wisdom is that you should keep as much as possible hidden away and only expose the minimum amount of functionality and data in order to maximize your freedom to refactor.

Here is the official docs page that you should have a thorough read of:

PHP Manual: Visibility

`https://www.php.net/manual/en/language.oop5.visibility.php`

Let's start looking into this by first of all understanding the three levels of visibility that PHP provides for our class properties and methods: private, protected, and public.

Private, protected, and public

By default, class properties and methods are public. This means that they are freely accessible for reading/writing/calling from inside and outside the class. This is very, *very* rarely the way you want it. Instead, we want to pull the curtains drawn and only expose the things that we really want to share.

By setting class properties and methods to *private*, we prevent any outside access at all. I would suggest this should be your default accessibility with all class members. Make everything private. If you want to allow people to read your properties, you can either define getter methods, or you can use some PHP magic to allow read-only access by implementing a __get method or __call method for properties and methods respectively.

> **What is a getter?**
>
> Quite simply, a getter is a method that "gets" a property. For mutable objects, you will often set a corresponding setter as well:
>
> getSomething():string
>
> setSomething(string $something)

If you have a child class, it will also not be able to read the properties or methods of your class. Once you get into inheritance, then you might find it easier to mark properties and methods as *protected*. This level of visibility is the same as private, but also allows child classes to have access.

The final, most open level – and therefore should be the least used – is *public* which allows full access to all comers. The door is wide open and everyone is invited. Generally, you should do this as infrequently as possible. If you fail to put a visibility modifier, then it defaults to public.

Access From	private	protected	public
Inside class	yes	Yes	yes
Child class	no	Yes	yes
Outside	no	No	yes

Now that you understand the difference between private, protected, and public, let's have a look at the way protected and public items can be inherited by child classes, and how inheritance works in general.

Inheritance–the classical parent, child, and "is a" style

Inheritance describes the way that PHP allows us to create formal and hierarchical graphs of related objects with a single-parent, multiple-child structure.

Even if you decide to avoid ever using inheritance in your own, lovingly crafted PHP, you will not be able to avoid the fact that inheritance plays a huge role in the built-in classes and interfaces and is also a major feature of big, must-have libraries such as PHPUnit.

To get a full understanding of the PHP inheritance model, your first port of call should be the official documentation:

PHP Manual – Object Inheritance

`https://www.php.net/manual/en/language.oop5.inheritance.php`

Inheritance in OOP refers to the fact that a class can inherit properties and methods from a parent class.

Have a look at the very simple demonstration that follows, which demonstrates one-level inheritance and also illustrates what is and is not accessible from the child class:

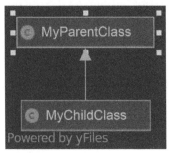

src/Part1/Chapter2/inheritance.php

Repo: `https://git.io/JRwQ5`

```php
<?php

declare(strict_types=1);

namespace Book\Part1\Chapter2;
```

```php
class MyParentClass
{
    protected int   $foo     = 1;
    private string $private = 'hidden';
}


class MyChildClass extends MyParentClass
{
    private int $bar = 2;

    public function getFoo(): int
    {
        // access parent class property
        return $this->foo;
    }

    public function getBar(): int
    {
        // access this class property
        return $this->bar;
    }

    public function getPrivate(): string
    {
        // THIS IS NOT POSSIBLE
        // return $this->private;
        return 'NOT POSSIBLE';
    }
}
```

The inheritance model in PHP is based on *single inheritance*. This means that a class can only have a single parent. Parent classes may have an unlimited number of child classes.

Some other languages support multiple inheritance, where a single class can have multiple parents. This can be more powerful but comes at the cost of significant extra complexity.

PHP does support multiple inheritance with interfaces. A single interface can extend multiple parent interfaces. A class can also implement multiple interfaces.

PHP Manual – Object Interfaces

`https://www.php.net/manual/en/language.oop5.interfaces.php`

src/Part1/Chapter2/interfaces.php

Repo: `https://git.io/JRwQd`

```php
<?php

declare(strict_types=1);

namespace Book\Part1\Chapter2;

interface GetsFoo
{
    public function getFoo(): string;
}

interface GetsBar
{
    public function getBar(): string;
}

final class MultipleInterfaces implements GetsFoo, GetsBar
{
    public function getFoo(): string
    {
        return 'foo';
    }

    public function getBar(): string
    {
        return 'bar';
    }
}
```

There can be multiple levels of parent-child relations, though generally, it is advisable to keep the number of levels as low as possible to avoid excessive complexity and coupling.

Have a look at the following code, where we can show that properties defined at the grandparent and parent level are both accessible from the child level:

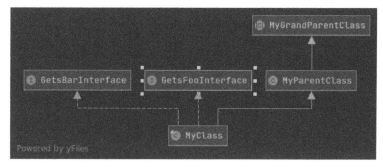

First, we have a grandparent class:

src/Part1/Chapter2/Inheritance/MyGrandParentClass.php

Repo: `https://git.io/JRwQF`

```php
<?php

declare(strict_types=1);

namespace Book\Part1\Chapter2\Inheritance;

abstract class MyGrandParentClass
{
    protected int $foo = 1;
}
```

Then we have a parent class, which extends the grandparent class and is also open for extension:

src/Part1/Chapter2/Inheritance/MyParentClass.php

Repo: `https://git.io/JRwQb`

```php
<?php

declare(strict_types=1);
```

```php
namespace Book\Part1\Chapter2\Inheritance;

class MyParentClass extends MyGrandParentClass
{
    protected int $bar = 2;
}
```

Next, we have two interfaces that both enforce a single getter method:

src/Part1/Chapter2/Inheritance/GetsBarInterface.php

Repo: https://git.io/JRwQN

```php
<?php

declare(strict_types=1);

namespace Book\Part1\Chapter2\Inheritance;

interface GetsBarInterface
{
    public function getBar(): int;
}
```

src/Part1/Chapter2/Inheritance/GetsFooInterface.php

Repo: https://git.io/JRwQA

```php
<?php

declare(strict_types=1);

namespace Book\Part1\Chapter2\Inheritance;

interface GetsFooInterface
{
    public function getFoo(): int;
}
```

Finally, we have our class that extends the parent (and thereby also the grandparent). It also implements both of our interfaces:

src/Part1/Chapter2/Inheritance/MyClass.php

Repo: https://git.io/JRwQx

```php
<?php

declare(strict_types=1);

namespace Book\Part1\Chapter2\Inheritance;

/**
 * Single Inheritance of Classes
 * Multiple Implementation of Interfaces.
 */
final class MyClass extends MyParentClass
    implements GetsBarInterface, GetsFooInterface
{
    public function getFoo(): int
    {
        return $this->foo;
    }

    public function getBar(): int
    {
        return $this->bar;
    }
}
```

Have a look through the following code, which, while still totally contrived, shows a bit more of a realistic selection of inheritance-based code:

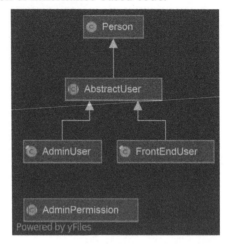

First, we have a simple class to represent a person. This class has been declared neither final nor abstract so it can both be extended and instantiated:

src/Part1/Chapter2/ForceInheritance/Person.php

Repo: `https://git.io/JRwQp`

```php
<?php

declare(strict_types=1);

namespace Book\Part1\Chapter2\ForceInheritance;

/**
 * Class CAN be instantiated and inherited from.
 */
class Person
{
    public function __construct(
        protected string $name
    ) {
    }
```

```
    /** Method CANNOT be overridden in child classes */
    final public function getName(): string
    {
        return $this->name;
    }
}
```

Now we extend that `Person` class, and we enforce that this new class *must* be extended as it is using the `abstract` keyword:

src/Part1/Chapter2/ForceInheritance/AbstractUser.php

Repo: `https://git.io/JRwQh`

```php
<?php

declare(strict_types=1);

namespace Book\Part1\Chapter2\ForceInheritance;

/**
 * Class CANNOT be instantiated, CAN be inherited from.
 */
abstract class AbstractUser extends Person
{
    public function __construct(
        protected int $id,
        protected string $name
    ) {
        parent::__construct($name);
    }

    // Abstract function - must be defined in child classes
    abstract public function __toString();
}
```

Our first implementation of the AbstractUser class is the contrived FrontEndUser. This class has been set as final, which ensures that this class cannot be extended:

src/Part1/Chapter2/ForceInheritance/FrontEndUser.php

Repo: https://git.io/JRw7e

```php
<?php

declare(strict_types=1);

namespace Book\Part1\Chapter2\ForceInheritance;

/**
 * Class CAN be instantiated, CANNOT be inherited from.
 */
final class FrontEndUser extends AbstractUser
{
    /** @var string[] */
    private array $recentlyViewedPages;

    public function __construct(
        protected int $id,
        protected string $name,
        string ...$recentlyViewedPages
    ) {
        parent::__construct($id, $name);
        $this->recentlyViewedPages = $recentlyViewedPages;
    }

    public function __toString(): string
    {
        $viewed = \print_r($this->recentlyViewedPages, true);

        return <<<STRING
            front end user {$this->name} ({$this->id}) has
recently viewed:
```

```
            {$viewed}
            STRING;
    }
}
```

Now we define an `abstract` admin permission class. This class must be extended, and the extending class must implement the `abstract` method, or be declared `abstract` itself:

src/Part1/Chapter2/ForceInheritance/AdminPermission.php

Repo: `https://git.io/JRw7v`

```php
<?php

declare(strict_types=1);

namespace Book\Part1\Chapter2\ForceInheritance;

/**
 * Class CANNOT be instantiated, CAN be inherited from.
 */
abstract class AdminPermission
{
    public const CAN_EDIT = 'canEdit';
    public const CAN_VIEW = 'canView';
    public const PERMS    = [
        self::CAN_EDIT,
        self::CAN_VIEW,
    ];

    abstract public function getPermName(): string;

    abstract public function isAllowed(): bool;
}
```

Next up is another implementation of AbstractUser, which is an admin user. Again, this is a final class and therefore cannot be extended. This class accepts a range of AdminPermission objects. We're starting to introduce some composition concepts here:

src/Part1/Chapter2/ForceInheritance/AdminUser.php

Repo: https://git.io/JRw7f

```php
<?php

declare(strict_types=1);

namespace Book\Part1\Chapter2\ForceInheritance;

/**
 * Class CAN be instantiated, CANNOT be inherited from.
 */
final class AdminUser extends AbstractUser
{
    /** @var array<string,AdminPermission> */
    private array $permissions;

    public function __construct(
        protected int $id,
        protected string $name,
        AdminPermission ...$permissions
    ) {
        parent::__construct($id, $name);
        \array_map(
            callback: function (AdminPermission $perm): void {
                $this->permissions[$perm->getPermName()] =
$perm;
            },
            array: $permissions
        );
    }
```

```php
    public function __toString(): string
    {
        $permissions = \implode(
            separator: "\n",
            array: \array_map(
                callback: static function (
                    AdminPermission $perm
                ): string {
                    $permName = $perm->getPermName();
                    $allowed  = ($perm->isAllowed() ? 'true' :
'false');

                    return "{$permName}: {$allowed}";
                },
                array: $this->permissions
            )
        );

        return <<<STRING

        admin user {$this->name} ({$this->id}) has these
permissions:
            {$permissions}

        STRING;
    }
}
```

Finally, we pull all this together and have a bit of top-level code to instantiate these classes and echo out the results.

Note that we are using anonymous classes to extend and implement the AdminPermission functionality:

src/Part1/Chapter2/force_inheritance.php

Repo: https://git.io/JRw7J

```php
<?php
```

```php
declare(strict_types=1);


namespace Book\Part1\Chapter2;


use Book\Part1\Chapter2\ForceInheritance\AdminPermission;
use Book\Part1\Chapter2\ForceInheritance\AdminUser;
use Book\Part1\Chapter2\ForceInheritance\FrontEndUser;


require __DIR__ . '/../../../vendor/autoload.php';


$frontEndUser = new FrontEndUser(
    2,
    'Steve',
    'http://php.com',
    'http://something.com'
);
echo $frontEndUser;


$adminUser = new AdminUser(
    1,
    'Joseph',
    new class() extends AdminPermission {
        public function getPermName(): string
        {
            return self::CAN_VIEW;
        }


        public function isAllowed(): bool
        {
            return true;
        }
    },
    new class() extends AdminPermission {
```

```php
        public function getPermName(): string
        {
            return self::CAN_EDIT;
        }

        public function isAllowed(): bool
        {
            return false;
        }
    },
);


echo $adminUser;
```

Output:

```
joseph@php-book: ~

joseph@php-book:~$ php force_inheritance.php
front end user Steve (2) has recently viewed:
Array
(
    [0] => http://php.com
    [1] => http://something.com
)

admin user Joseph (1) has these permissions:
canView: true
canEdit: false
```

So, hopefully, now you are clear on some of the techniques and features PHP provides so that you can enforce and control an inheritance chain. You can mark classes as abstract and enforce that they must be inherited from. You can also mark classes as final and enforce that they cannot be inherited from. By using these two language features, you make clear the intentions in your code and thereby keep things simple.

Let's have a quick look at another language feature in PHP, constructor promotion.

Constructor promotion

PHP 8 brings in a shorthand approach to defining class properties that are set at construction time. Properties defined with a visibility modifier in the __construct argument list will automatically be set as properties with the specified access level. This saves a bit of boilerplate and is something you should definitely use:

```php
class OldBoiler {
    private string $foo;
    private int $bar;
    public function __construct(string $foo, int $bar){
        $this->foo=$foo;
        $this->bar=$bar;
    }
}

class ShinyNew {
    public function __construct(
        private string $foo,
        private int $bar
    ){}
}
```

PHP Manual – Constructors and Destructors

```
https://www.php.net/manual/en/language.oop5.decon.php
```

Class Constants

In the previous code, you might have noted the use of class constants, as defined with the const keyword:

```php
public const CAN_EDIT = 'canEdit';
public const CAN_VIEW = 'canView';
public const PERMS    = [
    self::CAN_EDIT,
    self::CAN_VIEW,
];
```

Class constants have the same PPP access rules as everything else, though they are by definition read-only, and so generally it is perfectly safe to have them marked as `public`. I strongly encourage the use of class constants as the mechanism for storing your "magic strings" – those important strings that are meaningful and important and are often reused across your code base. The general guidance is to avoid using magic strings directly and instead refer to the class constant:

```
new AdminPermission(permName: AdminPermission::CAN_VIEW, can:
true);
```

PHP Manual – Class constants

https://www.php.net/manual/en/language.oop5.constants.php

Function/method arguments

Another thing you might have seen in the preceding examples are some different approaches to function arguments, namely the splat operator . . . and named arguments `AdminPermission(permName: AdminPermission::CAN_VIEW, can: true)`.

Have a read of the official docs here:

PHP Manual – Function arguments

https://www.php.net/manual/en/functions.arguments.php

Splat...

I love the onomatopoeic name of this operator. I admit to not knowing where it comes from. Apparently, the name comes from Ruby. Who cares – PHP has a proud history of pulling the best ideas from other languages, and the name of this operator is up there.

Using the splat operator is like throwing your array at the function, so it "splats" open into its component pieces. Splat…

The splat operator implies a typed array in many ways. It allows a function/method to be called with a variable number of arguments and inside the function body, the arguments are presented as an array. The splat operator also lets us pass an array to a method and unpack it into separate arguments, for example:

src/Part1/Chapter2/splat.php

Repo: https://git.io/JRw7U

```
<?php
```

```php
declare(strict_types=1);

namespace Book\Part1\Chapter2;

(static function (string ...$numbers): void {
    echo \implode("\n", $numbers);
})(...['one', 'two', 'three']);
```

Output:

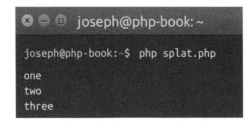

```
joseph@php-book: ~

joseph@php-book:~$ php splat.php

one
two
three
```

Named arguments

Named arguments allow us to create much better self-documenting code, by not only passing values into a method/function call but also describing what the values are for. Another feature of named arguments is that they allow us to pass function/method arguments in an arbitrary order. My hope is that this can put to bed the inane moaning about PHP argument order. It can also generally improve readability, which can only be a good thing.

In the following example, you can see that we take two functions that take an array and a callback as params, but by default the order is different. If this bothers you, then named params allow you to change the order of parameters so that they are both the same.

Alternatively (and the practice I suggest you adopt) is to continue to use the standard argument order, but improve the clarity by naming the arguments so that even if you do accidentally get them in the incorrect order, the code will still work. Fixing the argument order is something that can be done automatically by your IDE or in an automated QA/CI process:

src/Part1/Chapter2/named_args.php

Repo: `https://git.io/JRw7T`

```php
<?php

declare(strict_types=1);
```

```php
namespace Book\Part1\Chapter2;

/*
 * array_filter ( array $array , callable|null $callback = null
, int $mode = 0 ) : array
 */
\array_filter(
    array: [
        true,
        false,
        true,
    ],
    callback: static function ($item): bool {
        return $item === true;
    }
);


/*
 * array_map ( callable|null $callback , array $array , array
...$arrays ) : array
 */
\array_map(
    array: [
        true,
        false,
        true,
    ],
    callback: static function ($item): bool {
        return !$item;
    }
);
```

Static and late static binding

While you are likely to normally interact with classes in the form of objects that represent an instance of the specific class, there is also a style that allows you to call methods and access properties and constants directly on the class, without creating an instance. This can be useful for a variety of things, *though is not something you want to overuse.*

Static properties and methods do not require the class to be instantiated. If the property or method is public, then it can be accessed directly from the class. What this means is that static methods do not have the concept of $this as they are not aware of and do not interact with any specific instance of the class as an object.

PHP Manual – Static Keyword

`https://www.php.net/manual/en/language.oop5.static.php`

Static methods cannot access instance variables and instance methods. Static methods can only access static variables, class constants, and other static methods within the same class because static methods assume that the class is not instantiated. Static methods also cannot use $this because $this refers to "this" instance of a class.

When working with classes in an inheritance hierarchy and accessing static properties or methods, you have the choice of using self, which will access precisely the class that the code is in, or static, which will be the class that the code is being executed from – quite possibly a child class.

PHP Manual – Late Static Bindings

`https://www.php.net/manual/en/language.oop5.late-static-bindings.php`

Have a look at the following code, which briefly illustrates the difference between self and static.

First, we have a parent and child class:

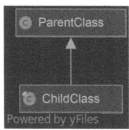

The parent class defines two methods, one accessing itself with self and the other with static:

src/Part1/Chapter2/StaticAccess/ParentClass.php

Repo: `https://git.io/JRw7k`

```php
<?php
```

```php
declare(strict_types=1);

namespace Book\Part1\Chapter2\StaticAccess;

class ParentClass
{
    private const ZIP          = '123';
    private static string $foo = 'bar';

    public static function getStringSelf(): string
    {
        return self::$foo . self::ZIP;
    }

    public static function getStringStatic(): string
    {
        return static::$foo . static::ZIP;
    }
}
```

A child class simply extends the parent and overrides the values of the properties we are working with:

src/Part1/Chapter2/StaticAccess/ChildClass.php

Repo: `https://git.io/JRw7I`

```php
<?php

declare(strict_types=1);

namespace Book\Part1\Chapter2\StaticAccess;

final class ChildClass extends ParentClass
{
    protected const ZIP          = '567';
    protected static string $foo = 'boo';
}
```

Here is some code so you can see how this works. Notice that we do not actually instantiate the classes into objects; we are working with the classes directly, calling static methods that access static properties:

src/Part1/Chapter2/static.php

Repo: `https://git.io/JRw7L`

```php
<?php

declare(strict_types=1);

namespace Book\Part1\Chapter2;

use Book\Part1\Chapter2\StaticAccess\ChildClass;
use Book\Part1\Chapter2\StaticAccess\ParentClass;

require __DIR__ . '/../../../vendor/autoload.php';

echo "\n\nParentClass::getStringSelf   = " .
ParentClass::getStringSelf();
echo "\n\nParentClass::getStringStatic = " .
ParentClass::getStringStatic();
echo "\n\nChildClass::getStringSelf    = " .
ChildClass::getStringSelf();
echo "\n\nChildClass::getStringStatic  = " .
ChildClass::getStringStatic();
```

Output:

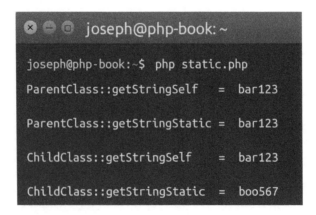

```
joseph@php-book:~$ php static.php
ParentClass::getStringSelf   = bar123

ParentClass::getStringStatic = bar123

ChildClass::getStringSelf    = bar123

ChildClass::getStringStatic  = boo567
```

As you can see, in the parent class, `static` and `self` work the same way; however, when called from the context of the child class, we get different values due to the fact that `static` refers to property values in the context of the child class.

In summary, if you want to prevent overriding, use `self`. If you want to allow overriding, use `static`.

To reiterate, static properties and methods are only useful in certain circumstances. Overuse of static access can bring unnecessary coupling to your code, making it harder to test and refactor. By default, you should always use instance methods and properties.

Let's move on to looking at another way of structuring code that avoids inheritance but still aims to allow easy code reuse: composition.

Composition–the modern, flexible "has a" style

So, inheritance seems great, doesn't it? You can keep your code really **DRY** by defining commonly used functionality in a parent or abstract class and then share that across a huge number of children. That's what a lot of people thought a few years ago, and then they worked on Magento…

What does DRY mean?

DRY stands for "don't repeat yourself" and with regards to coding, it means avoid copy-pasting and duplicating code and instead structure things so that any code that needs to be reused is packaged up in a way that facilitates that. It could be as simple as a global function or constant or could be a full-blown class that encapsulates the bundle of functionality that you want to share.

If we went with the hugely overused analogy of animals when discussing inheritance, then we could define a whole taxonomy with `AbstractOrganism` at the top and then child classes all the way down… `AbstractVertebrate` would have a huge number of child classes, and right at the bottom, we might have the actual plants and animals defined as `final` classes.

The challenge with this kind of structure is that it can be very complicated to understand and very difficult and brittle to work on. A change somewhere high up the chain of inheritance could have unexpected consequences. If you have seen Jurassic Park, then you no doubt remember the discussion where the mathematician is trying to explain chaos. "It simply deals with unpredictability in complex systems," he says. "The shorthand is 'the butterfly effect.' A butterfly can flap its wings in Peking, and in Central Park, you get rain instead of sunshine." You make a minor change in a middle-tier class and cause weird bugs in far-flung areas of your project.

So how can we avoid this kind of complexity? By using composition instead of inheritance. This simply means that we build our classes by composing them from other classes. We remove inheritance as a way of sharing functionality and instead we put that piece of functionality in a class and share that class everywhere the functionality is required. The goal of this approach is to reduce complexity and increase testability.

Have a look at the following code. Do you prefer it?

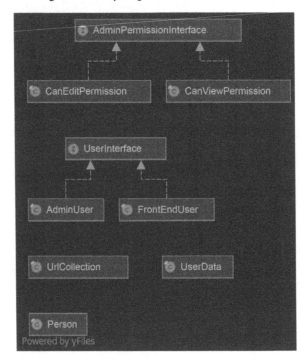

First up, we have a small, final – so not extensible but very easy to read and understand – Person class:

src/Part1/Chapter2/Composition/Person.php

Repo: https://git.io/JRw7q

```php
<?php

declare(strict_types=1);

namespace Book\Part1\Chapter2\Composition;

final class Person
```

```
{
    public function __construct(
        private string $name
    ) {
    }

    public function getName(): string
    {
        return $this->name;
    }
}
```

Next, we have another `final` class. This time, it's a simple collection of strings that represent URLs:

src/Part1/Chapter2/Composition/UrlCollection.php

Repo: `https://git.io/JRw7m`

```php
<?php

declare(strict_types=1);

namespace Book\Part1\Chapter2\Composition;

final class UrlCollection
{
    /** @var string[] */
    private array $urls;

    public function __construct(string ...$urls)
    {
        $this->urls = $urls;
    }

    /** @return string[] */
    public function getUrls(): array
    {
```

```
        return $this->urls;
    }
}
```

Now we have an interface. When using composition over inheritance, the interface becomes a crucial building block that allows us to define a *type* of class. Most importantly, it guarantees that the class must implement a method with a defined signature. In this case, we are using it to store constants related to this type of class (often a good place to keep them), and we define two methods:

src/Part1/Chapter2/Composition/AdminPermission/AdminPermissionInterface.php

Repo: https://git.io/JRw7Y

```php
<?php

declare(strict_types=1);

namespace Book\Part1\Chapter2\Composition\AdminPermission;

interface AdminPermissionInterface
{
    public const CAN_EDIT = 'canEdit';
    public const CAN_VIEW = 'canView';
    public const PERMS    = [
        self::CAN_EDIT,
        self::CAN_VIEW,
    ];

    public function getPermName(): string;

    public function isAllowed(): bool;
}
```

Now we have two implementations of the interface. Of course, this is totally contrived, but hopefully, you can see the point here. First, we have a "can edit" permission:

src/Part1/Chapter2/Composition/AdminPermission/CanEditPermission.php

Repo: https://git.io/JRw7O

```php
<?php

declare(strict_types=1);

namespace Book\Part1\Chapter2\Composition\AdminPermission;

final class CanEditPermission implements
AdminPermissionInterface
{
    public function __construct(
        private bool $allowed
    ) {
    }

    public function getPermName(): string
    {
        return self::CAN_EDIT;
    }

    public function isAllowed(): bool
    {
        return $this->allowed;
    }
}
```

And then we have a "can view" permission, also implementing the interface:

src/Part1/Chapter2/Composition/AdminPermission/CanViewPermission.php

Repo: https://git.io/JRw73

```php
<?php

declare(strict_types=1);
```

```php
namespace Book\Part1\Chapter2\Composition\AdminPermission;

final class CanViewPermission implements
AdminPermissionInterface
{
    public function __construct(
        private bool $allowed
    ) {
    }

    public function getPermName(): string
    {
        return self::CAN_VIEW;
    }

    public function isAllowed(): bool
    {
        return $this->allowed;
    }
}
```

Now we define UserInterface and for the purposes of this silly demo, the classes simply need to implement the magic __toString method:

PHP Manual – Magic Methods

https://www.php.net/manual/en/language.oop5.magic.php

src/Part1/Chapter2/Composition/User/UserInterface.php

Repo: https://git.io/JRw7s

```php
<?php

declare(strict_types=1);

namespace Book\Part1\Chapter2\Composition\User;

interface UserInterface
{
```

```php
    public function __toString();
}
```

To store general data about a user, we have the `UserData` class, which is also composed of a `Person` class. You will hopefully start to see how a kind of inheritance can be built up. `UserData` is another DTO. DTOs can and should be composed of other DTOs:

> **What is a DTO?**
>
> **DTO** stands for **Data Transfer Object**. It is simply an object that has no behavior and whose sole purpose is to be instantiated with data and then passed around. Generally, you would expect a DTO to be immutable, which means that once instantiated, it cannot be updated. This makes it incredibly simple. Simplicity is a good thing and so DTOs are good. Have a go at using them instead of arrays and notice how much more comprehensible your code is when you come back to it.

src/Part1/Chapter2/Composition/User/UserData.php

Repo: `https://git.io/JRw7G`

```php
<?php

declare(strict_types=1);

namespace Book\Part1\Chapter2\Composition\User;

use Book\Part1\Chapter2\Composition\Person;

final class UserData
{
    public function __construct(
        private int $id,
        private Person $person
    ) {
    }

    public function getId(): int
    {
        return $this->id;
```

```
    }

    public function getName(): string
    {
        return $this->person->getName();
    }
}
```

Finally, we have our two `User` implementations. They are this `AdminUser`:

src/Part1/Chapter2/Composition/User/AdminUser.php

Repo: https://git.io/JRw7Z

```php
<?php

declare(strict_types=1);

namespace Book\Part1\Chapter2\Composition\User;

use Book\Part1\Chapter2\Composition\AdminPermission\
AdminPermissionInterface;

final class AdminUser implements UserInterface
{
    /** @var array<string,AdminPermissionInterface> */
    private array $permissions;

    public function __construct(
        private UserData $userData,
        AdminPermissionInterface ...$permissions
    ) {
        \array_map(
            callback: function (AdminPermissionInterface
$perm): void {
                $this->permissions[$perm->getPermName()] =
$perm;
            },
            array: $permissions
```

```php
        );
    }

    public function __toString(): string
    {
        return "\n\nadmin user {$this->userData->getName()}
({$this->userData->getId()}) has these permissions: \n" .
            \implode(
                "\n",
                \array_map(
                    callback: static function (
                        AdminPermissionInterface $perm
                    ): string {
                        $permName = $perm->getPermName();
                        $allowed  = ($perm->isAllowed() ?
'true' : 'false');

                        return "{$permName}: {$allowed}";
                    },
                    array: $this->permissions
                )
            ) . "\n";
    }
}
```

And then our `FrontEndUser`. The point here is that as these are both `User` types, they can share some functionality and data types but are also quite different. By using composition instead of inheritance, we can keep them totally decoupled from each other while still sharing basic functionality through the use of simpler component classes:

src/Part1/Chapter2/Composition/User/FrontEndUser.php

Repo: `https://git.io/JRw7n`

```php
<?php

declare(strict_types=1);

namespace Book\Part1\Chapter2\Composition\User;
```

```php
use Book\Part1\Chapter2\Composition\UrlCollection;

final class FrontEndUser implements UserInterface
{
    public function __construct(
        private UserData $userData,
        private UrlCollection $recentlyViewedPages
    ) {

    }

    public function __toString(): string
    {
        return "front end user {$this->userData->getName()}
({$this->userData->getId()}) has recently viewed: " .
                \print_r($this->recentlyViewedPages->getUrls(),
true);
    }
}
```

And finally, we have the frontend code that pulls all this together:

src/Part1/Chapter2/composition_over_inheritance.php

Repo: https://git.io/JRw7c

```php
<?php

declare(strict_types=1);

namespace Book\Part1\Chapter2;

use Book\Part1\Chapter2\Composition\AdminPermission\
CanEditPermission;
use Book\Part1\Chapter2\Composition\AdminPermission\
CanViewPermission;
use Book\Part1\Chapter2\Composition\Person;
use Book\Part1\Chapter2\Composition\UrlCollection;
use Book\Part1\Chapter2\Composition\User\AdminUser;
```

```php
use Book\Part1\Chapter2\Composition\User\FrontEndUser;
use Book\Part1\Chapter2\Composition\User\UserData;

require __DIR__ . '/../../../vendor/autoload.php';

$frontEndUser = new FrontEndUser(
    new UserData(id: 2, person: new Person(name: 'Steve')),
    new UrlCollection('http://php.com', 'http://something.com')
);
echo $frontEndUser;

$adminUser = new AdminUser(
    new UserData(id: 1, person: new Person(name: 'Joseph')),
    new CanEditPermission(allowed: true),
    new CanViewPermission(allowed: true)
);
echo $adminUser;
```

Output:

```
joseph@php-book: ~

joseph@php-book:~$ php composition_over_inheritance.php
front end user Steve (2) has recently viewed: Array
(
    [0] => http://php.com
    [1] => http://something.com
)


admin user Joseph (1) has these permissions:
canEdit: true
canView: true
```

What you will notice is that, firstly, there is no inheritance at all. All classes are marked as final. What we do have is objects containing (being composed of) other objects by injection in the __construct method. We also have the use of interfaces, which is the way to achieve some of the benefits of inheritance without actually using inheritance. Let's have a closer look at interfaces and how they can be used instead of abstract classes and methods to enforce an API without incurring the complexity of inheritance.

Interfaces instead of abstract classes

You might have noticed that in this code, we have replaced the concept of the `abstract` method with `interface` instead. An interface is a bit like an abstract class, but it contains no functionality at all. Instead, it simply acts as a blueprint of what the class should do. This is defined by the method names, the arguments to those methods, and the return types. You can also specify public constants on interfaces, which can be very useful.

Interfaces can extend other interfaces, and a class can implement one or more interfaces. When we are type hinting in methods and properties, we can hint for the interface rather than the class. This allows us to build really flexible code that can be easily reused across different projects and within different sections of a single project. This is because we don't couple our code to a specific implementation and instead simply define the rules that code must adhere to in order to work with our code but leave the implementation open.

> **What is coupling?**
>
> We use the term "coupling" or "coupled" to describe code that is intrinsically linked to other code in a system. This could be through inheritance, property access, or method/function calls between different classes and code sections.
>
> When code is coupled, changes to one piece are likely to have an effect on other pieces. This can be a source of bugs and lost hours. Talking about changes, we mean changes to the code itself and also changes to the object at runtime.
>
> It's impossible to completely avoid coupling, but it is generally advisable to keep the level of coupling in your code as low as possible.

Due to the fact that interfaces can only hint methods and not properties, we are forced to adopt the style of creating "getters" for all the private or protected properties that we want to expose for public reading. A getter is simply a method that returns the property and by convention is called `getPropertyName`. Thankfully, modern IDEs generally make this very simple with a built-in function to automatically generate getters, so this is no particular hardship.

PHP Manual – Object Interfaces

https://www.php.net/manual/en/language.oop5.interfaces.php

Summary

And this concludes our second chapter. In this chapter, we aimed to learn as much as possible within the space available about the core OOP features of PHP. Firstly, we looked at what encapsulation means and the differences between `private`, `protected`, and `public`. We encouraged you to use `private` as your default, only relaxing this to `protected` as required. `public` properties are not normally encouraged as they break encapsulation.

Next, we looked at how inheritance works in PHP. We started with a very simple example and then built up to a more complex example using `abstract` and `final` to force or prevent inheritance as required. We also used interfaces to enforce classes implementing defined methods.

Finally, we looked at an alternative approach to building a graph of related classes that avoids using inheritance features and instead uses a technique called composition, whereby classes inherit functionality through dependency injection – the class defines what objects it depends on and these are set as constructor parameters, which enforces that they are provided to the class. This is often a much more flexible, easier to test, and less brittle approach and is generally the style that I encourage you to use.

In the next chapter, we are going to have a look at some more advanced OOP topics and features, including the **Standard PHP Library** (**SPL**) and metaprogramming using Reflection.

3
Advanced OOP Features

In this third chapter, we're going to look at some of the more advanced object-oriented language features within PHP 8.

First, we're going to explore the **Standard PHP Library – SPL** for short. This is a collection of built-in classes, interfaces, and functions that provide some highly useful functionality and are guaranteed to be available in your PHP installation.

Next up, we're going to take a look at exceptions and error handling in general. We're going to learn what exceptions are and how we can use them to provide safety and easier debugging for our projects.

Finally, we're going to dip our toes into the mystical and powerful world of meta-programming. This is going to introduce you to the awesome power of reflection, and you will learn how it can empower you to regard code as data and thereby increase your power as a programmer dramatically.

This chapter will cover the following main topics:

- SPL – the Standard PHP Library
- Exceptions and error handling
- Meta-programming with reflection and attributes

As usual, you can find all the code samples for this chapter in the main repo for the book available on GitHub at `https://github.com/PacktPublishing/The-Art-of-Modern-PHP-8`.

SPL – the Standard PHP Library

PHP ships with something called the SPL. Generally, this includes a set of built-in classes, interfaces, and functions that provide foundational features and functionality that you can then use in your own code. The SPL is designed to offer solutions to common problems and is guaranteed to be present in any PHP installation.

Probably the single most utilized SPL feature is `spl_autoload_register`, which we will learn more about later in the book.

As with anything PHP, your first point of reference should be to read the official documentation, which for SPL is located at:

PHP: SPL - Manual

`https://www.php.net/manual/en/book.spl.php`

Data structures

The first items listed in the docs are the SPL data structures:

PHP: Datastructures - Manual

`https://www.php.net/manual/en/spl.datastructures.php`

These are designed to offer more advanced features than the simple array, such as heaps, queues, and linked lists.

Unfortunately, these are not very commonly used. It doesn't take a lot of searching to find articles that can explain why the SPL's data structures are generally avoided. PHP 7 brought big performance improvements to the PHP array, which removed a lot of the pain that might have tempted you to use the SPL data structures.

Generally, the only time you would look at using these would be when you are juggling huge amounts of data and need to find some ways of improving performance and reducing resource usage. If you do need performance because you're working with big data then you could take a look at ext-ds, which is an extension you can add to PHP that provides some performance-optimized data structures. Although it does not have the advantage of being built in by default, it generally performs a lot better than SPL and standard arrays:

GitHub - php-ds/ext-ds: An extension providing efficient data structures for PHP 7

```
https://github.com/php-ds/ext-ds
```

If you really need to go off the deep end in the search for extreme performance, you might want to look at the PHP **Foreign Function Interface** (**FFI**), which allows you to utilize custom C code directly in your PHP code. That means that you could find a particularly performance-sensitive aspect of your app and decide to write it in hugely efficient C.

PHP: FFI - Manual

```
https://www.php.net/manual/en/class.ffi.php
```

Iterators

The most commonly used SPL feature, in my experience, is the iterators. These are like superpowers for the humble `foreach` loop and allow us to iterate over a number of different things, though I have generally seen it being used when iterating over the filesystem in some form.

An iterator is an object that allows data structures to be traversed—to be looped over—in the same way as we can with a normal array.

Unfortunately, like many things in SPL, iterators are not particularly well documented, so you are likely to need to use Stack Overflow to learn more, and do some of your own experiments. But as always, start with the official documentation:

PHP: Iterators - Manual

```
https://www.php.net/manual/en/spl.iterators.php
```

Have a read through the following classes and a final bit of frontend code to see the kinds of things you can do with iterators. It's only scratching the surface, but I think the filesystem is where you are most likely to see them in action.

First up, we have a basic Config **Data Transfer Object** (**DTO**), which is used in the code.

src/Part1/Chapter3/IteratorFun/Config.php

Repo: `https://git.io/JRw7g`

```php
<?php

declare(strict_types=1);
```

```php
namespace Book\Part1\Chapter3\IteratorFun;

final class Config
{
    /** @var string[] */
    private array $subDirs;

    public function __construct(private string $baseDir, string
...$subDirs)
    {
        foreach ($subDirs as $subDir) {
            if (\str_starts_with(
                haystack: $subDir,
                needle: $this->baseDir
            ) === false) {
                $subDir = "{$this->baseDir}/{$subDir}";
            }
            $this->subDirs[] = $subDir;
        }
    }


    /** @return string[] */
    public function getSubDirs(): array
    {
        return $this->subDirs;
    }


    public function getBaseDir(): string
    {
        return $this->baseDir;
    }
}
```

Next, we have a very small trait that can be used to force filesystem iterators to be configured to return the SplFileInfo object. By wrapping this into a trait, we can embed it into any class extending any iterator we need to as required, with no concerns about inheritance.

Traits are an alternative approach to sharing code between classes. They can be quite tricky to understand, but when you need them they can be very useful indeed. Generally, the only time you should use traits is when you need $this to be the current class, and you need to ensure you have access to all private properties and methods.

PHP: Traits - Manual

https://www.php.net/manual/en/language.oop5.traits.php

src/Part1/Chapter3/IteratorFun/CurrentIsFileInfoTrait.php

Repo: https://git.io/JRw72

```php
<?php

declare(strict_types=1);

namespace Book\Part1\Chapter3\IteratorFun;

use RuntimeException;
use SplFileInfo;

trait CurrentIsFileInfoTrait
{
    public function getCurrent(): SplFileInfo
    {
        $current = parent::current();
        if ($current instanceof SplFileInfo) {
            return $current;
        }
        throw new RuntimeException('unexpected current value '

                                        . \var_export($current,
true));
    }
}
```

The next class is a solution to an age-old problem in PHP: how to remove a directory that might not be empty. Unfortunately, there isn't a built-in rm -rf (though people have been known just to exec to that).

PHP: exec - Manual

`https://www.php.net/manual/en/function.exec.php`

Instead, we have to carefully remove all the files and directories inside a directory before trying to remove the directory itself. This class is a solution for this, and it is using iterators, as you can see.

src/Part1/Chapter3/IteratorFun/DirectoryRemover.php

Repo: `https://git.io/JRw7a`

```php
<?php

declare(strict_types=1);

namespace Book\Part1\Chapter3\IteratorFun;

use FilesystemIterator;
use RuntimeException;
use SplFileInfo;

/**
 * Unfortunately PHP has no built in equivalent to rm -rf
 * We can't remove directories that have contents so we have to
actually go
 * and remove all directory contents before we can remove the
directory.
 *
 * This class will handle that recursively, and we're using an
Iterator to
 * help, along with the SplFileInfo
 */
final class DirectoryRemover
{
    public function removeDir(string $path): void
    {
        if (!\is_dir($path)) {
            return;
        }
```

```
        $traversable = $this->getIterator($path);
        foreach ($traversable as $item) {
            if (false === ($item instanceof SplFileInfo)) {
                throw new RuntimeException(
                    message: 'Iterator badly configured,
                    must be set to return SplFileInfo objects
with CURRENT_AS_FILEINFO'
                );
            }
            if ($item->isDir()) {
                // at this point, we start to recurse
                $this->removeDir($item->getPathname());
                // then the directory is empty and we can
remove it
                \rmdir($item->getPathname());
            }
            if ($item->isFile()) {
                \unlink($item->getPathname());
            }
        }
    }

    private function getIterator(string $path):
FilesystemIterator
    {
        /**
         * The CURRENT_AS_FILEINFO informs the
FileSystemIterator to give us SplFileInfo objects
         * instead of plain path strings.
         *
         * The SKIP_DOTS flag means that it skips the ./ and
../ items
         */
        $flags = FilesystemIterator::CURRENT_AS_FILEINFO |
FilesystemIterator::SKIP_DOTS;

        /*
```

```
        * Creating a new anonymous class that extends the SPL
FilesystemIterator
            * and allows us to include our trait
        */
        return new class(directory: $path, flags: $flags)
extends FilesystemIterator {
            /*
            * We are overriding the FileSystemIterator and
enforcing that current()
            * will always return the SplFileInfo
            * and for brevity this is using an anonymous class
and a trait
            */
            use CurrentIsFileInfoTrait;
        };
    }
}
```

Now we have a class that will create files for us. It will recurse through the directory tree and create a file at each level. We have implemented a simple toggle so that we have a roughly even split of files prefixed with blue_ or green_.

src/Part1/Chapter3/IteratorFun/FileCreator.php

Repo: https://git.io/JRw7V

```php
<?php

declare(strict_types=1);

namespace Book\Part1\Chapter3\IteratorFun;

use RecursiveDirectoryIterator;
use RecursiveIteratorIterator;
use RuntimeException;
use SplFileInfo;

final class FileCreator
{
```

```php
    private bool $toggle = false;


    /** @var bool[] */
    private array $visited;


    /**
     * First we create our working directories
     * Then we loop over our iterator and create a file in each
nested
     * directory We include some sanity checks to ensure that
we don't hit
     * the same directory twice, and that we don't wander
outside the base
     * directory for any reason.
     *
     * Our return value is an array of the paths to all the
files that we
     * have created
     *
     * @return string[]
     */
    public function createNestedFiles(Config $config): array
    {
        $this->makeDirs($config);
        $created = [];
        foreach ($this->getIterator($config) as $fileInfo) {
            /** @var SplFileInfo $fileInfo */
            if ($this->visited($fileInfo) === true) {
                continue;
            }
            if ($this->valid($fileInfo, $config) === false) {
                continue;
            }
            $created[] = $this->createFile($fileInfo);
        }

        return $created;
```

```php
    }

    private function makeDirs(Config $config): void
    {
        foreach ($config->getSubDirs() as $subDir) {
            $this->makeDir($subDir);
        }
    }

    private function makeDir(string $path): void
    {
        if (
            !\mkdir($path, 0777, true)
            && !\is_dir($path)
        ) {
            throw new RuntimeException(
                \sprintf(
                    'Directory "%s" was not created',
                    $path
                )
            );
        }
    }

    /**
     * @return
RecursiveIteratorIterator<RecursiveDirectoryIterator>
     */
    private function getIterator(Config $config):
RecursiveIteratorIterator
    {
        /*
         * First we create a RecursiveDirectoryIterator which
will allow us
         * to iterate over a nested structure of files and
folders.
         */
```

```php
        $directoryIterator = new RecursiveDirectoryIterator(
            directory: $config->getBaseDir(),
            flags: RecursiveDirectoryIterator::SKIP_DOTS
        );

        /*
         * Then we build an instance of
RecursiveIteratorIterator which is required
         * to allow us to iterate over the
RecursiveDirectoryIterator
         *
         * The SELF_FIRST flag means that we list the directory
and then the files in there.
         */
        return new RecursiveIteratorIterator(
            iterator: $directoryIterator,
            mode: RecursiveIteratorIterator::SELF_FIRST
        );
    }

    /**
     * As we are actively creating files, it can cause us to
hit the same
     * path multiple times This check ensures we only hit a
single directory
     * once.
     */
    private function visited(SplFileInfo $fileInfo): bool
    {
        $path = $fileInfo->getPathname();
        if (isset($this->visited[$path])) {
            return true;
        }
        $this->visited[$path] = true;

        return false;
    }
```

```php
    /**
     * We check to confirm the file is in the right place and
also that it is
     * a directory.
     */
    private function valid(SplFileInfo $fileInfo, Config
$config): bool
    {
        return \str_starts_with(
            haystack: $fileInfo->getPathname(),
            needle: $config->getBaseDir()
        ) && $fileInfo->isDir() === true;
    }


    /**
     * We create a file in the specified directory path
     * with a known prefix of blue/green and then some random
characters.
     */
    private function createFile(SplFileInfo $fileInfo): string
    {
        $path   = $fileInfo->getPathname();
        $prefix = ($this->toggle = !$this->toggle) ? 'blue_' :
'green_';

        $filename = \tempnam($path, $prefix);
        if ($filename === false) {
            throw new RuntimeException('Failed creating file at
' . $path);
        }

        return $filename;
    }
}
```

And now we have a class that will loop through the files and directories we have created and filter them so that we get a list of the files prefixed with `blue_`.

src/Part1/Chapter3/IteratorFun/FilterBlueFiles.php

Repo: `https://git.io/JRw7w`

```php
<?php

declare(strict_types=1);

namespace Book\Part1\Chapter3\IteratorFun;

use FilterIterator;
use RecursiveDirectoryIterator;
use RecursiveIteratorIterator;
use SplFileInfo;

final class FilterBlueFiles
{
    public const FILTER_MATCH = 'blue';

    /** @return SplFileInfo[] */
    public function getFilteredFiles(Config $config): array
    {
        $filterIterator = $this->getIterator($config);

        /*
         * The iterator to array function effectively loops
         * through our iterator and provides the result as an
array
         */
        return \iterator_to_array($filterIterator);
    }

    private function getIterator(Config $config):
FilterIterator
    {
```

```php
        $directoryIterator = new RecursiveDirectoryIterator(
            directory: $config->getBaseDir()
        );


        /*
         * Creating a new anonymous class that is inheriting from
         * the SPL FilterIterator abstract class
         */
        return new class(new
RecursiveIteratorIterator($directoryIterator)) extends
FilterIterator {
            /**
             * Implementing the abstract method in FilterIterator
             * with our custom logic to only accept blue files.
             */
            public function accept(): bool
            {
                $current = $this->current();
                if ($current->isDir()) {
                    return false;
                }

                return $this->isBlue(filename: $current->getBasename());
            }

            private function isBlue(string $filename): bool
            {
                return \str_contains(
                    haystack: $filename,
                    needle: FilterBlueFiles::FILTER_MATCH
                );
            }
        };
```

```
        }
    }
```

And finally, the frontend code to pull all of this together is as follows.

src/Part1/Chapter3/iterator.php

Repo: `https://git.io/JRw7r`

```php
<?php

declare(strict_types=1);

namespace Book\Part1\Chapter3;

use Book\Part1\Chapter3\IteratorFun\Config;
use Book\Part1\Chapter3\IteratorFun\DirectoryRemover;
use Book\Part1\Chapter3\IteratorFun\FileCreator;
use Book\Part1\Chapter3\IteratorFun\FilterBlueFiles;
use Book\Part1\Chapter3\IteratorFun\Tree;
use RuntimeException;

require __DIR__ . '/../../../vendor/autoload.php';

const TMP_DIR = __DIR__ . '/../../../var/';
if (!\is_dir(filename: TMP_DIR)
    && \mkdir(directory: TMP_DIR, recursive: true)
    && !\is_dir(filename: TMP_DIR)
) {
    throw new RuntimeException(
        \sprintf(
            'Directory "%s" was not created',
            TMP_DIR
        )
    );
}

$config = new Config(TMP_DIR . '/iterator-fun', 'foo/bar/baz',
```

```php
'doo/dar/daz');

/*
 * First we use the DirectoryRemover to clean up any previous
run
 */
(new DirectoryRemover())->removeDir($config->getBaseDir());

/*
 * Next we recreate our directory structure
 * And we iterate through the nested structure and create a
temp file in each level
 */
(new FileCreator())->createNestedFiles($config);

/*
 * Tree after first recursive pass through and creating temp
files:
 */
echo "\nCreated File Tree:\n";
echo (new Tree())->getAsciiTree($config->getBaseDir());

/**
 * Now we're going to loop over the directory again using a
filter to pull
 * out blue only.
 */
$files = (new FilterBlueFiles())->getFilteredFiles($config);
echo "\n\nFiltered Blue Files:\n";
foreach ($files as $i) {
    echo "\n " . $i->getRealPath();
}
```

Output:

```
joseph@php-book: ~

joseph@php-book:~$ php iterator.php
Created File Tree:

|-/foo
|  |-/foo/blue_VfaMz2
|  \-/foo/bar
|     |-/foo/bar/baz
|     |  \-/foo/bar/baz/blue_zsOgSm
|     \-/foo/bar/green_XX60IH
\-/doo
   |-/doo/green_NADx11
   \-/doo/dar
      |-/doo/dar/daz
      |  \-/doo/dar/daz/green_DLw7jm
      \-/doo/dar/blue_LgfPaH

Filtered Blue Files:

 /home/book_ops/php-book-code/var/iterator-fun/foo/blue_VfaMz2
 /home/book_ops/php-book-code/var/iterator-fun/foo/bar/baz/blue_zsOgSm
 /home/book_ops/php-book-code/var/iterator-fun/doo/dar/blue_LgfPaH
```

And so ends our whistle-stop tour of iterators and the SPL. There is much more to learn here, and I encourage you to go and play with these features.

Now, let's move on to learning about what happens when things go wrong. Let's learn all about exceptions.

Exceptions and error handling

An exception in modern PHP is an object that represents the data for a particular error condition. Exceptions are not generally created with `create` but instead they are thrown, as in they are created and unleashed with one magic keyword: `throw`.

If you don't know about exceptions, it's time to hit the docs:

PHP: Exceptions - Manual

`https://www.php.net/manual/en/language.exceptions.php`

Once an exception is thrown, then it must be caught or it will become a `Fatal Error`. I always imagine it a bit like setting off the timer on a bomb. The bomb gets passed from handler to handler until it either hits someone who has the right tools to disable it, or we run out of `layers` that can possibly handle it and it goes off… boom.

We catch exceptions with the `catch` keyword. The `catch` keyword is always used with a type hint for what kind of exceptions it will catch. This can be quite specific, or can be totally general by hinting for `Throwable`, which is the interface implemented by all PHP exceptions and built-in error classes.

If you want to see the full tree of built-in classes and interfaces that descend from the root `Throwable` interface, this code snippet will show you the full hierarchy:

src/Part1/Chapter3/throwables.php

Repo: `https://git.io/JRw7o`

```php
<?php

declare(strict_types=1);

namespace Book\Part1\Chapter3;

$tree = [];
foreach (\get_declared_classes() as $item) {
    $implements = \class_implements($item);
    if ($implements === false) {
        continue;
    }
    if (\array_key_exists(key: 'Throwable', array:
$implements)) {
        $parent          = (string)\get_parent_class($item);
        $tree[$parent][] = $item;
    }
}
/** @param array<string, mixed> $tree */
function printTree(array $tree, string $parent = '', int $level
= 0): void
{
    if (isset($tree[$parent]) === false) {
        return;
    }
    $leaves = $tree[$parent];
    \natcasesort($leaves);
```

```
    $pad    = \str_repeat(' ', $level);
    foreach ($leaves as $leaf) {
        echo "{$pad}  {$leaf}\n";
        printTree($tree, $leaf, $level + 1);
    }
}

printTree($tree);
```

Output:

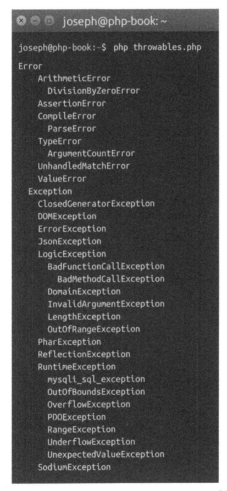

```
joseph@php-book: ~

joseph@php-book:~$ php throwables.php
Error
    ArithmeticError
        DivisionByZeroError
    AssertionError
    CompileError
      ParseError
    TypeError
        ArgumentCountError
    UnhandledMatchError
    ValueError
  Exception
    ClosedGeneratorException
    DOMException
    ErrorException
    JsonException
    LogicException
        BadFunctionCallException
            BadMethodCallException
        DomainException
        InvalidArgumentException
        LengthException
        OutOfRangeException
    PharException
    ReflectionException
    RuntimeException
        mysqli_sql_exception
        OutOfBoundsException
        OverflowException
        PDOException
        RangeException
        UnderflowException
        UnexpectedValueException
    SodiumException
```

The mechanism for catching exceptions is to use a `try`/`catch` block, optionally with a `finally` on the end.

Have a look at the following code to see how you can define your own exception classes and hopefully understand how they can be caught by specifying catch blocks with specified types to catch.

We defined two custom Exception classes, the first of which is BarException.

src/Part1/Chapter3/ExceptionSimple/BarException.php

Repo: https://git.io/JRw7K

```php
<?php

declare(strict_types=1);

namespace Book\Part1\Chapter3\ExceptionSimple;

use Exception;

final class BarException extends Exception
{
}
```

Then we define FooException. Yes, I'm being creative with the naming. I hope you are enjoying it.

src/Part1/Chapter3/ExceptionSimple/FooException.php

Repo: https://git.io/JRw76

```php
<?php

declare(strict_types=1);

namespace Book\Part1\Chapter3\ExceptionSimple;

use Exception;

final class FooException extends Exception
{
}
```

We also have a standalone class that implements the magic __invoke method, meaning it operates like a `callable`, or basically like a function.

PHP: Magic Methods - Manual

`https://www.php.net/manual/en/language.oop5.magic.php`

src/Part1/Chapter3/ExceptionSimple/Dumper.php

Repo: `https://git.io/JRw7i`

```php
<?php

declare(strict_types=1);

namespace Book\Part1\Chapter3\ExceptionSimple;

use Throwable;

/**
 * This is a special kind of object. It acts just like a function as it
 * implements the magic __invoke method.
 */
final class Dumper
{
    public function __invoke(Throwable $throwable): string
    {
        return "
Caught {$this->getClass($throwable)} with message:

{$throwable->getMessage()}

Stack Trace:
{$throwable->getTraceAsString()}
";
    }

    private function getClass(Throwable $throwable): string
```

```
    {
        return $throwable::class;
    }
}
```

To illustrate the point and use the previous exceptions, we have some code that is going to bring in those custom classes and then throw a BarException, which will then get caught in the first block, which is configured to catch either of our custom exceptions.

I have included the extra catch blocks purely to illustrate how your catch blocks would generally widen in scope until you finally try to catch Throwable, which basically means any catchable error. It is the broadest thing you can try to catch in PHP.

We have a finally block, which will always get executed no matter which catch is utilized. You might use this for things such as gracefully closing database connections, writing session and log data, and that kind of thing.

src/Part1/Chapter3/exception_simple.php

Repo: https://git.io/JRw7P

```php
<?php

declare(strict_types=1);

namespace Book\Part1\Chapter3;

use Book\Part1\Chapter3\ExceptionSimple\BarException;
use Book\Part1\Chapter3\ExceptionSimple\Dumper;
use Book\Part1\Chapter3\ExceptionSimple\FooException;
use Exception;
use Throwable;

require __DIR__ . '/../../../vendor/autoload.php';

$dumper = new Dumper();

try {
```

```php
        throw new BarException('something went wrong');
    } catch (FooException | BarException $superCustomException) {
        echo '
This block is going to be executed, because we have caught one
of the specific exception types we are catching
';
        echo $dumper($superCustomException);
    } catch (Exception $exception) {
        echo 'This block will not be executed, because the
exception has already been caught';
        echo $dumper($exception);
    } catch (Throwable $throwable) {
        echo 'This block will not be executed, because the
exception has already been caught';
        echo $dumper($throwable);
    } finally {
        echo '
The finally block always happens..
';
    }
```

Output:

```
joseph@php-book: ~

joseph@php-book:~$ php exception_simple.php
This block is going to be executed, because we have caught one of the
specific exception types we are catching

Caught Book\Part1\Chapter3\ExceptionSimple\BarException with message:

something went wrong

Stack Trace:
#0 {main}

The finally block always happens..
```

Note that we can define multiple exception classes to be caught in a single catch block using the | symbol to separate them.

Yoda and Pokemon exception handling

Something that is *infuriating* when you find it after spending hours to debug something is the silenced exception.

These are sometimes called the following:

- **Yoda exception handling** – *"Do or do not. There is no try."*
- **Pokemon exception handling** – *"Pokemon - gotta catch 'em all"*

To describe what this looks like, have a look at this:

src/Part1/Chapter3/yoda.php

Repo: `https://git.io/JRw7X`

```php
<?php

declare(strict_types=1);

namespace Book\Part1\Chapter3;

try {
    echo "\nStarting process";
    echo "\nAbout to do something really silly...";
    $ohno = \substr([], 1);
} catch (\Throwable) {
    // do nothing,
    // leave no trace in debug logs,
    // no breadcrumbs for weary developer to find their way
    // literally no way to figure out what is going on than to
read the code
    // or step through debug to figure out what is going on
}
echo "\nAnd continue, just assuming everything is fine...";
```

Output:

```
joseph@php-book: ~

joseph@php-book:~$ php yoda.php

Starting process
About to do something really silly...
And continue, just assuming everything is fine...
```

If I work with you and you do this, you probably won't be working with me for much longer...

Now you have learned a bit about exceptions, let's see how we can ensure that we never have to deal with legacy PHP errors/warnings/notices anymore.

Exception and error handling best practices

Once you start to use exceptions, you will realize that they are amazing and you will want to ensure that all your errors are exceptions. Most internal PHP errors are now exceptions and, generally, frameworks and platforms will ensure all errors are exceptions.

PHP: Errors in PHP 7 - Manual

```
https://www.php.net/manual/en/language.errors.php7.php
```

However, due to PHP's long life and incumbent legacy, that is not the case by default. If you want to ensure that all errors become exceptions that you can handle, then you need to implement some boilerplate. Every single OOP framework or project I have seen does this for you, but it is worth knowing how to do it and what is going on.

The trick here is the use of two built-in functions. `set_error_handler` allows us to define some custom userland code to be called whenever an old-fashioned PHP error/warning/notice is triggered.

PHP: set_error_handler - Manual

```
https://www.php.net/manual/en/function.set-error-handler.php
```

`set_exception_handler` allows us to define some custom userland code to be called whenever an exception or `Throwable` is not caught anywhere else and has bubbled through all the way to becoming a `Fatal Error`.

PHP: set_exception_handler - Manual

```
https://www.php.net/manual/en/function.set-exception-handler.
php
```

src/Part1/Chapter3/custom_error_handler.php

Repo: https://git.io/JRw7D

```php
<?php

declare(strict_types=1);

namespace Book\Part1\Chapter3;

use ErrorException;
use stdClass;
use Throwable;

/*
 * This bit of magic boilerplate will turn any old fashioned PHP error
 * into an ErrorException which you can then catch in your code.
 */
\set_error_handler(static function (
    int $severity,
    string $message,
    string $file,
    int $line
): bool {
    if (0 === (\error_reporting() & $severity)) {
        return true;
    }
    throw new ErrorException($message, 0, $severity, $file, $line);
});

/*
```

```php
 * This bit of magic boilerplate becomes your ultimate fallback
 * should any exceptions bubble past all the catch blocks in
your code.
 */
\set_exception_handler(static function (
    Throwable $throwable
): void {
    if (isset($_SERVER['DEBUG_MODE']) === false) {
        echo '

    An error has occurred,


        please look at a happy picture whilst our engineers fix
this for you :)


';


        return;
    }
    echo '


You are clearly a developer, please see a load of useful debug
info:

' . \var_export($throwable, true);
});


echo '


And now to do something silly to trigger a PHP error....

';
echo \substr(string: new stdClass(), offset: 'cheese');
```

Output:

```
🅧 ⊖ ⊟    joseph@php-book: ~

joseph@php-book:~$ php custom_error_handler.php
And now to do something silly to trigger a PHP error....


        An error has occurred,

        please look at a happy picture whilst our engineers fix this
for you :)
```

What the previous code is doing is transforming any old-fashioned PHP error/warning/ notice into a proper exception and then also defining a catch-all exception handler. With this kind of approach, we can ensure that users will always get something usable, even if it's just a silly "under construction" animated GIF, or a picture of a whale, or a confused robot...

Further, we can intelligently log and notify of the error, capturing large amounts of information that is hugely useful when debugging.

We could also at this point do things like sending Slack notifications or even automatically creating issues in an issue tracker.

While this is educational, I strongly suggest you don't reinvent the wheel and instead have a look at an existing implementation.

Have a look at the following:

GitHub - symfony/error-handler: The ErrorHandler component provides tools to manage errors and ease debugging PHP code.

```
https://github.com/symfony/error-handler
```

And also take a look at this:

GitHub - filp/whoops: PHP errors for cool kids

```
https://github.com/filp/whoops
```

Another library worth a mention with regard to modernizing PHP error handling is this one:

GitHub - thecodingmachine/safe: All PHP functions, rewritten to throw exceptions instead of returning false

```
https://github.com/thecodingmachine/safe
```

Now that you have learned a bit about exceptions, let's get to the last topic for this chapter and dip our toes into meta-programming.

Meta-programming with reflection and attributes

The phrase "meta-programming" describes a technique where your code and runtime become data that you can work with. It can be a bit mind-bending, but also awesomely powerful.

Reflection

PHP comes with something called reflection, which allows you to examine your code and objects at runtime.

PHP: Reflection - Manual

`https://www.php.net/manual/en/book.reflection.php`

I think the name "reflection" is really apt. It brings to mind a monk, meditating on their own nature and searching for a path to enlightenment.

Reflection is most useful in library code and is used extensively in projects such as Doctrine ORM (which you really should have a look at if you want to work with databases).

GitHub - doctrine/orm: Doctrine Object Relational Mapper (ORM)

`https://github.com/doctrine/orm`

Let's have a look at some simple code using reflection to meddle with a simple PHP class.

First, we have our simple PHP class.

src/Part1/Chapter3/ReflectionFun/Kid.php

Repo: `https://git.io/JRw7y`

```php
<?php

declare(strict_types=1);

namespace Book\Part1\Chapter3\ReflectionFun;
```

```php
final class Kid
{
    public function __construct(
        private string $name,
        private int $age
    ) {
    }

    public function getName(): string
    {
        return $this->name;
    }

    public function getAge(): int
    {
        return $this->age;
    }

    private function nameChange(string $newName): void
    {
        $this->name = $newName;
    }
}
```

And now we have some code that will create an instance of `ReflectionObject` from the instance of the `Kid` class, and from there demonstrate some of the power of this kind of programming.

PHP: ReflectionObject - Manual

https://www.php.net/manual/en/class.reflectionobject.php

Code Executable Snippet

```php
<?php

declare(strict_types=1);

namespace Book\Part1\Chapter3;
```

```php
use Book\Part1\Chapter3\ReflectionFun\Kid;
use ReflectionObject;


require __DIR__ . '/../../../vendor/autoload.php';


echo "
We're going to take an example object, nothing fancy
";
$instance = new Kid('Anna', 9);


$reflection = new ReflectionObject($instance);


echo '
You can get information about a class/object, such as the class
methods
';
foreach ($reflection->getMethods() as $method) {
    echo "\n - {$method->name}";
}
echo "

And now watch as we do things that you would not normally think
is possible,


We're taking a private method and invoking it from outside the
scope of the object.


";


echo '
Her name is ' . $instance->getName();


$method = $reflection->getMethod('nameChange');
$method->setAccessible(true);
$method->invoke($instance, 'Gwenn');
```

```
echo '
And now her name is ' . $instance->getName();
```

Output:

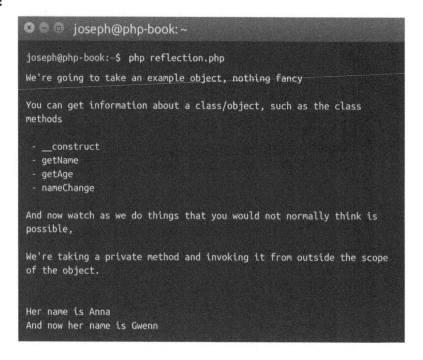

Attributes

If you want to take your meta-programming to the next level, then it is time to take a look at attributes, a new feature that has come in with PHP 8.

PHP: Attributes overview - Manual

https://www.php.net/manual/en/language.attributes.overview.php

Attributes allow you to attach real PHP code to your code to create dynamic metadata and empower all kinds of interesting things.

Let's have a look at some code.

First up, we have our attribute class itself. Note that this also has an attribute that marks this class to PHP as being one that can be used as an attribute on other classes.

src/Part1/Chapter3/Attributes/WrittenByAttribute.php

Repo: `https://git.io/JRw7S`

```php
<?php

declare(strict_types=1);

namespace Book\Part1\Chapter3\Attributes;

use Attribute;

/*
 * This class is the attribute itself. It has the magical
`#[Attribute]` attribute which marks it as such
 */

#[Attribute]
final class WrittenByAttribute
{
    public function __construct(
        private string $name
    ) {
    }

    public function getName(): string
    {
        return $this->name;
    }
}
```

Then we have three simple classes that define `WrittenByAttribute`.

src/Part1/Chapter3/Attributes/Bar.php

Repo: `https://git.io/JRw79`

```php
<?php

declare(strict_types=1);

namespace Book\Part1\Chapter3\Attributes;

#[WrittenByAttribute('Jane')]
final class Bar
{
}
```

src/Part1/Chapter3/Attributes/Baz.php

Repo: `https://git.io/JRw7H`

```php
<?php

declare(strict_types=1);

namespace Book\Part1\Chapter3\Attributes;

#[WrittenByAttribute('Steve')]
final class Baz
{
}
```

src/Part1/Chapter3/Attributes/Foo.php

Repo: `https://git.io/JRw7Q`

```php
<?php

declare(strict_types=1);
```

```php
namespace Book\Part1\Chapter3\Attributes;


#[WrittenByAttribute('Joseph')]
final class Foo
{
}
```

And finally, we have some code to loop over these classes, reflect on them, and get an instance of the attribute class.

src/Part1/Chapter3/attributes.php

Repo: `https://git.io/JRw77`

```php
<?php


declare(strict_types=1);


namespace Book\Part1\Chapter3;


require __DIR__ . '/../../../vendor/autoload.php';


use Book\Part1\Chapter3\Attributes\Bar;
use Book\Part1\Chapter3\Attributes\Baz;
use Book\Part1\Chapter3\Attributes\Foo;
use Book\Part1\Chapter3\Attributes\WrittenByAttribute;
use ReflectionClass;
use RuntimeException;


/*
 * Now we can loop over the classes
 * and dynamically pull out the attribute,
 * get an instance of the attribute
 * and then call methods on it
 */
foreach ([Foo::class, Bar::class, Baz::class] as $class) {
    $reflectionAttributes = (new ReflectionClass($class))->getAttributes(WrittenByAttribute::class);
```

```
    $reflectionAttribute = $reflectionAttributes[0]
                            ?? throw new
 RuntimeException('Failed getting attribute for ' . $class);


    $writtenBy = $reflectionAttribute->newInstance();


    /** @var WrittenByAttribute $writtenBy */
    echo "\nClass " . $class . ' was written by ' . $writtenBy-
>getName();
}
```

Output:

```
joseph@php-book: ~

joseph@php-book:~$ php attributes.php
Class Book\Part1\Chapter3\Attributes\Foo was written by Joseph
Class Book\Part1\Chapter3\Attributes\Bar was written by Jane
Class Book\Part1\Chapter3\Attributes\Baz was written by Steve
```

So, as you can see, we defined three classes and used the `WrittenBy` attribute to provide meta-information for us when we reflect on that code. Of course, this example is contrived, but hopefully you can appreciate the power and utility of this new feature in PHP 8.

Annotations

Many of you might have come across structured comment-based annotations in PHP code. These have been in common usage for some time. The library that is generally used to parse these is Doctrine Annotations.

GitHub - doctrine/annotations: Annotations Docblock Parser

```
https://github.com/doctrine/annotations
```

Doctrine Annotations was always a very clever solution to emulate a language feature that PHP didn't provide but there was a clear use case for.

Doctrine Annotations are amazing, although, being based on comments, they suffered from various pitfalls due to the fact that they are, at the end of the day, just comments. Here's some examples:

- Certain opcache configurations will simply remove comments from code before caching, which will break your annotations.

- When refactoring, you may find that your IDE does not do a great job of tracking down annotations that reference class names.

- You might find that IDEs and other tools will remove seemingly unused use statements that are actually required for your annotation to work.

These are all symptoms of the fact that the annotations approach is really pushing the limits of what comments are really for and, at the end of the day, they simply are not a first-class language feature.

I fully expect attributes to become the standard approach for this kind of meta programming and expect comment-based annotations to gradually wither away once code bases can demand PHP 8 as a minimum version. You can already see modern frameworks such as Symfony adding attribute support.

New in Symfony 5.2: PHP 8 attributes (Symfony Blog)

```
https://symfony.com/blog/new-in-symfony-5-2-php-8-attributes
```

Summary

That brings us to the end of this chapter and the end of *Part 1*. Let's have a quick reminder of what we have covered in this part and this chapter.

We started with a very quick overview of what **object-oriented programming** (**OOP**) actually means, and we clarified this by comparing it with some other programming styles. Next, we looked at some existing frameworks and platforms that you might work with that are written in OO PHP.

Then we had a good explore of how the inheritance model works, touched on how abstract, final classes and methods can be used to allow or prohibit inheritability, and looked at a contrived example of some inheritance-based code.

In contrast to inheritance, we explored composition, building classes using instances of other classes, and trying to keep classes small and tightly focused. More modern PHP tends to favor this approach as it brings multiple benefits in legibility, testability, and flexibility.

We moved then to have a very quick look at the SPL, with a deeper dive into iterators. Though we really only scratched the surface, I hope you took the opportunity to further familiarize yourself with this built-in functionality.

Next up was a look at what happens when things go wrong, with a particular focus on the more modern OO style of error conditions being handled as exceptions, and the ways we can catch them. We looked at the basic strategy employed by most modern PHP to ensure that all error conditions become exceptions, even if there is some deeper legacy PHP internal code that throws old-fashioned warnings or notices.

And finally, we had a very brief look at meta-programming, utilizing the built-in reflection functionality. We had a quick look at the new-to-PHP 8 attributes that transform the meta-programming style into a first-class feature of PHP.

I hope you found it useful and managed to take it in. In the next part of this book, we are going to explore types—something that has become integral to modern PHP.

Section 2 – PHP Types

Modern PHP, since version 7, is very much about types. In this section, you will learn all about the different types and the type system in PHP. Note that PHP 8 brought in some specific changes that we will cover. By the end of this section, you should have an excellent overall understanding of types in modern PHP.

This section contains the following chapters:

- *Chapter 4, Scalar, Arrays, and Special Types*
- *Chapter 5, Object Types, Interfaces, and Unions*
- *Chapter 6, Parameter, Property, and Return Types*

4
Scalar, Arrays, and Special Types

Welcome to *Section 2*. In this part of the book, we are going to look at something that has become much more of a first-class feature in modern PHP: types.

The release of PHP 7 marked a significant turning point in the history of PHP. It ended a long period of stagnation that included the abandonment of a whole version – PHP 6. With PHP 7, we got some significant and highly useful changes to the language, and one of those was the introduction of scalar type declarations:

PHP: New features - Manual

```
https://www.php.net/manual/en/migration70.new-features.php
```

PHP 7 brought the advent of scalar type hints and strict type checking. This allowed us to write code with a clearer API and built-in assurances that parameters are at least of the correct type, which allowed a significant reduction in boilerplate code to confirm parameters are correct. It also brought in the concept of return types. These two added features tipped the balance quite significantly and made modern PHP a much safer, clearer, and less verbose language.

In this chapter, we will look in detail at scalar types, arrays, and iterables, and the "nothing" nullable, void, and uninitialized types, and we will briefly look at resources.

In *Chapter 5, Object Types, Interfaces and Unions,* we will look at object types, object type inheritance, and object references. We will learn about the difference between object equality and object identity and will learn about how object variables are really just references to a single instance.

In *Chapter 6, Parameter, Property and Return Types,* we will look at parameter and return types and try to get our head around the concepts of contravariance and covariance, including trying to remember which is which.

Alongside reading this part of the book, you are strongly encouraged to have a thorough read through the official docs:

PHP: Introduction - Manual

`https://www.php.net/manual/en/language.types.intro.php`

With a proper understanding of types and type hinting in PHP, you can write code that is clear and self-documenting. You can also help to avoid numerous pitfalls and hairloss-inducing bugs that are inherent to a loosely typed language such as PHP.

If you are not clear what we are talking about when referring to types, we suggest you have a look at this Wikipedia page:

> **Data type - Wikipedia**
> `https://w.wiki/wow`
>
> In computer science and computer programming, a data type, or simply type, is an attribute of data that tells the compiler or interpreter how the programmer intends to use the data.

While PHP has only relatively recently started to bring typing concepts more strongly to the fore, it has always been true that any variable, at any time, has a specific type. You can always get the type of any variable with the `gettype` function. *Well, apart from resources, but we'll get to that...*

PHP: gettype - Manual

`https://www.php.net/manual/en/function.gettype.php`

This chapter will cover the following main topics:

- Scalar types
- Arrays and iterables
- Nullable, void, and uninitialized
- Resources

As usual, you can find all the code samples for this chapter in the main repo for the book available on GitHub at `https://github.com/PacktPublishing/The-Art-of-Modern-PHP-8`

Let's kick off with the basics and look at scalar types.

Scalar types

The first kind of type to get your head around is what is called "scalar." This is a fancy way of saying "simple." The best way to think of "scalar" types is as opposed to "compound" types. A scalar is not made of anything else; it is the smallest unit of data.

According to someone more learned than me on Stack Overflow, the term "scalar" comes from linear algebra, where it means a single number as opposed to a vector or matrix. I'm not a linear algebra specialist, so let's just take it that scalar means the opposite of complex.

The scalar types are as follows:

- `string`
- `int`
- `float`
- `bool`

If you want to check dynamically whether a variable is scalar, PHP has a function for that:

PHP: is_scalar - Manual

`https://www.php.net/manual/en/function.is-scalar.php`

Let's have a quick look through the scalar types in PHP.

Strings

String is the name for textual content. You tend to use strings a lot and being a language that is mostly used to spit out HTML strings, PHP comes with a lot of ways of working with strings.

Have a look at the docs page dedicated to strings:

PHP: Strings - Manual

`https://www.php.net/manual/en/language.types.string.php`

Creating strings

As the docs show, there are four ways to directly create a new string variable. The first thing you should decide when creating your string is whether you intend to embed other things in it, or you are happy for it to just be hardcoded text.

If you want to define hardcoded text, then you should use one of the following:

- `single quoted`
- `NOWDOC:`

src/Part2/Chapter4/string_create_single_quoted_nowdoc.php

Repo: `https://git.io/JRwd3`

```php
<?php

declare(strict_types=1);

namespace Book\Part2\Chapter4;

/**
 * Don't want to embed anything in the string.
 */
$singleQuoted =
    'This is a single quoted string. It can contain all kind of
characters such as $"\n#, '
    . ';nothing will happen, the raw characters will just be
included in your string.'
    . ' This makes it a very safe one to use. The main time it
gets annoying, '
    . 'is when you want your string to contain \' characters, '
    . 'as then you have to remember to escape them with \\';
echo "\n{$singleQuoted}\n";

$nowDoc = <<<'DELIM'
    This is a NOWDOC string. The definition looks more verbose
than single quoted, and you have to type a few more characters.
    What you get in return though is that you can include all
''' you want with no escaping.
    You can include all the $%"\n' special characters you want
```

```
and they will just be included in the string as is
    DELIM;
echo "\n{$nowDoc}\n";
```

Output:

```
joseph@php-book: ~

joseph@php-book:~$ php string_create_single_quoted_nowdoc.php

This is a single quoted string. It can contain all kind of characters
such as
quot;\n#, ;nothing will happen, the raw characters will just be
included in your string. This makes it a very safe one to use. The
main time it gets annoying, is when you want your string to contain '
characters, as then you have to remember to escape them with \

This is a a NOWDOC string. The definition looks more verbose than
single quoted, and you have to type a few more characters.
What you get in return though is that you can include all ''' you want
with no escaping.
You can include all the $%"\n' special characters you want and they
will just be included in the string as is
```

If you want to embed variables directly in the string, you should use one of the following:

- double quoted

- HEREDOC:

src/Part2/Chapter4/string_create_double_quoted_heredoc.php

Repo: https://git.io/JRwds

```php
<?php

declare(strict_types=1);

namespace Book\Part2\Chapter4;

/**
 * Do want to embed things directly in the string.
 */
$thingToEmbed = ' [embed me pls] ';
$otherThing   = new class() {
```

```
    public function getStuff(): string
    {
        return ' (some stuff) ';
    }
};
$doubleQuoted = "
A double quoted string can include other variables directly
such as {$thingToEmbed}.
You can also directly embed more complex things if you wrap it
in curly braces, like this {$otherThing->getStuff()}
As with single quoted strings, you have to escape any \"
characters you want to include.
\nOne nice feature of this kind of string is that you can
easily\n embed \n\t special\n\t\t characters
";
echo "\n{$doubleQuoted}\n";


$hereDoc = <<<DELIM
    A heredoc is exactly like the double quoted string, but
comes with the benefit of " and ' being included with no
hassle.
    You can also embed things like {$thingToEmbed} and
{$otherThing->getStuff()}.
    HEREDOC strings will also let you \n embed\n\t special\n\
t\t characters.
    DELIM;
echo "\n{$hereDoc}\n";
```

Output:

```
joseph@php-book: ~

joseph@php-book:~$ php string_create_double_quoted_heredoc.php

A double quoted string can include other variables directly such as
[embed me pls] .
You can also directly embed more complex things if you wrap it in
curly braces, like this  (some stuff)
As with single quoted strings, you have to escape any " characters you
want to include.

One nice feature of this kind of string is that you can easily
 embed
         special
                 characters


A heredoc is exactly like the double quoted string, but comes with the
benefit of " and ' being included with no hassle.
You can also embed things like  [embed me pls]  and  (some stuff) .
HEREDOC strings will also let you
 embed
         special
                 characters.
```

In the preceding code snippet, you can see the four types of string creation being used and hopefully can see the pros and cons of each one. The exact right one to use in a given situation is generally more a matter of opinion or coding standard.

Escape sequences

With the double-quoted and HEREDOC styles, you can also embed special characters by using escape sequences:

```
\n  Newline
\r  Carriage Return
\t  Tab
\$  A literal dollar characters
\"  A literal double quote, in a double quoted string
\'  A literal single quote, in a single quoted string
\\  A literal backslash
```

Here is the link for the full table of escape sequences:

PHP: Strings - Manual

```
https://www.php.net/manual/en/language.types.string.
php#language.types.string.syntax.double
```

Working with strings

If you want to do anything with strings, before you write your own userland function, you would be advised to go and see whether there's already a function for it:

PHP: String Functions - Manual

```
https://www.php.net/manual/en/ref.strings.php
```

One thing that is new with PHP 8 is the introduction to some fairly innocuous but extremely useful functions for checking whether a string starts with or ends with another string:

src/Part2/Chapter4/string_functions.php

Repo: `https://git.io/JRwdG`

```php
<?php

declare(strict_types=1);

namespace Book\Part2\Chapter4;

/** @see http://officeipsum.com/ */
$officeWisdom = "
How much bandwidth do you have get six alpha pups in here for a
focus group no scraps hit the floor, we need this overall
  to be busier and more active. Deploy to production we are
running out of runway yet cross functional teams enable out
  of the box brainstorming we've got to manage that low hanging
fruit and curate, but synergistic actionable.
  Ladder up / ladder back to the strategy have bandwidth. Best
practices post launch for globalize crisp ppt obviously
  are we in agreeance get six alpha pups in here for a focus
group.
";
```

```php
// true
$stringContains = \str_contains(haystack: $officeWisdom,
needle: 'active');


// false, because this is case sensitive
$stringStartWith = \str_starts_with(haystack: $officeWisdom,
needle: 'how');


// true
$stringEndsWith = \str_ends_with(haystack: $officeWisdom,
needle: 'focus group.');
```

As you can see, it is in the same style as the str_contains function we've had for some time. One thing to pay particular attention to is the case sensitivity of the PHP string functions. As a rule, the functions are case-sensitive, though some have case-insensitive variants that are notable by the extra i in the name.

For example, here are some case-sensitive and -insensitive functions:

Case-Sensitive	Case-Insensitive
strpos	stripos
strrpos	strripos
str_replace	str_ireplace

Strings as arrays?

In some languages, strings are regarded as compound types as they are composed of a sequence of single characters. In fact, in PHP, you can access characters in a string using array syntax:

src/Part2/Chapter4/string_as_array.php

Repo: https://git.io/JRwdZ

```php
<?php

declare(strict_types=1);

namespace Book\Part2\Chapter4;
```

```
$string = <<<'TEXT'
    this is a string
    TEXT;
```

```
echo "\n\n{$string[0]}\n\n";
```

Output:

```
joseph@php-book: ~
joseph@php-book:~$ php string_as_array.php
t
```

Numeric strings

If you decide to do some math with strings, then PHP will try valiantly to do something sane by converting the string to a number.

It is important to note that the exact behavior has changed in PHP 8.

First, go read the docs page, which tries to explain how PHP handles strings in numeric contexts:

PHP: Numeric strings - Manual

https://www.php.net/manual/en/language.types.numeric-strings.php

Hopefully, you can now see that PHP will do its best, but will also raise an error. The actual error raised has been increased in seriousness in PHP 8 from notice to warning or even a TypeError exception.

Have a look at the following to illustrate the point:

src/Part2/Chapter4/string_maths.php

Repo: https://git.io/JRwdn

```
<?php

declare(strict_types=1);
```

```
namespace Book\Part2\Chapter4;

echo "\n1 + 1 = " . \var_export(1 + 1, true) . "\n\n";

echo "\n1 + '1 or something like that' = " .
    \var_export(1 + '1 or something like that', true);
```

Output:

```
joseph@php-book: ~

joseph@php-book:~$ php string_maths.php
1 + 1 = 2

PHP Warning:  A non-numeric value encountered in
/home/book_ops/php-book-code/src/Part2/Chapter4/string_maths.php on
line 10

1 + '1 or something like that' = 2
```

As you can see, PHP does figure out what was a reasonable thing to do, but not without complaining.

Generally, trying to feed strings into mathematical operations is not the most sensible thing you could do, and I suggest you avoid it.

Ints

`int` is short for `integer` and it means a whole number, such as 100. It can be a positive or negative number. Where we are talking about decimal (normal) numbers, it is basically any number that does not have a decimal point (.) in there:

PHP: Integers - Manual

https://www.php.net/manual/en/language.types.integer.php

Gotcha

Where ints can get a bit more interesting is when we start to see cryptic-looking non-decimal number formats. You are just as likely to meet these by accident as on purpose. For example, if you accidentally have what you wanted to be a normal decimal int prefixed with a zero, then you have now got an octal number on your hands, and it does not mean anything close to what you originally intended. Oh, the joy of hunting down these kinds of bugs:

src/Part2/Chapter4/int_eresting.php

Repo: `https://git.io/JRwdc`

```php
<?php

declare(strict_types=1);

namespace Book\Part2\Chapter4;

echo "\n100 = 0100? " . \var_export(100 === 0100, true) . "\n";

echo "\n100 = 0144? " . \var_export(100 === 0144, true) . "\n";
```

Output:

```
joseph@php-book: ~

joseph@php-book:~$ php int_eresting.php

100 = 0100? false

100 = 0144? true
```

Floats

Floats are simply just ints with a decimal point (.). Pretty simple, until they aren't!

PHP: Floating point numbers - Manual

`https://www.php.net/manual/en/language.types.float.php`

The massive red box on the PHP docs page should give you a hint that things might not be as simple as they seem. The issue with floats is that they are not really accurate at all. Once you really need to know exactly what value they represent, things get a bit hand-wavy and ambiguous.

Floats are deliberately intended to represent real numbers as an approximation. This is a compromise that opts to improve computation speed in exchange for precision. The reason that floats are inherently imprecise is that they're based on binary (base 2) fractions rather than a normal decimal (base 10). As a result, floats may not always accurately represent what you expect, as you'll see in the following code:

src/Part2/Chapter4/float_your_boat.php

Repo: `https://git.io/JRwdC`

```php
<?php

declare(strict_types=1);

namespace Book\Part2\Chapter4;

// seems OK...
echo "\n(0.2+0.2) = 0.4? " . \var_export((0.2 + 0.2) === 0.4,
true) . "\n";

// wait, what?
echo "\n(0.7+0.1) = 0.8? " . \var_export((0.7 + 0.1) === 0.8,
true) . "\n";
```

Output:

```
joseph@php-book: ~
joseph@php-book:~$ php float_your_boat.php
(0.2+0.2) = 0.4? true

(0.7+0.1) = 0.8? false
```

As you can see, things with floats are often not the way you would like them to be.

If you need to work with floating-point numbers, then you should take a look at BCMath, which works at a defined precision and will help you to avoid the accuracy issues inherent with true float values:

PHP: BCMath - Manual

`https://www.php.net/manual/en/book.bc.php`

Have a look at the following code, where you can see that with BCMath, the world does make sense, even for highly complex calculations such as 0.7 + 0.1:

src/Part2/Chapter4/bcmath.php

Repo: `https://git.io/JRwdW`

```php
<?php

declare(strict_types=1);

namespace Book\Part2\Chapter4;

echo "\n(0.7+0.1) = 0.8? "
    . ((\bccomp(
        \bcadd(num1: '0.7', num2: '0.1', scale: 1),
        num2: '0.8',
        scale: 1
    ) === 0) ? 'yes' : 'no');
```

Output:

```
joseph@php-book: ~
joseph@php-book:~$ php bcmath.php
(0.7+0.1) = 0.8? yes
```

Scenarios where you might decide to use floats are basically those where you don't really care too much about it being exactly correct. For example, you might be calculating the width to display a page element, or perhaps you are timing something and used the built-in microtime, which has a `$as_float` Boolean parameter, so that you get a `bool` return. It's a measurement but we don't really care about absolute correctness:

PHP: microtime - Manual

`https://www.php.net/manual/en/function.microtime.php`

A common scenario where developers use floats is to work with currency. This is a very common but terrible misapplication of floats. Generally, when working with currency calculations, it is really quite important that the maths is reliable – people don't tend to appreciate being charged the wrong amount or having invoices that don't tally up correctly. If you are working with currency and require a robust solution, then I really suggest taking a look at this library:

GitHub - moneyphp/money: PHP implementation of Fowler's Money pattern

`https://github.com/moneyphp/money`

This library uses BCMath internally, but wraps it in a friendly and currency-focused abstraction layer, which makes your life as a developer very easy but gives you confidence that the math behind the scenes is precise.

Bools

Bools can only represent one of two values – `true` or `false`. This binary nature makes them incredibly predictable and safe to use. Whenever you are making a logical decision such as in an `if` block, you are ultimately asking `if ( condition === true)`. What this means is that when you pass in a variable that is not a bool, then you are triggering type juggling to get the bool value from whatever variable or statement you include in your `if` block.

For safety, it is always better to explicitly declare your bool in some way to ensure expected behaviors and avoid type-juggling gotchas.

Bools are great, you should use them as much as possible, the reason being they are very simple indeed:

```php
<?php
$boolGood=true;

if($boolGood){
    useMoreBools();
}
```

Type juggling

So, did you know PHP can juggle?

Unfortunately, we're not talking about throwing more things in the air than we have hands for the amusement of small children. We are in fact talking about converting a variable from one type to another, and updating the value of the variable as we do that.

As you can no doubt appreciate, it is not possible to convert a variable from one type to another without generally incurring some data loss.

Have a look at the docs:

PHP: Type Juggling - Manual

```
https://www.php.net/manual/en/language.types.type-juggling.php
```

There are predictable rules about how type juggling works, but they are not simple and frankly, relying on your accurate understanding of the type juggling rules to determine whether your code works as expected is not a great idea.

Type and value comparison

In PHP, you have two choices when it comes to checking values for equality, namely the following:

- Identical (=== !==)
- Equal (== !=)

Identical in this sense means the same *type* and the same *value*.

Equal means the same value after *type* juggling has taken place to make both values the same *type*.

Have a look at the page on comparison operators, and note the big red box for floats!

PHP: Comparison Operators - Manual

```
https://www.php.net/manual/en/language.operators.comparison.
php
```

Identical (===) is the simplest form of comparison and the most predictable; however, it will always return `false` if the types don't match up. This means that you need to be responsible for juggling any mismatching types before you do your comparison. Ideally, you will use strict types and type hints to ensure that you know exactly what your types are before you even try to do a comparison.

In contrast, the equals (==) comparison will automatically type juggle for you, and the result can sometimes be surprising. In particular, things such as strings beginning with numbers can get converted into numbers. Basically, when you use ==, a lot of things are equal to each other when it is unlikely that you want them to be.

If you have never seen it before, I really suggest you take a look at the full tables of PHP types comparisons:

PHP: PHP type comparison tables - Manual

`https://www.php.net/manual/en/types.comparisons.php`

When comparing things in PHP, you really should use === all the time. If you can get in the habit of using ===, then you will avoid a whole category of bugs. Just following this advice, though, is not enough; you also need to watch out for functions that will do a loose comparison.

Let's have a look at the following code, where we are going to use `TruthDumper` to examine how various PHP mechanisms calculate the truthiness of a specific type and value:

src/Part2/Chapter4/Truthy/TruthDumper.php

Repo: `https://git.io/JRwdl`

```php
<?php

declare(strict_types=1);

namespace Book\Part2\Chapter4\Truthy;

final class TruthDumper
{
    private const HEADERS = [
        'item ',
        'equal',
        'identical',
        'if',
        'empty',
        'isset',
        'switch',
        'match',
    ];
```

```php
    public static function createTable(mixed ...$inputs):
string
    {
        $rows   = [];
        $header = implode(separator: ' | ', array:
self::HEADERS);
        $rows[] = $header;
        $line   = str_repeat(string: '-', times:
strlen($header));
        $rows[] = $line;
        foreach ($inputs as $input) {
            $rows[] = self::row($input);
        }

        return "\n" . implode(separator: "\n", array: $rows) .
"\n";
    }

    private static function row(mixed $input): string
    {
        $items   = [self::pad(var_export($input, true), 'item
')];
        $items[] = self::equal($input);
        $items[] = self::identical($input);
        $items[] = self::if($input);
        $items[] = self::empty($input);
        $items[] = self::isset($input);
        $items[] = self::switch($input);
        $items[] = self::match($input);

        return implode(' | ', $items);

    }

    private static function equal(mixed $input): string
    {
```

```php
        $truthy = ($input == true);

        return self::pad((string)(int)$truthy, 'equal');
    }

    private static function identical(mixed $input): string
    {
        $truthy = ($input === true);

        return self::pad((string)(int)$truthy, 'identical');
    }

    private static function if(mixed $input): string
    {
        $truthy = ($input ? true : false);

        return self::pad((string)(int)$truthy, 'if');
    }

    private static function empty(mixed $input): string
    {
        $truthy = (empty($input) === false);

        return self::pad((string)(int)$truthy, 'empty');
    }

    private static function isset(mixed $input): string
    {
        $truthy = (isset($input));

        return self::pad((string)(int)$truthy, 'isset');
    }

    private static function switch(mixed $input): string
    {
        switch (true) {
```

```php
                case $input:
                    $truthy = true;
                    break;
            default:
                $truthy = false;
        }

        return self::pad((string)(int)$truthy, 'switch');
    }

    private static function pad(string $string, string $key):
string
    {
        $pad = strlen($key);

        return sprintf("%${pad}s", $string);
    }

    private static function match(mixed $input): string
    {
        $truthy = match (true) {
            $input => true,
            default => false,
        };

        return self::pad((string)(int)$truthy, 'match');
    }
}
```

src/Part2/Chapter4/truthy.php

Repo: `https://git.io/JRwd8`

```php
<?php

declare(strict_types=1);

namespace Book\Part2\Chapter4;
```

```php
require __DIR__ . '/../../../vendor/autoload.php';

use Book\Part2\Chapter4\Truthy\TruthDumper;

echo TruthDumper::createTable(
    null,
    0,
    0.0,
    '0',
    '',
    false,
    true,
    1,
    'a',
    01,
    -1,
    0.1
);
```

Output:

```
joseph@php-book:~

joseph@php-book:~$ php truthy.php
item  | equal | identical | if | empty | isset | switch | match
----------------------------------------------------------------
NULL  |   0   |     0     | 0  |   0   |   0   |   0    |   0
   0  |   0   |     0     | 0  |   0   |   1   |   0    |   0
 0.0  |   0   |     0     | 0  |   0   |   1   |   0    |   0
 '0'  |   0   |     0     | 0  |   0   |   1   |   0    |   0
  ''  |   0   |     0     | 0  |   0   |   1   |   0    |   0
false |   0   |     0     | 0  |   0   |   1   |   0    |   0
true  |   1   |     1     | 1  |   1   |   1   |   1    |   1
   1  |   1   |     0     | 1  |   1   |   1   |   1    |   0
 'a'  |   1   |     0     | 1  |   1   |   1   |   1    |   0
   1  |   1   |     0     | 1  |   1   |   1   |   1    |   0
  -1  |   1   |     0     | 1  |   1   |   1   |   1    |   0
 0.1  |   1   |     0     | 1  |   1   |   1   |   1    |   0
```

As you can see, relying on truthiness can be a bit unpredictable and requires you to memorize the comparison table if you want to be able to code reliably. Strict comparison will generally fail faster and in a more understandable way when you inadvertently have an unexpected value in your code.

Always try to use the stricter variant:

Loose	Strict
==	===
!=	===
switch	match
in_array	in_array with true as third argument
$value ?: $fallback	$value===true ? $value : $fallback

Hopefully, you get the idea that strict comparison of scalars is crucial if you want to have an easy life. It's just an extra = most of the time, and generally the tiny bit of extra time and care you need to put into writing stricter code is hugely outweighed by the time-saving in not having to hunt down weird bugs. Let's move on and look at arrays and iterables.

Arrays and iterables

Now that we have looked at the simple scalar types, we should look at the single most utilized compound type in PHP – the array – and its close relation, iterables.

Arrays

Arrays in PHP are hugely powerful and useful. You can use it to pass a handful of values around, or you can let it grow to tremendous sizes and eat all your system's RAM if you so choose.

Have a look at the official docs for arrays:

PHP: Arrays - Manual

```
https://www.php.net/manual/en/language.types.array.php
```

What the docs say, in more words than me, is that arrays are the single tool that ticks a load of data structure boxes. An array consists of keys and associated values. The keys can be int or string. If they are not specified, then they are int starting at 0.

There are a huge number of built-in functions that assist with efficiently processing arrays. You should always try to use the built-in functions instead of creating your own, so try to learn the array functions:

PHP: Array Functions - Manual

https://www.php.net/manual/en/ref.array.php

Here is a very brief play with arrays – just scratching the surface of the things you can do:

src/Part2/Chapter4/array.php

Repo: https://git.io/JRwd4

```php
<?php

declare(strict_types=1);

namespace Book\Part2\Chapter4;

// if we don't specify keys, they are ints starting from 0
$intKeysStringValues = ['a', 'b', 'c'];
echo "\n\$intKeysStringValues =" . \var_
export($intKeysStringValues, true);

// we can specify string keys
$stringKeysFloatValues = ['one' => 1.0, 'two' => 2.0, 'three'
=> 3.0];
echo "\n\$stringKeysFloatValues =" .
    \var_export($stringKeysFloatValues, true);

// we can extract arrays into variables
[$a, $b, $c] = [1, 2, 3];
echo "\n\$a is {$a}";

// we can quickly create arrays with built in functions
$numbers = \range(start: 1, end: 5);
echo "\n\$numbers =" . \var_export($numbers, true);

$letters = \str_split(string: 'abcde');
echo "\n\$letters=" . \var_export($letters, true);
```

Output:

```
joseph@php-book: ~

joseph@php-book:~$ php array.php
$intKeysStringValues =array (
  0 => 'a',
  1 => 'b',
  2 => 'c',
)
$stringKeysFloatValues =array (
  'one' => 1.0,
  'two' => 2.0,
  'three' => 3.0,
)
$a is 1
$numbers =array (
  0 => 1,
  1 => 2,
  2 => 3,
  3 => 4,
  4 => 5,
)
$letters=array (
  0 => 'a',
  1 => 'b',
  2 => 'c',
  3 => 'd',
  4 => 'e',
)
```

One thing that I want to use the brief space we have for arrays to do is to warn you of a really common gotcha:

src/Part2/Chapter4/array_merge.php

Repo: https://git.io/JRwdB

```php
<?php

declare(strict_types=1);

namespace Book\Part2\Chapter4;

/**
 * Simulating the kind of scenario this happens in.
 *
```

```php
 * @return string[]
 */
function loadFromDb(): array
{
    return \array_fill(0, 10, 'foo');
}


$howManyRows = 1000;
$result      = [];
$start       = \microtime(true);
for ($row = 0; $row < $howManyRows; ++$row) {
    $result = \array_merge($result, loadFromDb());
}
$takenLoop = \microtime(true) - $start;
echo "\nArray merge in a loop took " . \round($takenLoop, 4);

$toMerge = [];
$start   = \microtime(true);
for ($row = 0; $row < $howManyRows; ++$row) {
    $toMerge[] = loadFromDb();
}
$result     = \array_merge(...$toMerge);
$takenSplat = \microtime(true) - $start;
echo "\nSingle array merge with splat took " . \
round($takenSplat, 4);

$percentSlower = \round((($takenLoop / $takenSplat) * 100),
precision: 2);
echo "\nThat means that array merge in a loop is
{$percentSlower}% slower!";
```

Output:

```
joseph@php-book:~

joseph@php-book:~$ php array_merge.php
Array merge in a loop took 0.0097
Single array merge with splat took 0.0006
That means that array merge in a loop is 1687.83% slower!
```

What you can see is that you should be cautious of rebuilding arrays in a loop. Calling `array_merge` in a loop here is hugely slower than building up an array of arrays and then merging it all in one go at the end using good old `splat`...

Iterables

Iterables is the name for objects and other things in PHP that try their best to act exactly like arrays when it comes to being compatible with the humble yet awesomely powerful `foreach` loop.

I just don't have the space to do a deep dive into iterables and generators – which is a shame as this is a great topic. However, I will try to cover them briefly and give you the jump-off points you need to fully understand.

First, have a read of the docs page here:

PHP: Iterables - Manual

```
https://www.php.net/manual/en/language.types.iterable.php
```

`iterable` is a special type that you can use in parameter or return types to indicate that the value may be one of the following:

- A standard PHP array.

- An internal object that implements the special `Traversable` interface, such as the SPL iterators we saw in the last chapter:

    PHP: Traversable - Manual

    ```
    https://www.php.net/manual/en/class.traversable.php
    ```

- A userland object that implements the `Iterator` interface:

    PHP: Iterator - Manual

    ```
    https://www.php.net/manual/en/class.iterator.php
    ```

    This is an object that allows itself to be treated as an array and be `foreach` looped over. Inside the object, you can control exactly what is returned on each iteration and when the iteration is completed.

- The return of a function that is a generator:

    PHP: Generators overview - Manual

    ```
    https://www.php.net/manual/en/language.generators.
    overview.php
    ```

Generators are especially cool, and I really encourage you to go and have a play with them. The generator is a return value that can be iterated over, and on each iteration, it will jump back into the function or method that it was returned from and will run until it hits a `yield` statement or the end of the function.

A generator can return only values or can return keys and values.

Here is a taster:

src/Part2/Chapter4/generator.php

Repo: `https://git.io/JRwdR`

```php
<?php

declare(strict_types=1);

namespace Book\Part2\Chapter4;

use Generator;

/** @return Generator<int> */
function gener8(int $num): Generator
{
    // be careful doing this kind of thing :)
    while (true) {
        // square
        $num *= $num;
        // check for modulus 8 and if found,
        if (($num % 8) === 0) {
            // yield a single value ready to start all over
again
            yield $num;
        }
    }
}

foreach (gener8(num: 2) as $x) {
    echo "\n{$x}";
    if ($x > 2000) {
```

```
        break;
    }
}
```

Output:

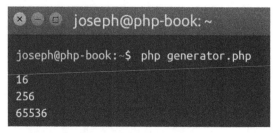

I tend to use generators a lot with PHPUnit data providers:

2. Writing Tests for PHPUnit — PHPUnit 9.5 Manual

`https://phpunit.readthedocs.io/en/9.5/writing-tests-for-phpunit.html#data-providers`

I prefer the syntax over a nested multidimensional array, for example, this provider taken from one of the tests for a later chapter:

```
/**
 * this is a data provider, providing values to be used
 * in the hasReturnsTrueForValidServiceIds test.
 *
 * @dataProvider
 *
 * @return Generator<string, array<int,string>>
 */
public function provideValidServiceIds(): Generator
{
    yield EchoStuffInterface::class =>
[EchoStuffInterface::class];
    yield MathsInterface::class => [MathsInterface::class];
    yield LevelOneService::class =>
[LevelOneService::class];
    yield LevelTwoService::class =>
[LevelTwoService::class];
```

```
      yield LevelThreeService::class =>
[LevelThreeService::class];
   }
```

Another place you may want to use generators is when it would be very resource-intensive to return all of the items at once and instead it will be much more efficient to return them one at a time. Imagine, for example, reading and filtering lines from a humongous file and returning the ones that match. If the file is GB in size, then you would need GB of RAM to return the filtered result, whereas by using a generator, you could return the filtered result a line at a time.

DocBlock types

One way that PHP developers have always used to document the types that their code will work with is to use specially formatted comments called **DocBlocks**.

First, make sure you are clear about what we mean by comments:

PHP: Comments - Manual

```
https://www.php.net/manual/en/language.basic-syntax.comments.php
```

If you are not clear what DocBlocks are, you might want to have a look at the documentation for PHPDoc, the de facto standard for PHP DocBlocks (though the true range of DocBlocks has now grown beyond this official spec):

phpDocumentor

```
https://docs.phpdoc.org/3.0/guide/references/phpdoc/index.html
```

Also, take a look at this proposed standard for writing DocBlocks:

fig-standards/phpdoc.md at master · php-fig/fig-standards · GitHub

```
https://github.com/php-fig/fig-standards/blob/master/proposed/phpdoc.md
```

It is important to note that **PHP itself does not read DocBlocks or infer anything from them**. The only things that read DocBlocks are the following:

- Developers
- IDEs
- Static analysis tools
- Userland PHP code that reads DocBlocks using reflection

The risk with DocBlocks is that they can be completely incorrect and misleading; however, there are circumstances where it is the best you can do to document things with DocBlocks. In PHP 8, the circumstances that require DocBlocks for types to be inferred are mercifully few and are generally around arrays and iterables.

For example, in the `ModernClass` you have already seen, you might have noticed that we declared one property the old-fashioned way, and used a DocBlock to hint at the type. That is because the type, as PHP knows, is simply an array, which, while correct, is not the whole story. What we really need to know is what is it an array of?

DocBlocks give us two ways to achieve this, simply by declaring the type of values with `[]`, or we can specify the key type as well with `array<{key_type}, {value_type}>`. If you are going to stick to one, use the `<key,value>` syntax because more information is always better:

```php
/** @var string[] | array<int,string> */
$arrayOfStrings=['a','b','c'];


/**
 * This function expects an array of strings with int keys
 * and returns an iterator that contains SplFileInfo objects to
iterate over
 *
 * @param array<int,string> $arrayOfStrings
 * @return IteratorIterator<int,SplFileInfo>
 */
function getIterator(array $arrayOfStrings):IteratorIterator{
    // get an iterator and return it
}
```

As you can see, we can use this notation for properties and variables, parameters, and return types.

The reason for doing this is largely so that IDE autocompletion works correctly, and also so that static analysis tools can pick up on it and check for errors in code that uses the iterable or array.

As you can see, there is a bit of nuance to arrays and iterables in PHP. We start to bump up against the limits of the language. Next, we're going to look at three different ways of expressing nothing. Sounds a bit zen-like, but hopefully you will be able to gain understanding without having to reach nirvana.

Nullable, void, and uninitialized

There are three special types in PHP that represent no value at all. The first is null; it is something that is expected as a valid value for your properties and return types, though it is something that you need to account for.

Another one is void and it really does mean nothing. It is only used as a return type and it defines that the function or method does not return anything at all.

The final one is uninitialised, which is a special limbo state that has been introduced along with PHP 8 constructor property promotion. We will explore how all of these work.

Null and nullable

First, let's have a look at null. null behaves like a scalar value in that you can assign it, check for it, and return it as an option on any other type.

Have a look at this code:

src/Part2/Chapter4/null.php

Repo: https://git.io/JRwd0

```php
<?php

declare(strict_types=1);

namespace Book\Part2\Chapter4;

// assigning null as a value
$foo = null;

// short function syntax to return a null
$bar = (static fn (): ?string => null)();

// short function syntax to return a null using union type
$baz = (static fn (): string | null => null)();

echo "\n\$foo===\$bar? " . \var_export($foo === $bar, true);
echo "\n\$foo===\$baz? " . \var_export($foo === $baz, true);
```

Output:

```
joseph@php-book: ~

joseph@php-book:~$ php null.php
$foo===$bar? true
$foo===$baz? true
```

So, you can see we can directly assign null as a value. We can define functions and methods as optionally returning null by prefixing any other type with a ?. Note that we cannot return null as a standalone type; it is only available as an option. If you always want to return null, you must return void instead. Let's explore that next.

It is worth knowing at this point that there are some very useful shorthand operators that you can use when possibly dealing with nulls. Have a look at the following code snippet:

src/Part2/Chapter4/shorthand.php

Repo: https://git.io/JRwdE

```php
<?php

declare(strict_types=1);

namespace Book\Part2\Chapter4;

use Book\Part2\Chapter4\ShortHand\Container;
use Book\Part2\Chapter4\ShortHand\SmallClass;

require __DIR__ . '/../../../vendor/autoload.php';

$object = new Container(
    new SmallClass('foo val'),
    null
);

/*
 * First lets compare some classic if/else code with a ternary
operator
```

```php
 */
// Classic if/else code checking
if ($object->bool1 === true) {
    $value1 = 'bool 1 is true';
} else {
    $value1 = 'bool 1 is false';
}


// Ternary
// Note - if your variable or value is not a bool, it will be
type juggled to one.
// You can make ternary strict by checking for identity (===)
with true/false directly
$value2 = $object->bool1 === true ? 'bool 1 is true' : 'bool 1
is false';


echo "\n" . '$value1===$value2? ' . \var_export($value1 ===
$value2, true);


// classic null checking monstrosity (deliberately verbose)
if ($object->property2 === null) {
    if ($object->property1 === null) {
        $value3 = null;
    } else {
        if ($object->property1->foo === null) {
            $value3 = null;
        } else {
            $value3 = $object->property1->foo;
        }
    }
} else {
    if ($object->property2->foo === null) {
        $value3 = null;
    } else {
        $value3 = $object->property2->foo;
    }
}
```

```php
// null coalesce & nullsafe operator
$value4 = $object->property2?->foo ?? $object->property1?->foo;

echo "\n" . '$value3===$value4? ' . \var_export($value3 ===
$value4, true);
```

Output:

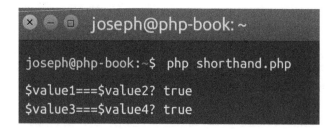

So, what you can see in this code is that we have two pieces of code that work the same way when calculating value 1 and value 2; however, value 2 is a bit less verbose. Ternaries are sometimes contentious and can definitely be overused, but for quick one-liners, I personally think they are great. I definitely advise against ever thinking of nesting ternaries though.

When you see the difference between the classic null checking with ifs versus using the null coalesce and nullsafe operator, I think you can agree that the code is not only much less verbose but also much easier to read and comprehend.

Check out the official docs:

PHP: Comparison Operators - Manual

https://www.php.net/manual/en/language.operators.comparison.php#language.operators.comparison.coalesce

Void

void is a special type, only usable for return typing. It simply defines and enforces that a function or method does not return anything. In this context, it basically means null, as this is what any function returns when there is not an explicit return value.

Have a look at the following code, where we have one function with a void return type, and another with no return type and no return:

Src/Part2/Chapter4/void.php

Repo: `https://git.io/JRwdu`

```php
<?php

declare(strict_types=1);

namespace Book\Part2\Chapter4;

function returnsNull(): ?string
{
    return null;
}

function noReturn(): void
{
}

$void = returnsNull();

$noReturn = noReturn();

echo "\n\$void=" . \var_export($void, true);

echo "\n\$noReturn=" . \var_export($noReturn, true);

echo "\n\$void === \$noReturn? " . \var_export($void ===
$noReturn, true);
```

Output:

```
joseph@php-book:~$ php void.php

$void=NULL
$noReturn=NULL
$void === $noReturn? true
```

As you can see, void and returning nothing with no type defined both give us `null`. For the sake of type safety though, you should always define functions with no return as `void`; this way, if they do return something, you will get a type error and will quickly realize your code is broken.

Uninitialized

The final no-value type we are going to look at is `uninitialised`. This comes into play when we are dealing with typed properties in classes or objects and before the property value has been set.

There is no way to get or assign the value of an `uninitialised` property; trying to access it throws a fatal error, so you need to be very careful with this one, and ensure that your type properties (and all class properties really) are properly initialized before any code may access them

Have a look at the following simple demo:

src/Part2/Chapter4/uninitialised.php

Repo: `https://git.io/JRwdz`

```php
<?php

declare(strict_types=1);

namespace Book\Part2\Chapter4;

$untyped = new class() {
    public $uninitialised;
};

echo "\nYou can access untyped properties and the value is: " .
    \var_export($untyped->uninitialised, true);

$typed = new class() {
    public string $uninitialised;
```

```
};
```

```
echo "\nHowever, try this with typed properties..\n and it
goes:\n\n";
```

```
echo $typed->uninitialised;
```

Output:

```
joseph@php-book: ~

joseph@php-book:~$ php uninitialised.php

You can access untyped properties and the value is: NULL
However, try this with typed properties..
 and it goes:

PHP Fatal error:  Uncaught Error: Typed property
class@anonymous::$uninitialised must not be accessed before
initialization in
/home/book_ops/php-book-code/src/Part2/Chapter4/uninitialised.php:19
Stack trace:
#0 {main}
   thrown in
/home/book_ops/php-book-code/src/Part2/Chapter4/uninitialised.php on
line 19
```

As you can see, typed class properties come with a responsibility to ensure that the property has the correct type before any access happens.

Hopefully, you now understand the subtle differences between null, void, and uninitialised. They are all nothing more than different kinds of nothing. The final type is even more special in that it doesn't really exist; it is only a reference to something beyond – we're going to have a look at resources.

Resources

Resources are the weird kid in the corner of the PHP types party. Maybe you can relate?

If you call gettype on a resource, you will get null. This is because they are a bit special. They are like wormholes into the dimension beyond the realms of PHP. All we know is they exist, but what goes on beyond their event horizon we can only speculate…

Resources that you are likely to have already come across on a regular basis are file pointers when using `fopen` and database connections. There are in fact numerous resources that you can open in PHP and you can read all about them in the manual:

PHP: List of Resource Types - Manual

`https://www.php.net/manual/en/resource.php`

The good news is that in PHP 8, the resource types are gradually being hunted down and replaced with more useful types – namely objects. Already, the `curl_init` function now returns a `CurlHandle` class. You still can't really get anything useful from it, but you can at least do basic sanity checks on it:

src/Part2/Chapter4/resource.php

Repo: `https://git.io/JRwdg`

```php
<?php

declare(strict_types=1);

namespace Book\Part2\Chapter4;

function info(mixed $resource): string
{
    $var    = \var_export($resource, true);
    $type   = \gettype($resource);
    $empty  = \var_export(empty($resource), true);
    $isset  = \var_export(isset($resource), true);

    return "\nVar: {$var}" .
           "\n Type: {$type} | Empty: {$empty} | Isset: {$isset}\n";
}

$file = \fopen(__FILE__, 'r');
echo info($file);

$curl = \curl_init();
echo info($curl);
```

The output is as follows:

```
joseph@php-book: ~

joseph@php-book:~$ php resource.php
Var: NULL
 Type: resource | Empty: false | Isset: true

Var: CurlHandle::__set_state(array(
))
 Type: object | Empty: false | Isset: true
```

You can see that `curl_init` now returns an object; it has no methods or properties, but at least it has a name. The file pointer resource is `null` if you try to get its value, but otherwise is truthy.

There's not really much else to say about resources. By their very nature, you can't really do much with them.

Summary

That brings us to the end of Chapter 4. Let's provide a quick recap for you.

First, we looked at all the scalar types – the simple fundamental data. We learned as well about type juggling between these scalar types and how it can be quite complex and tricky to predict if you rely on automatic type juggling. We learned about the difference between identical and equal and the corresponding operators, `===` and `==`. The gist here was that you are always better off using checks for identity wherever possible so you can avoid the pitfalls of type juggling.

After that, we looked at arrays and iterables, including a quick peek at generators – go and play with them, they are awesome. We also looked at the use of DocBlocks to cover the current lack of rich type information in the language itself when dealing with arrays and iterables and how we can supplement this so that IDEs and QA tools can understand what our arrays and iterators actually contain.

We looked at the "nothing" types of `null`, `void`, and `uninitialised` and had a look at the ways that they can be useful, and also the gotchas that you need to watch out for.

Finally, we had a quick look at resources. There's not loads to say about them, but you are certain to use them and so you need to know what they are.

In the next chapter, we are going to take a look at objects, classes, and interfaces and understand the way types and operators work with them.

5

Object Types, Interfaces, and Unions

In this chapter, we're going to look specifically at object and class types.

Objects, like scalars, have types. Unlike scalars, though, a single object can be regarded as one of a potentially large number of types. Let's explore how this works.

We'll begin by looking at object type inheritance. Then, we are going to understand how object comparison works and the difference between identity (===) and equality (==) when it comes to objects.

Finally, in this chapter, we're going to look at the relationship between object variables and instances and look to understand the way that in PHP, objects are passed by reference by default.

The topics in this chapter are interdependent and so it is tricky to find the correct order to explain things. If this is all new to you, it might be useful to read through the chapter twice so that it all properly makes sense to you.

The following topics will be covered in this chapter:

- Object type inheritance
- Object comparison
- Passing objects by reference
- Making new objects

As usual, you can find all the code samples for this chapter in the main repo for the book available on GitHub at `https://github.com/PacktPublishing/The-Art-of-Modern-PHP-8`.

Let's kick off with a look into object type inheritance, so we can understand how a single object can be regarded as multiple types.

Object type inheritance

Each class and interface is a type. There are also various types that PHP has built-in and that your class or interface might also incorporate.

Any object is an instance of a specific class – the class that it was created from using the `new` keyword. This is the most obvious type for the object. After that, it is the class's parent class (if it has one), and then its grandparent class (again if it has one)… all the way up to the grandest-parentiest class at the top of the hierarchical chain.

Further to this, each class is also every interface it implements, and the parent and grandparent (and so on) interfaces of those interfaces, again all the way to the top. Remember, a single class can implement multiple interfaces and those interfaces can all extend further interfaces.

As you can imagine, this can get confusing, and it's one reason why massive inheritance chains can be a bad thing when it comes to having comprehensible code. If you adopt composition over inheritance as your primary style, then you can avoid much of this complexity.

Let's take the following classes and interfaces:

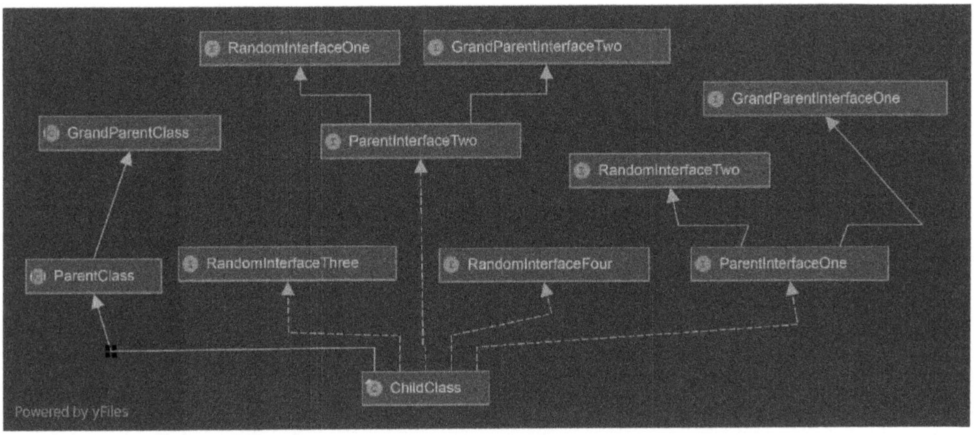

First, we have two grandparent interfaces. Remember, interfaces support multiple inheritance, so multiple grandparents at the same level is absolutely fine:

src/Part2/Chapter5/TypeInheritance/GrandParentInterfaceOne.php

Repo: `https://git.io/JRw5N`

```
<?php

declare(strict_types=1);

namespace Book\Part2\Chapter5\TypeInheritance;

interface GrandParentInterfaceOne
{
}
```

src/Part2/Chapter5/TypeInheritance/GrandParentInterfaceTwo.php

Repo: `https://git.io/JRw5A`

```
<?php

declare(strict_types=1);

namespace Book\Part2\Chapter5\TypeInheritance;

interface GrandParentInterfaceTwo
```

```php
{
}
```

Next, we have two parent interfaces. Each of these is extending grandparent interfaces and also extending another random interface:

src/Part2/Chapter5/TypeInheritance/ParentInterfaceOne.php

Repo: https://git.io/JRw5x

```php
<?php

declare(strict_types=1);

namespace Book\Part2\Chapter5\TypeInheritance;

interface ParentInterfaceOne extends GrandParentInterfaceOne,
RandomInterfaceTwo
{
}
```

src/Part2/Chapter5/TypeInheritance/ParentInterfaceTwo.php

Repo: https://git.io/JRw5p

```php
<?php

declare(strict_types=1);

namespace Book\Part2\Chapter5\TypeInheritance;

interface ParentInterfaceTwo extends GrandParentInterfaceTwo,
RandomInterfaceOne
{
}
```

Now we have four random interfaces that do not extend anything else but stand alone:

src/Part2/Chapter5/TypeInheritance/RandomInterfaceOne.php

Repo:: `https://git.io/JRw5h`

```php
<?php

declare(strict_types=1);

namespace Book\Part2\Chapter5\TypeInheritance;

interface RandomInterfaceOne
{
}
```

src/Part2/Chapter5/TypeInheritance/RandomInterfaceTwo.php

Repo: `https://git.io/JRw5j`

```php
<?php

declare(strict_types=1);

namespace Book\Part2\Chapter5\TypeInheritance;

interface RandomInterfaceTwo
{
}
```

src/Part2/Chapter5/TypeInheritance/RandomInterfaceThree.php

Repo: `https://git.io/JRwde`

```php
<?php

declare(strict_types=1);

namespace Book\Part2\Chapter5\TypeInheritance;

interface RandomInterfaceThree
{
}
```

src/Part2/Chapter5/TypeInheritance/RandomInterfaceFour.php

Repo: `https://git.io/JRwdv`

```php
<?php

declare(strict_types=1);

namespace Book\Part2\Chapter5\TypeInheritance;

interface RandomInterfaceFour
{
}
```

Now we've defined all our interfaces, let's create some classes. We'll start off with an abstract grandparent class:

src/Part2/Chapter5/TypeInheritance/GrandParentClass.php

Repo: `https://git.io/JRwdf`

```php
<?php

declare(strict_types=1);

namespace Book\Part2\Chapter5\TypeInheritance;

abstract class GrandParentClass
{
}
```

Here is a mid-level abstract parent class that extends from the grandparent abstract class:

src/Part2/Chapter5/TypeInheritance/ParentClass.php

Repo: `https://git.io/JRwdJ`

```php
<?php

declare(strict_types=1);

namespace Book\Part2\Chapter5\TypeInheritance;
```

```php
abstract class ParentClass extends GrandParentClass
{
}
```

Now we have a final child class that extends the parent abstract class (and thereby the grandparent class) and also implements the two parent interfaces, the grandparent interfaces that they extend, and another random interface as well:

src/Part2/Chapter5/TypeInheritance/ChildClass.php

Repo: `https://git.io/JRwdU`

```php
<?php

declare(strict_types=1);

namespace Book\Part2\Chapter5\TypeInheritance;

/**
 * Can only inherit from a single parent class
 * but can implement multiple interfaces, each of which can
have their own inheritance chain.
 */
final class ChildClass extends ParentClass implements
ParentInterfaceOne, ParentInterfaceTwo, RandomInterfaceThree
{
}
```

As you can imagine, `ChildClass` now represents not only itself as a type, but also every single other thing that it inherits from, all the way up the inheritance chain.

Now we have the following code, which will create an instance of the final `ChildClass` and then determine the parents and interfaces, and finally, do some explicit `instanceof` checks against a sequence of class and interface **fully qualified names** (**FQNs**):

src/Part2/Chapter5/class_parents.php

Repo: `https://git.io/JRwdT`

```php
<?php

declare(strict_types=1);
```

```php
namespace Book\Part2\Chapter5;

require __DIR__ . '/../../../vendor/autoload.php';

use Book\Part2\Chapter5\TypeInheritance\ChildClass;
use Book\Part2\Chapter5\TypeInheritance\RandomInterfaceFour;
use stdClass;

$child                = new ChildClass();
$childFqn             = $child::class;
$childClassParents    = \array_values(\class_parents($child));
$childClassInterfaces = \array_values(\class_
implements($child));

echo "\nClass Parents of {$childFqn}:\n" .
    \var_export($childClassParents, true);

echo "\nInterfaces of {$childFqn}:\n" .
    \var_export($childClassInterfaces, true);

function isInstanceOf(object $object, string $item): string
{
    $format = "\n%-60s %s\n";
    $result = \var_export($object instanceof $item, true);

    return \sprintf($format, "{$item}?", $result);
}

echo "\n\n{$childFqn} instance of checks:\n";

foreach ($childClassParents + $childClassInterfaces as $item) {
    echo isInstanceOf($child, $item);
}

$otherTypes = [RandomInterfaceFour::class, stdClass::class];
```

```php
foreach ($otherTypes as $item) {
    echo isInstanceOf($child, $item);
}
```

Output:

```
joseph@php-book: ~

joseph@php-book:~$ php class_parents.php
Class Parents of Book\Part2\Chapter5\TypeInheritance\ChildClass:
array (
  0 => 'Book\\Part2\\Chapter5\\TypeInheritance\\ParentClass',
  1 => 'Book\\Part2\\Chapter5\\TypeInheritance\\GrandParentClass',
)
Interfaces of Book\Part2\Chapter5\TypeInheritance\ChildClass:
array (
  0 => 'Book\\Part2\\Chapter5\\TypeInheritance\\ParentInterfaceOne',
  1 => 'Book\\Part2\\Chapter5\\TypeInheritance\\ParentInterfaceTwo',
  2 => 'Book\\Part2\\Chapter5\\TypeInheritance\\RandomInterfaceThree',
  3 => 'Book\\Part2\\Chapter5\\TypeInheritance\\RandomInterfaceTwo',
  4 =>
'Book\\Part2\\Chapter5\\TypeInheritance\\GrandParentInterfaceOne',
  5 => 'Book\\Part2\\Chapter5\\TypeInheritance\\RandomInterfaceOne',
  6 =>
'Book\\Part2\\Chapter5\\TypeInheritance\\GrandParentInterfaceTwo',
)

Book\Part2\Chapter5\TypeInheritance\ChildClass instance of checks:

Book\Part2\Chapter5\TypeInheritance\ParentClass?              true

Book\Part2\Chapter5\TypeInheritance\GrandParentClass?         true

Book\Part2\Chapter5\TypeInheritance\RandomInterfaceThree?     true

Book\Part2\Chapter5\TypeInheritance\RandomInterfaceTwo?       true

Book\Part2\Chapter5\TypeInheritance\GrandParentInterfaceOne? true

Book\Part2\Chapter5\TypeInheritance\RandomInterfaceOne?       true

Book\Part2\Chapter5\TypeInheritance\GrandParentInterfaceTwo? true

Book\Part2\Chapter5\TypeInheritance\RandomInterfaceFour?      false

stdClass?                                                    false
```

The preceding code has shown us the fact that an instance of `ChildClass` passes as an instance of all of its parent items all the way up the inheritance tree. The following code snippet will illustrate how this type information affects how the instance of `ChildClass` can be passed into functions that are hinting for those parent types:

src/Part2/Chapter5/function_hints.php

Repo: `https://git.io/JRwdk`

```php
<?php

declare(strict_types=1);

namespace Book\Part2\Chapter5;

require __DIR__ . '/../../../vendor/autoload.php';

use Book\Part2\Chapter5\TypeInheritance\ChildClass;
use Book\Part2\Chapter5\TypeInheritance\GrandParentInterfaceTwo;
use Book\Part2\Chapter5\TypeInheritance\RandomInterfaceFour;
use Book\Part2\Chapter5\TypeInheritance\RandomInterfaceTwo;
use ReflectionClass;
use stdClass;
use TypeError;

$child     = new ChildClass();
$callables = [
    ChildClass::class                => (static fn (ChildClass $classn) => true),
    stdClass::class                  => (static fn (stdClass $class) => true),
    GrandParentInterfaceTwo::class => (static fn (GrandParentInterfaceTwo $class) => true),
    RandomInterfaceFour::class       => (static fn (RandomInterfaceFour $class) => true),
    RandomInterfaceTwo::class        => (static fn (RandomInterfaceTwo $class) => true),
    ReflectionClass::class           => (static fn (ReflectionClass $class) => true),
```

```
];
foreach ($callables as $hintFqn => $callable) {
    try {
        $result = $callable($child);
    } catch (TypeError) {
        $result = false;
    }
    echo \sprintf("\n%-60s %s", $hintFqn, $result ? 'true' :
'false');
}
```

Output:

```
joseph@php-book: ~
joseph@php-book:~$ php function_hints.php
Book\Part2\Chapter5\TypeInheritance\ChildClass                true
stdClass                                                      false
Book\Part2\Chapter5\TypeInheritance\GrandParentInterfaceTwo   true
Book\Part2\Chapter5\TypeInheritance\RandomInterfaceFour       false
Book\Part2\Chapter5\TypeInheritance\RandomInterfaceTwo        true
ReflectionClass                                               false
```

Now you understand that objects and classes in PHP do not have a single type, but in fact, they have their own type and that of each of their ancestral types via both class inheritance and interface implementation. Let's move on to looking at how comparison works with objects.

Object comparison

It is important to understand how comparison works with PHP. Just as with scalars, we have the choice of comparing objects by identity (===) or equality (==). While in PHP you might have two distinct variables that can be identical, this is not the case with objects. For objects to be identical, they must not only be of the same class, but also be the exact same *instance*.

What do we mean by instance?

When we call a new ClassName in PHP, we are creating a new instance of that class. I like to think of it as like starting a mini program. It has a bit of functionality and data and takes up a bit of memory. We can choose to start more than one instance if we want, and a bit like Chrome tabs, they will each consume resources.

As usual, I really suggest you read through the official docs if you are not already completely familiar with this topic:

PHP: Comparing Objects - Manual

`https://www.php.net/manual/en/language.oop5.object-comparison.php`

Have a look at the following code to see this illustrated simply:

src/Part2/Chapter5/object_comparison.php

Repo: `https://git.io/JRwdI`

```php
<?php

declare(strict_types=1);

namespace Book\Part2\Chapter5;

use stdClass;

// Create new instance
$instanceOne = new stdClass();

// Create another new instance
$instanceTwo = new stdClass();

// Create a reference to the first instance
$referenceOne = $instanceOne;

echo "\n" .
    '$instanceOne identical to $instanceTwo?  ' .
    \var_export($instanceOne === $instanceTwo, true) .
    "\n";

echo "\n" .
```

```
        '$instanceOne equal to $instanceTwo?          ' .
        \var_export($instanceOne == $instanceTwo, true) .
        "\n";

echo "\n" .
        '$instanceOne identical to $referenceOne? ' .
        \var_export($instanceOne === $referenceOne, true) .
        "\n";

$instanceOne->foo = 'bar';

echo "\n" .
        '$instanceOne with foo equal to $instanceTwo?          ' .
        \var_export($instanceOne == $instanceTwo, true) .
        "\n";
```

Output:

```
joseph@php-book: ~

joseph@php-book:~$ php object_comparison.php
$instanceOne identical to $instanceTwo?  false

$instanceOne equal to $instanceTwo?        true

$instanceOne identical to $referenceOne? true

$instanceOne with foo equal to $instanceTwo?        false
```

So, as you can see, while the equality operator will return when the objects are instances of the same class and have the same property values, two separate instances will always fail the identical operator. Also, once one object has different property values, then they are no longer equal.

What you can also see is that if we assign an instance to another variable and then compare that with the identical operator, this passes as true.

To pass the strictest identical check, it simply has to be the same "instance" of the class, though it can be a different "reference." Let's go on to exploring references in a bit more detail.

Passing objects by reference

References in PHP refer to the ability for multiple `$variable` variables to actually refer to a single value. You can read about this in detail in the official docs, something I suggest you always do:

PHP: References Explained - Manual

`https://www.php.net/manual/en/language.references.php`

To create references to scalar values, we have to use the `&` reference modifier. This can be in function arguments, `function(&$foo)`, and it can also be by assignment, `$foo=&$bar;`.

As opposed to scalar references, which have to be explicitly created, PHP object variables are references by default. When dealing with objects in PHP, the expectation is that you are almost always dealing with them by reference. This means that as you pass an object into a method of another class, for example, you have not copied it – it is still the same object instance. If you do any kind of value assignment of an object in PHP, you are simply creating another reference to the single instance of the object. This includes both assigning to variables and also passing the instance into other methods.

It's worth having a read through the basic docs on object references:

PHP: Objects and references - Manual

`https://www.php.net/manual/en/language.oop5.references.php`

Have a look at the following code, which illustrates briefly how object instances are passed by reference by default:

src/Part2/Chapter5/reference.php

Repo: `https://git.io/JRwdL`

```php
<?php

declare(strict_types=1);

namespace Book\Part2\Chapter5;

//For non object variables, we have to use the & sign to
declare references
```

```php
$a = 1;
echo "\n\$a is {$a}";


// $b is a reference to $a
$b =&$a;


// by updating $b, we actually update $a
$b = 2;
echo "\nAnd now \$a is {$a}";


//A simple object that gives its object ID when we cast it to
string
$instance = new class() {
    public function __toString(): string
    {
        return (string)\spl_object_id($this);
    }
};
echo "\n\$instance ID: {$instance}";


// Now creating a simple reference to that instance
// Note that we do not include a &, it is all automatic
$reference1 = $instance;
echo "\n\$reference1 ID: {$reference1}";


// Now creating a function and calling, passing in the instance
(static function (object $reference2): void {
    echo "\n\$reference2 ID: {$reference2}";
})($reference1);


// Finally, getting a new instance
$newInstance = clone $instance;
echo "\n\$newInstance ID: {$newInstance}\n";
```

Output:

So, what we have learned is that PHP allows us to work by "reference" as opposed to by "value." For scalar values, creating and working with references is done explicitly by using the & modifier.

When working with objects, the opposite is true and object variables are always "references" to an instance. When we say $instance=new stdClass(), we are creating the instance and we are assigning a reference for that instance to $instance. If we then assign $instance to another variable, $foo=$instance, we have simply created another reference; there is still only one instance of the class.

Let's now have a look at how we can make new objects in PHP.

Making new objects

We've already seen how we can create objects using the new keyword, but there are other ways of creating them, and it is worth knowing about them as we learn about comparing objects.

Have a look at the following code, and then we will look further into each of the methods.

First, a simple class that implements the magic __clone method is as follows:

src/Part2/Chapter5/NewInstance/Cloner.php

Repo: https://git.io/JRwdt

```php
<?php

declare(strict_types=1);

namespace Book\Part2\Chapter5\NewInstance;
```

```php
final class Cloner
{
    public string $state = 'limbo';

    public function __construct()
    {
        $this->state = 'constructed';
    }

    public function __clone()
    {
        $this->state = 'cloned';
        echo "\nI am multiplying: hey me, meet me";
    }

    /** The actual ID for the unique object instance */
    public function getObjectId(): int
    {
        return \spl_object_id($this);
    }
}
```

Cloning is a way of creating a new instance by copying a current instance. We will discuss it in more detail shortly.

Now we have a simple class that implements __serialize and __unserialize:

src/Part2/Chapter5/NewInstance/Sleeper.php

Repo: https://git.io/JRwdq

```php
<?php

declare(strict_types=1);

namespace Book\Part2\Chapter5\NewInstance;

use RuntimeException;
```

```php
final class Sleeper
{
    private string $foo = 'bar';
    private int $boo    = 123;
    /** @var resource */
    private $fp;

    public function __construct()
    {
        $this->openResource();
    }


    /**
     * Handle any cleanup tasks before going down for
serialisation,
     * then return the data need to actually store in
serialised form.
     *
     * @return array<int, mixed>
     */
    public function __serialize(): array
    {
        echo "\nI am going to sleep";

        //deliberately excluding our resource as it can not be
serialised
        return [$this->foo, $this->boo];
    }


    /**
     * Handle setting the data of our new instance by unpacking
the
     * serialised data array and assigning it as required. Any
resources can
     * be reestablished as required.
     *
     * @param array<int, mixed> $data
```

```php
    */
    public function __unserialize(array $data): void
    {
        echo "\nI have awoken!";
        [$this->foo, $this->boo] = $data;
        //reconnecting to our resource
        $this->openResource();
    }

    private function openResource(): void
    {
        $fp = \fopen(__FILE__, 'rb');
        if ($fp === false) {
            throw new RuntimeException('Failed opening file');
        }
        $this->fp = $fp;
    }
}
```

Serialization is a way of converting values into storable strings and conversely converting the special string format back into values or objects. Again, we will discuss this in more detail shortly.

The following example illustrates how we can use these code samples to create new instances via cloning, reflection, and serialization:

src/Part2/Chapter5/new_instance.php

Repo: `https://git.io/JRwdm`

```php
<?php

declare(strict_types=1);

namespace Book\Part2\Chapter5;

require __DIR__ . '/../../../vendor/autoload.php';

use Book\Part2\Chapter5\NewInstance\Cloner;
```

```php
use Book\Part2\Chapter5\NewInstance\Sleeper;
use ReflectionClass;

echo "\nSome cloning:";
$cloner  = new Cloner();
$cloner2 = clone $cloner;
echo "\nCloner ID: {$cloner->getObjectId()}, Cloner2 ID:
{$cloner2->getObjectId()}";
echo "\n\$cloner == \$cloner2? " . \var_export($cloner ===
$cloner2, true);
echo "\n This is false because \$cloner state is {$cloner-
>state} but \$cloner2 state is {$cloner2->state}  ";

echo "\n\nAnd some reflection";
$clonerReflection = (new ReflectionClass(Cloner::class))-
>newInstance();
echo "\n\$cloner == \$clonerReflection? " .
    \var_export($cloner === $clonerReflection, true);
$clonerReflNoConstruct =
    (new ReflectionClass(Cloner::class))->newInstanceWithoutCon
structor();
echo "\n\$cloner == \$clonerReflNoConstruct? " .
    \var_export($cloner === $clonerReflNoConstruct, true);
echo "\n This is false because \$cloner state is
{$cloner->state} but \$clonerReflNoConstruct state is
{$clonerReflNoConstruct->state}  ";

echo "\n\nAnd some serializing/unserializing";
$sleeper       = new Sleeper();
$sleeperAsleep = \serialize($sleeper);
echo "\nSleeper Asleep:\n{$sleeperAsleep}";

echo "\nNow unserializing with allowed classes:";
$sleeper2 =
    \unserialize($sleeperAsleep, ['allowed_classes' =>
[Sleeper::class]]);
echo "\n\$sleeper === \$sleeper2? " .
    \var_export($sleeper === $sleeper2, true);
```

Output:

```
😣 ● ⊡   joseph@php-book: ~

joseph@php-book:~$ php new_instance.php

Some cloning:
I am multiplying: hey me, meet me
Cloner ID: 2, Cloner2 ID: 4
$cloner == $cloner2? false
 This is false because $cloner state is constructed but $cloner2 state
is cloned

And some reflection
$cloner == $clonerReflection? false
$cloner == $clonerReflNoConstruct? false
 This is false because $cloner state is constructed but
$clonerReflNoConstruct state is limbo

And some serializing/unserializing
I am going to sleep
Sleeper Asleep:
O:39:"Book\Part2\Chapter5\NewInstance\Sleeper":2:{i:0;s:3:"bar";i:1;i:123;}
Now unserializing with allowed classes:
I have awoken!
$sleeper === $sleeper2? false
```

So, as you can see, when we create instances using cloning, reflection, and serialization, equality may not always be guaranteed, and you need to pay attention. For example, the instance of $sleeper is different because although the scalar values are the same, the file pointer is now different, as you can see when you inspect the values in xdebug.

```
∨ ≣ $sleeper = {Book\Part1\Chapter2\NewInstance\Sleeper} [3]
    🗆 foo = "bar"
    🗆 boo = {int} 123
    🗆 fp = {resource} resource id='118' type='stream'
∨ ≣ $sleeper2 = {Book\Part1\Chapter2\NewInstance\Sleeper} [3]
    🗆 foo = "bar"
    🗆 boo = {int} 123
    🗆 fp = {resource} resource id='119' type='stream'
```

sleeper-debug.png

Cloning

You can also clone an existing instance of an object, which will trigger the `__clone` method on the object if it is defined. Have a read of the docs:

PHP: Object Cloning - Manual

`https://www.php.net/manual/en/language.oop5.cloning.php`

Normal variables are *set by value* by default in PHP – for example, `$b=$a` copies the value of `$a` to a new variable, `$b`, unless we use `&`. With objects, it is reversed, and assignment simply creates a reference by default. If you want to actually create a new copy with the same values, then you need to use `clone`.

The magic `__clone` method is not meant to handle the cloning itself; it is designed to give you chance to fix any errant outcomes of cloning something.

Reflection

You can use reflection to get a new instance of an object, possibly bypassing the `__construct` method as well if you want to. Please note that in general, you do not want to use these methods; I am merely listing them here for completeness.

Have a look at the following three methods:

- Firstly, a simple new instance without any constructor arguments:

    - **PHP: ReflectionClass::newInstance - Manual**

        - `https://www.php.net/manual/en/reflectionclass.newinstance.php`

- The same, but with constructor arguments:

    - **PHP: ReflectionClass::newInstanceArgs - Manual**

        - `https://www.php.net/manual/en/reflectionclass.newinstanceargs.php`

- Finally, for special moves, a new instance without even calling the constructor:

    - **PHP: ReflectionClass::newInstanceWithoutConstructor - Manual**

        - `https://www.php.net/manual/en/reflectionclass.newinstancewithoutconstructor.php`

Here is a quick code example showing how these work:

src/Part2/Chapter5/reflection_creation.php

Repo: `https://git.io/JRwdY`

```php
<?php

declare(strict_types=1);

namespace Book\Part2\Chapter5;

use Book\Part2\Chapter5\ReflectionNewInstance\Foo;
use ReflectionClass;

require __DIR__ . '/../../../vendor/autoload.php';

$reflectionClass = new ReflectionClass(Foo::class);

// This is pretty much the same as just calling new Foo('new
instance with args');
// It becomes useful when you don't actually know what class
you are instantiating
// because you are deep into the world of meta programming
$newInstance = $reflectionClass->newInstance('new instance with
args');
echo "\n\$newInstance->bar = {$newInstance->bar}";

// This is almost the same as new instance, but we pass an
array rather than just listing arguments.
// This is less useful now that we have the splat operator, but
you might find it useful
// when you want to build an array before creating the instance
$newInstanceArgs = $reflectionClass->newInstanceArgs(['new
instance with array args']);
echo "\n\$newInstanceArgs->bar = {$newInstanceArgs->bar}";
```

```
// Finally, bypassing the constructor completely. This trick is
used by Doctrine extensively
// and is the first thing that confuses people who didn't know
this was possible.
// Clearly there are major risks in bypassing the constructor
as generally the constructor
// will be responsible for ensuring that the class properties
are all properly set up and valid.
// Bypassing this safety is not something to be done lightly!
$newInstanceWithoutConstructor = $reflectionClass->newInstanceW
ithoutConstructor();
echo "\n\$newInstanceWithoutConstructor->bar =
{$newInstanceWithoutConstructor->bar}";
```

Output:

```
joseph@php-book: ~

joseph@php-book:~$ php reflection_creation.php
$newInstance->bar = new instance with args
$newInstanceArgs->bar = new instance with array args
$newInstanceWithoutConstructor->bar = default
```

Serialization

The final method you could use to get a new instance of an object, but one you should be very wary of, is unserialize.

Serialization is the process of converting a data value into a storable string format. The special format can be unserialized back into an instance of the original data:

PHP: serialize - Manual

```
https://www.php.net/manual/en/function.serialize.php
```

There are caveats, though, in that not all forms of data can be serialized and not all class properties will be serialized. To get the full details on this, I suggest you hit the docs page:

PHP: Object Serialization - Manual

```
https://www.php.net/manual/en/language.oop5.serialization.php
```

However, the short version is that these things will generally not be serialized:

- Internal PHP objects
- Static class properties
- Resources

To convert the stored data back into a value or object, we use the `unserialize` function:

PHP: unserialize - Manual

`https://www.php.net/manual/en/function.unserialize.php`

This will take any previously serialized PHP variable and bring it back to life as a real variable. This can include class instances. This might seem awesomely powerful, and it can be, but with great power comes great responsibility.

It is your responsibility to ensure that only those classes you expect are instantiated. To be honest, this feature has become such a target for exploits that if you find yourself reaching for it, you should probably second guess yourself and consider using something less exploitable, such as JSON:

PHP Object Injection | OWASP

`https://owasp.org/www-community/vulnerabilities/PHP_Object_Injection`

To avoid unexpected classes being unserialized, *you really must* pass in a second argument of allowed classes as you can see in this line: `$sleeper2 = unserialize($sleeperAsleep, ['allowed_classes' => [Sleeper::class]]);`. Even better, don't use PHP serialization and use JSON instead.

Summary

That brings us to the end of Chapter 5, so here's a quick recap of what we have covered.

Firstly, we looked at the way objects and classes within an inheritance chain can be regarded as not only themselves but also all of their parents and interfaces.

We then had a look at the way comparison operators work when used with object instances and the difference between identity and equality.

Finally, we looked at the way PHP object variables are actually just references to a single instance and also looked at some different ways you can create a new instance.

In the next chapter, we are going to look at parameter and return types, which is where types gain most of their utility. We're also going to get our heads around covariance and contravariance – basically, the rules that define in what way you can tweak the parameter and return types when you are implementing or overriding methods from interfaces or parent classes, respectively.

6

Parameter, Property, and Return Types

Hopefully, after reading the preceding chapters and topping up your knowledge gaps by hitting the official docs pages, you now have a good understanding of how PHP types work. What we are going to explore in this chapter is the way that those types can be checked and enforced in function or method parameters and return types. This is where types really gain their utility and so it is important that you have a clear understanding of how this works.

We will start off by looking at the difference between the default "coercive" mode and the recommended but optional "strict" mode. Then, we are going to try to get our heads around covariance and contravariance and understand how they limit what we can do when extending parent classes or implementing interfaces.

This chapter will cover the following topics:

- Coercive and strict modes
- Covariance and contravariance

As usual, you can find all the code samples for this chapter in the main repo for the book available on GitHub at `https://github.com/PacktPublishing/The-Art-of-Modern-PHP-8`.

Coercive and strict modes

Type definitions give our code the guarantee that parameter and return types will be correct. They can operate in two modes. *Coercive* – the default – is basically as if a manual type cast is called on each parameter at the top of the function, and the return parameter before the variable is returned. This brings back a lot of the type-juggling pain and uncertainty we are trying to avoid.

The other approach, and the one I suggest you use, is strict. In strict mode, PHP will spit its dummy out (throw an exception) at the first sign of your code being misused (by you, no doubt). This early and robust failure allows you to quickly find issues in your code without having to wait for bugs to occur and then figuring out that the cause of the bug is an invalid value being passed further up the call chain.

To enable strict mode, you must include `declare(strict_types=1);` at the top of your PHP file. You have probably noticed that this is done in the various examples you have seen in this book. You should not even need to get in the habit of doing this; simply configure your IDE to always include this in the file templates that get used when creating new files. You should also enforce this with coding standard tools when you come to set up your **continuous integration (CI)** chain.

> **Coercive mode example**
>
> I was going to illustrate how coercive mode works, but I decided against it – let's just not go there. Hopefully, at some point, we will be able to configure strict mode at a more global or namespace level so we can cut down on the boilerplate of adding it to every file.
>
> For now, just imagine that in coercive mode, you generally won't get type errors, but you will get random type juggling happening.
>
> My advice is to use strict mode all the time.

I strongly suggest that you use strict mode in all your modern PHP code so that you catch meaningful errors early in your execution.

You can read about the full range of types that can be declared in the official docs:

PHP: Type declarations - Manual

`https://www.php.net/manual/en/language.types.declarations.php`

Have a look at the following code, which compares PHP 5 styles (both slack and defensive) with modern, strict PHP.

First, we have a classic, optimistic PHP 5 developer who has dutifully annotated their code with DocBlocks in the hopes that users of their code will stick to the expected parameter types. If you know the "Cheeto lock" meme, that's basically where we are at...

src/Part2/Chapter6/TypeDeclarations/YeOldeClass.php

Repo: `https://git.io/JRwd2`

```php
<?php

declare(strict_types=1);

namespace Book\Part2\Chapter6\TypeDeclarations;

use stdClass;

/**
 * Ye Olde Fashioned Class
 * Way back when we had to use a whole boat load of comments
and boilerplate
 * to define types. Unfortunately its about as defensively
useful as a
 * chocolate teapot.
 */
final class YeOldeClass
{
    /** @var int[] */
    private $anArray;
    /** @var stdClass */
    private $anObject;
    /** @var float|int */
    private $aNumber;
    /** @var string */
    private $aString;
    /** @var bool */
    private $aBool;
```

```php
/**
 * @param int[]     $anArray
 * @param int|float $aNumber
 * @param string    $aString
 * @param bool      $aBool
 */
public function __construct(
    array $anArray,
    stdClass $anObject,
    $aNumber,
    $aString,
    $aBool = true
) {
    $this->anArray  = $anArray;
    $this->anObject = $anObject;
    $this->aNumber  = $aNumber;
    $this->aString  = $aString;
    $this->aBool    = $aBool;
}


/** @return int[] */
public function getAnArray()
{
    return $this->anArray;
}


/** @return stdClass */
public function getAnObject()
{
    return $this->anObject;
}


/** @return int|float */
public function getANumber()
{
```

```php
        return $this->aNumber;
    }

    /** @return string */
    public function getAString()
    {
        return $this->aString;
    }

    /** @return bool */
    public function isABool()
    {
        return $this->aBool;
    }
}
```

Next, we have the wiser PHP 5 developer who doesn't trust users of their code (including, most of all, themself). This class properly checks the validity of the parameters passed in, though at the cost of 16 lines of boilerplate, which will need proper unit testing to ensure there are no gaps or issues:

src/Part2/Chapter6/TypeDeclarations/YeOldeDefensive.php

Repo: `https://git.io/JRwda`

```php
<?php

declare(strict_types=1);

namespace Book\Part2\Chapter6\TypeDeclarations;

use RuntimeException;
use stdClass;

/**
 * Ye Olde Fashioned Defensive Class
 * The only way to be truly defensive was to build in lots of
type checking
 * and enforcement.
```

```php
    */
final class YeOldeDefensive
{
    /** @var int[] */
    private $anArray;
    /** @var stdClass */
    private $anObject;
    /** @var float|int */
    private $aNumber;
    /** @var string */
    private $aString;
    /** @var bool */
    private $aBool;

    /**
     * @param int[]       $anArray
     * @param int|float $aNumber
     * @param string      $aString
     * @param bool        $aBool
     */
    public function __construct(
        array $anArray,
        stdClass $anObject,
        $aNumber,
        $aString,
        $aBool = true
    ) {
        $errors = [];
        if (false === (\is_int($aNumber) || \is_float($aNumber))) {
            $errors[] =
                'invalid $aNumber ' .
                $aNumber .
                ', must be an int or a float';
        }
        if (\is_string($aString) === false) {
```

```php
            $errors[] = 'invalid $aString ' . $aString . ',
must be a string';
        }
        if (\is_bool($aBool) === false) {
            $errors[] = 'invalid $aBool ' . $aBool . ', must be
a bool';
        }
        if ($errors !== []) {
            throw new RuntimeException('Errors in constructor
params: ' .
                                        \print_r($errors,
true));
        }
        $this->anArray  = $anArray;
        $this->anObject = $anObject;
        $this->aNumber  = $aNumber;
        $this->aString  = $aString;
        $this->aBool    = $aBool;
    }


    /** @return int[] */
    public function getAnArray()
    {
        return $this->anArray;
    }


    /** @return stdClass */
    public function getAnObject()
    {
        return $this->anObject;
    }


    /** @return int|float */
    public function getANumber()
    {
        return $this->aNumber;
    }
```

```php
    /** @return string */
    public function getAString()
    {
        return $this->aString;
    }


    /** @return bool */
    public function isABool()
    {
        return $this->aBool;
    }
}
```

Finally, we have the modern PHP developer. If they simply add the declare(strict_types=1) line at the top of their file and also make sure all parameters and return types are set, they can write much less code. Hardly any DocBlocks (wahey!) and no verbose type checking boilerplate (woo!):

src/Part2/Chapter6/TypeDeclarations/ModernClass.php

Repo: https://git.io/JRwdV

```php
<?php

declare(strict_types=1);

namespace Book\Part2\Chapter6\TypeDeclarations;

/**
 * The modern class requires nearly no docblocks for type
information,
 * everything it strongly defined in code apart from the
contents of arrays
 * and other iterables. We still don't have generics so we have
to docblock
 * that but we can at least get some type safety with the splat
operator.
 */
```

```php
final class ModernClass
{
    /** @var int[] */
    private array $anArray;

    public function __construct(
        private object $anObject,
        // notice union type, PHP 8 feature
        private int | float $aNumber,
        private string $aString,
        private bool $aBool = true,
        // choosing the type safety of splat over the
        // convenience of constructor promotion and named parameters
        int ...$anArray
    ) {
        $this->anArray = $anArray;
    }

    /** @return int[] */
    public function getAnArray(): array
    {
        return $this->anArray;
    }

    public function getAnObject(): object
    {
        return $this->anObject;
    }

    public function getANumber(): int | float
    {
        return $this->aNumber;
    }

    public function getAString(): string
    {
```

```php
        return $this->aString;
    }

    public function isABool(): bool
    {
        return $this->aBool;
    }
}
```

Here, we have some code that illustrates the way that strictly enforced types for all array, object, and scalar types bring huge amounts of safety:

src/Part2/Chapter6/type_declarations.php

Repo: `https://git.io/JRwdw`

```php
<?php

declare(strict_types=1);

namespace Book\Part2\Chapter6;

use Book\Part2\Chapter6\TypeDeclarations\ModernClass;
use Book\Part2\Chapter6\TypeDeclarations\YeOldeClass;
use Book\Part2\Chapter6\TypeDeclarations\YeOldeDefensive;
use ReflectionClass;
use RuntimeException;
use stdClass;
use Throwable;

require __DIR__ . '/../../../vendor/autoload.php';

/*
 * Notice how I can totally misuse this class,
 * despite YeOlde Developer's best efforts at clearly
documenting what I'm supposed to do,
 * like a classic user I can find weird and wonderful ways of
stabbing myself in the eye
 */
```

```php
echo "\nGetting new instance of YeOldeClass";
$yeOlde = new YeOldeClass([1, 2, 3], new stdClass(), '1', 123,
'yes');

echo "\nYeOlde number is a " . \gettype($yeOlde->getANumber())
.
    ' with a value of ' . \var_export($yeOlde->getANumber(),
true);

/*
 * I can't get past the defensive class, though
 */
echo "\n\nGetting new instance of YeOldeDefensiveClass";
try {
    $yeOldeDefensive =
        new YeOldeDefensive([1, 2, 3], new stdClass(), '1',
123, 'yes');
} catch (RuntimeException $runtimeException) {
    echo "\nFailed instantiating, got this error: " .
        $runtimeException->getMessage();
}
/*
 * Oh but wait, a determined user can always find a way to stab
themselves
 */
echo "\nNow trying to get an instance of YeOldeDefensiveClass
being sneaky and using reflection";
$yeOldeDefensive =
    (new ReflectionClass(YeOldeDefensive::class))->newInstanceW
ithoutConstructor();
echo "\nYeOldeDefensive number is a " .
    \gettype($yeOldeDefensive->getANumber()) .
    ' with a value of ' .
    \var_export($yeOldeDefensive->getANumber(), true);

/*
 * Now the same class in modern PHP, there are lots of barriers
to even the most determined user stabbing themselves
```

```php
*/
echo "\n\nTrying to get an instance of ModernClass with invalid
params";
try {
    $modern = new ModernClass(new stdClass(), '1', 123, 'yes',
...[1, 2, 3]);
} catch (Throwable $throwable) {
    echo "\nAnd failed, got an instance of " .
$throwable::class .
        " with an error message:\n {$throwable-
>getMessage()}";
}


echo "\n\nNow trying to get an instance of ModernClass being
sneaky and using reflection";
$modern =
    (new ReflectionClass(ModernClass::class))->newInstanceWitho
utConstructor();
try {
    echo "\nModern number is a " . \gettype($modern-
>getANumber()) .
        ' with a value of ' . \var_export($modern-
>getANumber(), true);
} catch (Throwable $throwable) {
    echo "\nAnd failed, got an instance of " .
$throwable::class .
        " with an error message:\n {$throwable-
>getMessage()}";
}
```

Output:

```
joseph@php-book: ~

joseph@php-book:~$ php type_declarations.php

Getting new instance of YeOldeClass
YeOlde number is a string with a value of '1'

Getting new instance of YeOldeDefensiveClass
Failed instantiating, got this error: Errors in constructor params:
Array
(
    [0] => invalid $aNumber 1, must be an int or a float
    [1] => invalid $aString 123, must be a string
    [2] => invalid $aBool yes, must be a bool
)

Now trying to get an instance of YeOldeDefensiveClass being sneaky and
using reflection
YeOldeDefensive number is a NULL with a value of NULL

Trying to get an instance of ModernClass with invalid params
And failed, got an instance of TypeError with an error message:
 Book\Part2\Chapter6\TypeDeclarations\ModernClass::__construct():
Argument #2 ($aNumber) must be of type int|float, string given, called
in
/home/book_ops/php-book-code/src/Part2/Chapter6/type_declarations.php
on line 55

Now trying to get an instance of ModernClass being sneaky and using
reflection
And failed, got an instance of Error with an error message:
 Typed property
Book\Part2\Chapter6\TypeDeclarations\ModernClass::$aNumber must not be
accessed before initialization
```

So, as you can see, the modern code will just not work if we don't instantiate it properly. Completely not working at all is good; it's better than working enough so that no one notices that it's actually broken. Also, notice that while the type options in PHP 8 are vastly improved, we still have compromises to make. In this instance, the modern developer has chosen type safety on the array of ints by utilizing splat, but that comes at the cost of constructor promotion and also forbids the use of named parameters. Type safety is better than syntactic sugar though, so we will take it whenever we can.

Hopefully, now you are clear that modern PHP supports type declarations for all property types apart from resources. By using `declare(strict_types=1)` on all of our PHP files, we ensure that any code that gets a type it was not expecting will throw an exception. This removes our need for writing lots of defensive checks and verbose DocBlocks and allows us to stop wasting our time writing boring boilerplate and focus on the real task at hand.

Let's move on to looking at some of the nuances of parameter and return types when working with interfaces and inheritance.

Covariance and contravariance

Covariance and contravariance is one of those topics that once you have got your head around it, then it becomes quite intuitive – however, explaining it is somewhat challenging. The worst thing about covariance and contravariance is the words used to describe them. I admit to always forgetting which one is which!

You can have a look at the Wikipedia page, though you may end up more confused than you were before:

Covariance and contravariance (computer science) - Wikipedia

`https://w.wiki/HJT`

A much better idea, and, as you have probably gathered, something I generally encourage, is to hit the official PHP docs:

PHP: Covariance and Contravariance - Manual

`https://www.php.net/manual/en/language.oop5.variance.php`

Covariance and contravariance refer to the rules for what parameter and return types you are allowed to use when extending classes or implementing interfaces.

The following points are quoted from the official docs:

- Contravariance allows a parameter type to be *less specific* in a child method, than that of its parent.

- Covariance allows a child's method to return a *more specific* type than the return type of its parent's method.

Let's look at contravariance in detail first.

Contravariance – that is, allowing less specific parameter types than the parent

Contravariance means that our implementation can differ from our parent implementation, but only in one direction – more permissive and open on the accepted types. If we have a hierarchical chain, we can only move up the chain toward the grandparents. If it's a scalar type hint, we can extend it with a union type.

So, what this means is that when extending classes, or implementing interfaces, we are allowed to change the types that the method will accept in parameters, but only by making them less specific. That could even include just removing type hinting altogether, or using the mixed type, which is basically the same thing.

If you think about this logically, then if the method was previously expected to take a string, but now takes anything, it will still work fine with code that calls it and passes a string. Therefore, it's an allowable change of API.

Next, let's take a dive into covariance.

Covariance – that is, allowing more specific return types than the parent

Covariance means that our implementation can differ from our parent implementation, but only in one direction – this time it's less permissive. We can only make our return type more specific. If it was a union type, it can only be one of the types in the union. If it was a hierarchical object type, then it can only move further down the hierarchical chain.

So, this means that when extending classes or implementing interfaces, we are allowed to change the return type, but only by making it more specific.

Again, this makes sense logically. Any code that deals with the return of this method call and can handle both the `int` and string returns is going to continue to work fine even though it will only ever get int. Therefore, it's an allowable change of API.

You might have noticed I'm being quite repetitive here. This is deliberate as I'm trying to hammer the point home. It's simple, but also easy to get muddled on.

Let's have a look at some code!

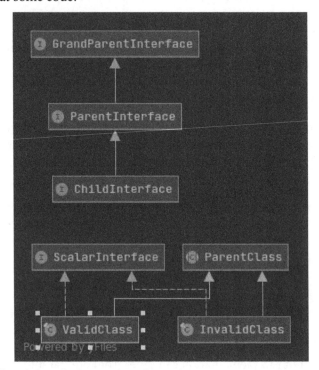

So, first up, there's a three-tier hierarchy of interfaces, imaginatively named
`GrandParent`, `Parent`, and `Child`:

src/Part2/Chapter6/CoContra/GrandParentInterface.php

Repo: `https://git.io/JRwdr`

```php
<?php

declare(strict_types=1);

namespace Book\Part2\Chapter6\CoContra;

interface GrandParentInterface
{
}
```

src/Part2/Chapter6/CoContra/ParentInterface.php

Repo: `https://git.io/JRwdo`

```php
<?php

declare(strict_types=1);

namespace Book\Part2\Chapter6\CoContra;

interface ParentInterface extends GrandParentInterface
{
}
```

src/Part2/Chapter6/CoContra/ChildInterface.php

Repo: `https://git.io/JRwdK`

```php
<?php

declare(strict_types=1);

namespace Book\Part2\Chapter6\CoContra;

interface ChildInterface extends ParentInterface
{
}
```

And now there's another interface that defines a method with scalar parameter and return type hints:

src/Part2/Chapter6/CoContra/ScalarInterface.php

Repo: `https://git.io/JRwdi`

```php
<?php

declare(strict_types=1);

namespace Book\Part2\Chapter6\CoContra;
```

```php
interface ScalarInterface
{
    public function doSomething(string | int $foo): string;
}
```

Now, we have an abstract parent class that defines a method that type hints for the mid-tier `ParentInterface` in both parameter and return types:

src/Part2/Chapter6/CoContra/ParentClass.php

Repo: `https://git.io/JRwdP`

```php
<?php

declare(strict_types=1);

namespace Book\Part2\Chapter6\CoContra;

abstract class ParentClass
{
    abstract public function getSomething(
        ParentInterface $thing
    ): ParentInterface;
}
```

Now, finally, we have two actual classes that are pulling all of the above together.

The first one is completely invalid and you can see in the DocBlocks why this is. Both methods have completely invalid parameter and return type modifications. You can't see it in the book, but in my IDE, `InvalidClass` has a lot of red squigglies:

src/Part2/Chapter6/CoContra/InvalidClass.php

Repo: `https://git.io/JRwdX`

```php
<?php

declare(strict_types=1);

namespace Book\Part2\Chapter6\CoContra;
```

```php
final class InvalidClass extends ParentClass implements
ScalarInterface
{
    /**
     * Invalid - have tried to make the param tighter by moving
it down the
     * hierarchical chain and also invalid as we have tried to
make the
     * return type wider by moving it up the hierarchical
chain.
     */
    public function getSomething(ChildInterface $thing):
GrandParentInterface
    {
        return $thing;
    }

    /**
     * Invalid - have tried to make the param tighter by
removing int as an
     * allowed type and also invalid as we have now tried to
widen the return
     * types by adding int as an allowed return type.
     */
    public function doSomething(string $foo): string | int
    {
    }
}
```

The second class is valid; all the parameter and return types have moved in the allowed direction and so while the API is different from parent implementations, it is entirely legal:

src/Part2/Chapter6/CoContra/ValidClass.php

Repo: `https://git.io/JRwd1`

```php
<?php

declare(strict_types=1);
```

```php
namespace Book\Part2\Chapter6\CoContra;


final class ValidClass extends ParentClass implements
ScalarInterface
{
    /**
     * Contravariant with ParentClass, param type moved up a
notch on the
     * hierarchical chain.
     *
     * Covariant with ParentClass, return type moved down
     * a notch on the hierarchical chain.
     */
    public function getSomething(GrandParentInterface $thing):
ChildInterface
    {
        return new class() implements ChildInterface {
        };
    }


    /**
     * Contravariant with Interface, types expanded to accept
ints.
     *
     * Covariant with Interface, return type has been tightened
and int has
     * been removed as an allowed type.
     */
    public function doSomething(string | int $foo): string
    {
        return (string)$foo;
    }
}
```

Remembering the rules

When extending classes or implementing interfaces, we are only allowed to do the following:

- Make parameters less specific
- Make return types more specific

You don't need to know what the correct term is, but **you must understand the rules**.

The reason it works this way is that it ensures that other code has a high chance of continuing to work even though you have changed the API. If you understand this reason why the rules are in place, it makes it a lot easier to remember what the rules are.

Summary

That brings us to the end of *Section 2*.

Let's have a quick reminder of what we have covered so far.

First of all, we made sure we understood what types are, and then we had a really good look at the scalar types: the fundamental types that form the basis of all of our data. We learned about the four different ways we can create strings and illustrated some of the pros and cons of each. We had a very brief look at some string functions, though I encourage you to really go back to the docs and see how many there are. We looked at ints and floats, and explained how floats can catch you out. And, of course, we touched on bools; there's not much to say about them other than that they are great.

After this exploration of scalars, we moved on to looking at type juggling and comparison. We looked at the difference between equality and identity when comparing things. We confirmed that the rules around type juggling are predictable but often complex and ideally should be avoided.

We had a brief look at resources and then touched upon arrays and iterables, though both of these topics really warrant your own further investigation as there is a huge amount there to learn. I especially encourage you to look at generators as they provide a very ergonomic way to do highly customized iteration without excessive boilerplate.

After this, we had a look at the "nothing" types in PHP, nullable, void, and the gotcha, which is the uninitialized type property.

Next, we moved on to object types and looked at class and interface inheritance and how this works with comparison – what the concepts of equal and identical mean when referring to objects. We learned a bit about references in PHP and the way that scalars can be optionally passed by reference, but objects are always by reference. We learned about different ways that objects can be instantiated and explored how this can impact object identity and equality.

Then, we moved on to looking at how PHP implements property, parameter, and return types. We had a look at strict and coercive mode and suggested you use strict mode by default.

We then looked at contravariance and covariance, hammering home the fact that when extending classes or implementing interfaces, we can only do the following:

- Make parameters less specific
- Make return types more specific

We understood that the reasoning behind these rules is to ensure that client code that is not aware of the customization in child classes will still work if it conforms to the API of the parent classes, which keeps things sane and safe.

In the next part, we're going to move away from learning about PHP language features and step into the world of clean code and design patterns, a huge and often contentious topic. I will do my best to steer you through it in three chapters; wish me luck!

Section 3 – Clean PHP 8 Patterns and Style

The previous two sections were about fundamental language features. This section is where we start looking at writing code rather than just understanding it. If you haven't already, you are **strongly encouraged** to clone or download the code from the GitHub repository hosted at `https://github.com/PacktPublishing/The-Art-of-Modern-PHP-8` as you really will benefit from seeing the code in your IDE when working through this section.

This section contains the following chapters:

- *Chapter 7, Design Patterns and Clean Code*
- *Chapter 8, Model, View, Controller (MVC) Example*
- *Chapter 9, Dependency Injection Example*

7

Design Patterns and Clean Code

In the previous two chapters, we have been looking at how to write modern, object-oriented, and typed PHP 8 code. That is all well and good, but there is always going to be a difference between writing valid code and writing clean, self-documenting, and easily testable code.

In this chapter, we are going to explore some ways you can move from writing code that works through to code that works and is also a pleasure to work with throughout its life cycle, from initial writing through to long-term maintenance.

This chapter will cover the following main topics:

- Clean code overview
- Design patterns

As usual, you can find all the code samples for this chapter in the main repo for the book available on GitHub at `https://github.com/PacktPublishing/The-Art-of-Modern-PHP-8`

Clean code overview

When we are writing code, there are always many ways of achieving the same goals. This means that it is possible to write perfectly functional code that achieves primary requirements but fails in other metrics. The other metrics are really important, and they include:

- Ease of reading
- Ease of comprehension
- Ease of testing
- Test coverage
- Ease of refactoring/changing

If your code scores badly on these factors, then we would regard it as having a high amount of *technical debt*.

What is technical debt?

This is one of my favorite terms because it's a metaphor that most clients can understand very quickly. Most people, and especially business owners, are generally very familiar with the concept of debt. You get something quickly, but it costs more than its initial value as you have to pay for it over time, often with significant interest.

Technical debt refers to taking shortcuts now to deliver working code quickly, but that code then has to be maintained and supported over time, and the costs of supporting technical debt-laden code are much higher than code with low technical debt.

Over time, the cost of maintaining code with high technical debt can be significantly greater than equally functional but more cleanly written code.

While writing your code, you are going to hit similar scenarios on a regular basis. Not only will you have likely met these scenarios before, but countless other developers have in the past. Rather than reinvent the wheel, it makes sense to reuse similar strategies that are proven to work well. That is the whole concept of design patterns – code strategies to meet particular requirements or scenarios that can be easily reused and are also easy for other developers to understand as they are familiar. We'll look at design patterns in their own section, later.

There are whole books written on the concept of clean coding. It can be something of a subjective topic, though there are certainly some rules and guidelines that have been almost universally acknowledged as correct in regard to writing code that is clear and clean – scoring as highly as possible on the metrics we outlined earlier.

In this section, we're going to have a very quick look at some clean code concepts, and to start with, we're going to try to understand some of the popular acronyms.

Clean Code Acronyms (CCA)

When talking about clean code, there are a few very famous acronyms that you probably want to familiarize yourself with if you don't already know them (ironically, as you will see, the use of acronyms is an anti-pattern).

SOLID

So, this is a big one. I think largely because, while very popular and neatly fitting into a meaningful acronym, the actual definitions are a bit obtuse and so have generated reams and reams of debate, blogs, articles, and books with pages and pages of text devoted to clarifying exactly what SOLID really means.

Be careful when reading about SOLID as the vague language of the principle has led to a wide range of interpretations, confusion, and misunderstanding. In fact, don't even take what I have written as anything more than "one guy's opinion" and please do read into this more to determine your own clear understanding.

SOLID – Wikipedia

```
https://w.wiki/JAz
```

Here is the Wikipedia summary of SOLID:

- **S**ingle-responsibility principle
  - "A class should have one and only one reason to change. A class should only have a single responsibility, that is, only changes to one part of the software's specification should be able to affect the specification of the class."

- **O**pen–closed principle
  - "Software entities ... should be open for extension, but closed for modification."

- **LSP**
  - "Objects in a program should be replaceable with instances of their subtypes without altering the correctness of that program." See also design by contract.

- Interface segregation principle

  - "Many client-specific interfaces are better than one general-purpose interface."

- Dependency inversion principle

  - One should "depend upon abstractions, (not) concretions."

My understanding of SOLID

Not the easiest concept to understand, I tend to distill this down to:

- **S**: Classes should only do or represent one specific feature or requirement.

  - Think of a very well-written and highly detailed specification. A single class should only ever represent a single feature in that detailed specification, never more than that.

  - If requirements change, this should affect only those classes or modules that are directly related to that change, which in turn requires that classes and modules are tightly focused on specific requirements.

- **O**: Split common and variable parts of a feature into separate classes and allow them to be combined to handle different scenarios.

  - So, you have a notification system that needs to send emails and Slack and SMS messages – you would create a `MessageSender` interface to handle the specific type of message, but keep the general message notification logic centralized in a class that simply uses the `MessageSender` and doesn't need to know or care exactly how the message is sent.

  - When the specification or requirements change, you should be able to adjust a minimal amount of code that really does need to be changed, without causing a ripple of required changes across unrelated parts of the code base.

- **L**: Where a class is expected to be a dependency or method argument, the class should implement an interface that can be type hinted for.

  - The calling or dependant class should not know or care about the implementation of the interface and should readily accept any class that implements the interface.

  - Any class implementing that interface should be sufficient for the system to work correctly and should not require any special handling or behavior – that is, you should not need to check for specific types beyond the interface.

- **I**: Interfaces should be tightly focused.

  - It is perfectly fine for a class to implement multiple interfaces.
  - Try to keep interfaces small enough so that they do not include features that may not be needed – it's better to split them into multiple interfaces.

- **D**: High-level abstractions should not depend on low-level implementations.

  - Where possible and sensible, abstractions should depend on other abstractions, not on specific implementations.
  - Where possible, class properties and method parameters should be interfaces, abstract classes, or scalar instead of specific classes.

Or to distill this down even further:

- Write small focused classes and interfaces with each only representing one feature or entity, delegating other tasks and data to other objects that are class properties of the current class.
- Where possible, type hint for the highest-level abstraction for methods and properties and allow these to be easily swapped out without any code changes to your class.

Let's discuss each of the points of SOLID in a little more detail.

The single-responsibility principle

The **Single-Responsibility Principle (SRP)** states that each software module should have one and only one reason to change.

There is a wealth of online discussion and articles about this point. It seems that there is widespread confusion about exactly what this point means. Some people take the phrase quite literally to say that a class should only do or represent one thing. This leads us toward a structure of very small, tightly focused classes. This is not necessarily a bad thing, but it is a misunderstanding of the principle.

Other interpretations regard this as more of a pointer toward "Separation of Concerns," where each class should be responsible for one, potentially changeable, part of the specification. If the specification changes, then those changes should largely be encapsulated inside the class.

You can read an article by Uncle Bob, the guy who actually created this principle, in which he tries to clarify exactly what he meant:

Clean Coder Blog

```
https://blog.cleancoder.com/uncle-bob/2014/05/08/
SingleReponsibilityPrinciple.html
```

In this article, he tries to clarify that the changes he meant were not runtime changes, but changes in the actual code due to changing specifications. He provides an alternative wording:

Gather together the things that change for the same reasons. Separate those things that change for different reasons.

And he goes further to explain that this is about allowing cohesion between things that change for the same reason, but reducing or removing coupling between things that change for different reasons. Remember, we are talking about changes to the specification, not changes to runtime data properties or state.

What the principle should mean to you is that, when structuring your application, you keep coupling between classes and modules as low as possible, but you do allow coupling or cohesion where those elements are all related to providing the same feature or functionality.

If someone changes the spec and says the `widget` should actually do a `wobble` instead of a `wibble`, then that should only require changes to the `widget` and there should not be widespread changes throughout your code base to reflect a change in this single area of the specification.

If you find that the easiest way for you to stick to this principle is to keep all your classes small and tightly focused on a single task or value – delegating other tasks or data storage to related classes that can be accessed as class properties or dependencies – then I would agree that it is a valid technique to meet the requirements of the SRP.

The open-closed principle

Here's the Wikipedia definition of the open-closed principle:

- A module will be said to be open if it is still available for extension. For example, it should be possible to add fields to the data structures it contains or new elements to the set of functions it performs.

- A module will be said to be closed if [it] is available for use by other modules. This assumes that the module has been given a well-defined, stable description (the interface in the sense of information hiding).

The open-closed principle – Wikipedia

```
https://w.wiki/3AG4
```

The open-closed principle is generally agreed to be related to the ability to inherit from parent definitions to extend their behavior without having to change the parent element.

What this means is that a single piece of code can be utilized but have its behavior changed without requiring changes to the code itself. This leads to a flexible and easier-to-manage code base that is generally more "future-proof" and makes changes much less risky as they do not require the kinds of global changes that often yield weird and wonderful bugs.

PHP provides two main mechanisms for this:

- Class inheritance
- Interfaces

Extensive use of class inheritance, as you have already seen, can lead to highly complex and coupled code structures, which become brittle. Interfaces are generally a better solution as the behavior is by definition completely up for interpretation.

A nice example of this would be logging. Imagine a class that does "something," and it also needs to log information as it runs. It shouldn't need to know or care exactly how those logs are handled, but we do need to easily change the logging behavior based on things such as the current environment (development or production).

To achieve this, we might define a `LoggerInterface`, which our class can require as a dependency. That logger interface will be called upon at various stages but exactly what happens when we call it is entirely dependent on the actual interface implementation. It might even just do nothing.

As this is such a common scenario, the PHP-FIG group have designed a standard `LoggerInterface`, which you can read about here:

PSR-3: Logger Interface – PHP-FIG

```
https://www.php-fig.org/psr/psr-3/
```

Any class that might need to log things can type-hint for this `LoggerInterface` but does not need to know or care exactly how the logging is implemented.

The `LoggerInterface` itself is a great example of the open-closed principle. It defines a clear API that must be adhered to. As it is an interface, it must be extended as it has no inherent implementation and purely defines the API that an actual implementation must adhere to. That API is closed for modification. While some covariant and contravariant (remember these?) changes in the API are allowed, these changes are valid implementations of the original API as defined in the interface, thanks to the specific co/contravariance rules enforced by PHP.

The Liskov substitution principle

Wikipedia defines the **Liskov substitution principle (LSP)** as: *A program that uses an interface must not be confused by an implementation of that interface.*

Liskov substitution principle – Wikipedia

`https://w.wiki/3AG5`

We saw in the open-closed principle that elements of a system should be changeable without needing to change the code of those elements. This can be done by injecting different implementations of a dependency such as a logger.

The LSP makes it clear that our class that does "something" should not need to know or care exactly which implementation of a logger has been included. It should be perfectly acceptable to simply call interface methods and any returned values should be correct and expected.

Taking the logger as an example, we should not need to check which kind of logger it is, nor do any special checks.

Imagine a badly written filesystem logger that writes to a log file. Imagine that this particular implementation tries to write to a folder but doesn't have any sanity checking to ensure the folder exists before trying to write to it. If our class needs to use that logger, then it will have to first check whether the logger implementation is this badly written one, and if it is, will need to perform the folder creation work to ensure that the system is stable or risk a fatal error at runtime.

This is a clear breach of the LSP. You will know if you are breaking the LSP if you ever have to do any `instanceof` checks on class dependencies.

The interface segregation principle

Clients should not be forced to depend upon interfaces that they do not use.

Interface segregation principle – Wikipedia

`https://w.wiki/3AG6`

What this means is that interfaces should be small and focused. A class that requires something, for example, a logger, should not have to also bring in lots of email-related functionality that it does not require. Instead, the logging and the emailing should be split out into separate interfaces that can be separately included as required.

The alternative to this structure is what are often called "God objects." The God object is like an entire toolbox when all you needed was a single spanner of a specific size. Taken to the extreme, the God object may be a toolbox with a generator and a shower head with running water, a TV screen, and a karaoke microphone with flashing LED lights.

What that would mean is that if your class needed a karaoke mic (hey, why not?), it has no choice but to fire up the entire God object and bring it all in, just to call one single method or access one single property (let it be, let it be…).

What we should be doing instead is splitting up all the things into discrete interfaces that can be separately brought into your class as dependencies on an "as needed" basis. This strategy aids in keeping things simple, can improve the performance and efficiency of your code, and also helps when it comes time to test and refactor your code.

This can lead to classes that have more dependencies, and that is fine. It is better to have five dependencies for five different requirements than one dependency that provides five things we need and five things we don't.

The dependency inversion principle

The principle states:

- High-level modules should not depend on low-level modules. Both should depend on abstractions (for example, interfaces).

- Abstractions should not depend on details. Details (concrete implementations) should depend on abstractions.

The dependency inversion principle – Wikipedia

`https://w.wiki/3AG7`

What this one means is that when composing your class and bringing in dependencies, you should generally not depend on a specific implementation but instead depend on an interface that provides the behaviors you require.

Your class should only care about what its dependency can do. Your class should not know, need to know, or care exactly how dependencies do the things your class needs them to do.

One word of caution, though. There can be a temptation to "interface all the things." This can lead to a lot of bloat in your code. I would suggest that if you are not sure, then feel free to take this approach. However, where there is a certainty that you will only ever use a single implementation, then it is OK to depend on that implementation.

Interfaces are very useful when there is even a small possibility that the dependency might need to be swapped out for an alternative implementation. Bear in mind, one place where dependencies are often swapped out is when testing.

The bottom line on SOLID

I've done my best to explain SOLID and clarify some of these principles. I hope you have found this useful. If you disagree with some of my interpretations of SOLID, that's great – it means you are fully engaging with the topic and I would encourage you to read further on this. If this is a topic you find interesting and would like to read more on, then I really encourage you to do so. My only word of caution is that this topic seems to yield many different opinions and so it makes sense to check your sources and try to get a balanced range of opinions. A good starting point for further reading is this summary article by Uncle Bob:

Clean Coder Blog

```
https://blog.cleancoder.com/uncle-bob/2020/10/18/Solid-
Relevance.html
```

Let's move on now to tackle a much simpler acronym, DRY.

DRY

This one is much easier to get your head around. It stands for:

- **Don't**
- **Repeat**
- **Yourself**

Quite simply, it means don't copy and paste code or values around, and instead find ways to move that code or value definition into a single reusable place.

For functionality, that would be into a class, class method, or perhaps a global function (if that is appropriate).

For values, then you would move them into a (class) constant unless it must be mutable, at which point you would assign them to a variable or class property. If you find yourself writing scalar values directly into method calls more than once, you almost certainly want to be moving that scalar value into a class or interface constant.

Next on our list of simpler acronyms: KICK.

KICK

- **Keep**
- **It**
- **Clear**
- **OK**

OK, I made this one up – perhaps you can tell by the dodgy acronym, but let's go with it…

What I wanted to mention here is the general principle of writing your code in a way that is optimal for comprehension. The next sections will outline ways in which you can do just that.

Clear naming

This is simple but vitally important to the legibility of your code. Use full, clear, and descriptive names that accurately describe what the item is or does.

Have a look at this variable – you have no doubt seen this kind of thing:

```
$isDME=false;
```

Then compare that with this next variable – it took a few seconds to type those extra few characters:

```
$isDebugModeEnabled=true;
```

The difference in comprehension time though is significant and could even be absolute. Future you, or some other hapless developer burdened with maintaining your code, could never truly know what you intended the first variable to mean…

- `isDarkMatterEngaged?`
- `isDubiousMaterialEnabled?`
- `isDoubleMegaExceptional?`

Often, the only way to decipher this kind of acronym-based variable naming is to go and look at how it is being used and thereby reverse engineer the original meaning. What a huge waste of time!

The same goes for class and method names – make them a bit longer and use the extra characters to document what they do. If you use an IDE, then autocompletion kicks in and means that it rarely costs you any more keystrokes anyway.

Also, when naming things, try to be boring. Just be clear; don't come up with your own vocabulary. Name it in a way that anyone reading it will have a very clear idea of what it does or is. The following table has a few basic examples of what could be considered good and bad naming:

Bad	Good
`$n`	`$name`
`unlink()`	`delete()`
`retrieveItem()`	`getItem()`

Ubiquitous language

This is a term from **domain-driven design (DDD)**. We don't have space to go into what DDD is all about, but this one aspect can be easily applied to any project. The term "ubiquitous language" describes the jargon that you have in a particular project.

Let's say you are building a CRM system for a client that is designed to replace a current manual system. As the client describes the workflow, they will have names for the statuses, documents, and other things that are involved that are already embedded within the company and form their internal jargon.

"Pass me the **RFP** from that new **Lead** would you, Janice?"

It is important that you understand this jargon and then repeat it in your code. If they refer to new inquiries as " leads," then in your code, you should have a `LeadEntity`, not an `EnquiryEntity`. If they refer to requests for quotes on client projects as "RFPs" (short for Requests for Proposals), then you should have a `RequestForProposalEntity`. I do suggest that in your code you unpack acronyms in ubiquitous language. It's very easy to cognitively compress an unpacked acronym back into its terse form as required.

This simple trick means that when you read client specifications and meeting notes, you can easily translate from corporate jargon into code, and more quickly and easily understand what the code is doing. Likewise, when you talk to the client about needing to extend the functionality around the `LeadEntity,` then they quickly understand what you are talking about.

The "ubiquitous" bit (which means "present, appearing, or found everywhere," if you didn't know) refers to the fact that the same jargon terms are used everywhere – in the code, in the client specs, in conversations, and meetings. Everyone from the client to developers refers to the same concepts with the same names.

More, smaller methods

One great way to make your intention clear is to have small clearly defined methods that have a very clear name. You can adopt the rule that all method names must begin with a verb:

- `getItem()`
- `validateItem()`
- `saveItem()`
- `isValid()`
- `hasItem()`

Though, like any rule, you also break it freely when it's the right thing to do, such as when creating fluent interfaces:

```
$queryBuilder->select('i')->from('Item', 'i')->where('i.id = ?1');
```

By using smaller methods with clear names, your code can become very readable and clear to understand.

Self-documenting

Done well, your code can read so clearly that docblocks become pointless as the method and variable names clearly explain what is going on. This is what we call "self-documenting code" and it looks something like this:

```
final class ThingProcessor implements ProcessorInterface {

    public function doTheProcess(ThingInterface $thing) :void{
        if($this->canProcess($thing) === false){
            throw new ProcessNotPossibleException('meaningful error message');
        }
        // do the process
    }
```

```php
    // public access in case client code wants to check if it
can process
    public function canProcess(ThingInterface $thing):bool{
        return $this->isValid($this) && $this->isNotAlreadyDone
($thing);
    }


    private function isNotAlreadyDone(ThingInterface
$thing):bool{
        // check if already done
        return $result;
    }


    public function isValid(ThingInterface $thing):bool{
        // check for validatity
        return $result;
    }
}
```

Hopefully, you agree that the preceding code does not require any extra documentation to describe what it is doing. The class, method, and variable names are all clear and do not require extra docblocks.

By prefixing methods with is and can, it is clear that the method answers a question and will return a boolean value.

Other methods are prefixed with verbs such as do or get, followed by the details of the action that will be taken. By making method and variable names a little longer and with names chosen to impart meaning, the requirement for explanatory docblocks can be reduced significantly, which ultimately saves keystrokes (assuming you were going to do those nice explanatory docblocks).

Early return and cyclomatic complexity

You might not have heard of cyclomatic complexity, but you have certainly tasted it. Quite simply, it is a score that includes the total number of *decision points* in a method, plus one for the entry.

A decision point is:

- Anything that causes a branch (usually demarked with curly braces), including `if`, `while`, `for`, `case`, and `match`

- `AND` `OR` conditionals as part of a compound statement

It is not simply the number of lines, so please don't try to reduce cyclomatic complexity by creating one-liners.

The higher the cyclomatic complexity, the more complex and difficult to read and understand the method is. Anything above 7 is high, with over 10 being *obscene*.

The solution for cyclomatic complexity is to break the large method up into smaller methods and also to utilize one awesome strategy called "early return:"

src/Part3/Chapter7/early_return.php

Repo: `https://git.io/JRw5n`

```php
<?php

declare(strict_types=1);

namespace Book\Part3\Chapter7;

/**
 * Note the error returns are towards the end of the function
 * - a dead giveaway that this should be returning early
 */
function isValidValueNested(int|float|null $value): bool
{                                           # cylomatic complexity 1
    if (is_int($value) || is_float($value)) {# cylomatic complexity 3
        if ($value > 10) {                  # cylomatic complexity 4
            if ($value < 200) {             # cylomatic complexity 5
                return true;
            } else {                        # cylomatic complexity 6
```

```
                return false;

            }
        } else {                              # cylomatic
complexity 7
            return false;

        }
    } else {                                  # cylomatic
complexity 8
        return false;

    }
}
```

```
/**
 * Trying to reduce this to a one liner can reduce cylomatic
complexity, but it
 * can also have a negative impact on legibility and clarity,
breaking the KICK rules.
 * It is generally not likely to be the lowest cyclomatic
complexity
 * and is not a strategy you should employ in general to reduce
cyclomatic complexity
 */
function isValidValueOneLiner(int|float|null $value): bool
{                                      # cylomatic complexity 1
    return (
        (null !== $value)      # cylomatic complexity 2
        && ($value > 10)       # cylomatic complexity 3
        && ($value < 200)      # cylomatic complexity 4
    );
}
```

```
/**
 * This function uses the "early return" style to expose and
wrap up decision points early in the function, returning
 * as soon as possible and thereby closing a decision tree.
 * By checking for errors and returning early, we can totally
avoid any nesting, and it is sooo
 * much easier to read
```

```
 * I would suggest this should be your default cyclomatic
complexity reducing strategy
 */
function isValidValueEarlyReturn(int|float|null $value): bool
{                               # cylomatic complexity 1
    if (null === $value) { # cylomatic complexity 2
        return false;
    }
    if ($value < 10) {      # cylomatic complexity 3
        return false;
    }
    if ($value > 200) {     # cylomatic complexity 4
        return false;
    }


    return true;
}


/**
 * The eagle eyed among you might have spotted that there are
unnecessary decision points in the above functions.
 * Removing these is another valid cyclomatic reduction
strategy and can be employed.
 * I would not generally recommend this unless you have good
unit test coverage to ensure you have not
 * inadvertently broken things, or you are really, really sure
you have read the code correctly :)
 */
function isValidLogicallyReduced(int|float|null $value): bool
{                                       # cylomatic complexity
1
    return $value > 10 && $value < 200; # cylomatic complexity
3
}


echo "\nisValidValueNested(20)===isValidValueOneLiner(20)? " .
    var_export(isValidValueNested(20) ===
isValidValueOneLiner(20), true);
```

```
echo "\nisValidValueNested(20)===isValidValueEarlyReturn(20)? "
.

    var_export(isValidValueNested(20) ===
isValidValueEarlyReturn(20), true);


echo "\nisValidValueNested(20)===isValidLogicallyReduced(20)? "
.

    var_export(isValidValueNested(20) ===
isValidLogicallyReduced(20), true);
```

Output:

```
joseph@php-book: ~

joseph@php-book:~$ php early_return.php
isValidValueNested(20)===isValidValueOneLiner(20)? true
isValidValueNested(20)===isValidValueEarlyReturn(20)? true
isValidValueNested(20)===isValidLogicallyReduced(20)? true
```

In the preceding code, you can see two functions that are totally equivalent to each other, but I'm sure you will agree that the second one is much easier on the eyes and easier to quickly understand. The reason it's so much nicer is that there is less indentation and way fewer curly braces. It also has lower cyclomatic complexity and so incurs a lower cognitive load.

The technique is simply to unpack ugly nested conditionals and try to return as early as possible in the method with any success or error condition. As soon as that condition has returned, that entire branch is finished and the remainder of the method or function can be much simpler. This can generally be repeated until all scenarios are covered. Implementing the early return technique to your code is probably the single best thing you can do to make your code much easier to read and have significantly lower cyclomatic complexity.

If you would like to see some real-life cyclomatic complexity improvements, you could take a look at this PR:

Reduce cyclomatic complexity in Problem Methods by sergeynezbritskiy · Pull Request #318 · magento/magento2-functional-testing-framework · GitHub

```
https://github.com/magento/magento2-functional-testing-
framework/pull/318/files
```

Favor immutability

One clean code trick that is easy to implement and can really help keep things tidy is to always try to keep mutability to a minimum. Mutability describes the ability to change the value(s) stored within an object instance after it has been created.

The easiest way to make an object immutable is to keep all properties private and to only allow values to be injected within the constructor. The access can then be restricted to get only by simply not providing any form of set method:

```php
final class Immutable{
    public function __construct(private string $value){}
    public function getValue():string{
        return $this->value;
    }
}
```

The classic example of a gotcha related to mutability is with DateTime versus DateTimeImmutable:

src/Part3/Chapter7/immutable.php

Repo: https://git.io/JRw5c

```php
<?php

declare(strict_types=1);

namespace Book\Part3\Chapter7;

use DateInterval;
use DateTime;
use DateTimeImmutable;

$start     = new DateTime('2020-02-23 09:16:00');
$oneMinute = new DateInterval('PT1H');
$end       = $start->add($oneMinute);

echo "Mutable started at {$start->format('H:i:s')} "
    . "\nand ended at {$end->format('H:i:s')}"
```

```php
        . "\na difference of " . $start->diff($end)->format('%h
hours');

$start     = new DateTimeImmutable('2020-02-23 09:16:00');
$oneMinute = new DateInterval('PT1H');
$end       = $start->add($oneMinute);

echo "\n\nImmutable started at {$start->format('H:i:s')} "
        . "\nand ended at {$end->format('H:i:s')}"
        . "\na difference of " . $start->diff($end)->format('%h
hours');
```

Output:

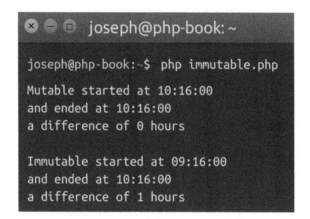

```
joseph@php-book: ~

joseph@php-book:~$ php immutable.php

Mutable started at 10:16:00
and ended at 10:16:00
a difference of 0 hours

Immutable started at 09:16:00
and ended at 10:16:00
a difference of 1 hours
```

As you can see, the fact that DateTime is mutable and is passed by reference can very easily catch out the unwary. Immutable objects will either totally prevent values from being changed or will return a brand-new instance of itself with the new value.

Maximize meaningful types

This one is somewhat related to the LSP in SOLID. One thing that I see sometimes that disappoints me is when class methods return meaningless types that provide no value or clarity.

Ensure that your interfaces provide enough information for your client classes to properly interact and for client developers to get proper and complete autocompletion without requiring them to actually run the code to figure out what the implementation actually is.

For example, imagine your system works with a `PersonInterface` that has a single method, `getName`. However, in your code, you actually have multiple implementations of `PersonInterface` and these all have a variety of useful behaviors that are not hinted at within the interface. The only way to know what methods can be called is to run `instanceof` checks, or if the code path determines a single implementation, to force your IDE to type-hint for a specific implementation using docblocks. If you are always going to return a `Customer` that has things like `getAccountNumber`, then you should be hinting for a `Customer` instead of a `PersonInterface`, thereby making things clearer and more robust.

You are likely to find it impossible to avoid these "vague interface" scenarios completely, but I would encourage you to keep them to a minimum.

If you do find yourself having to deal with broad types, try to minimize the code path where the real type is not known by enforcing or checking the type as early as possible so that the greatest amount of the code can be clearly typed. Ideally, this should be done with actual return types rather than docblocks to ensure correctness.

There will always be certain parts of your code that deal with very vague abstractions but try to determine and enforce the more precise type as early as possible to maximize comprehension and correctness, and to facilitate meaningful autocompletion and static analysis.

Minimize magic

In software engineering, there are things called "magic numbers" and also "magic strings." Sometimes these are grouped under the general term "magic constants." These are values that have an important meaning and effect on application behavior.

Magic number (programming) – Wikipedia

`https://w.wiki/3DQU`

When these values are specified directly within code, they are regarded as "magic." By using values directly, it is not possible for the reader to immediately know what the value actually represents.

Using magic numbers and strings is a clear violation of the DRY principles, as you generally have to repeat those magical values in multiple places. If for some reason, the magical values need to be changed, then generally this would require multiple code edits and hunting down the value across your code base.

First, have a look at this class – `WetWizard` is breaking the DRY rules and is using both magic numbers and magic strings:

src/Part3/Chapter7/Magic/WetWizard.php

Repo: `https://git.io/JRw5C`

```php
<?php

declare(strict_types=1);

namespace Book\Part3\Chapter7\Magic;

/**
 * The wet wizard is using magic strings and numbers directly
within code. These values would need to be individually
 * hunted down and replaced should we ever need to refactor.
 */
final class WetWizard
{
    public function getCurrencySymbol(): string
    {
        // magic string
        return '£';
    }

    public function formatPrice(int | float $price): string
    {
        // magic number
        return \number_format(num: $price, decimals: 2);
    }

    public function getDisplayPrice(int | float $price): string
    {
        // magic string and magic number
        return '£' . \number_format(num: $price, decimals: 2);
    }
```

```php
    public function isValidPrice(int | float $price): bool
    {
        // magic number
        return $price > 20;
    }

    public function ensureValidPrice(int | float $price): int |
float
    {
        if ($this->isValidPrice($price)) {
            return $price;
        }

        // magic number
        return 20;
    }
}
```

The equivalent but DRY and magic-free class, `DryMuggle`, demonstrates how to do this properly:

src/Part3/Chapter7/Magic/DryMuggle.php

Repo: `https://git.io/JRw5W`

```php
<?php

declare(strict_types=1);

namespace Book\Part3\Chapter7\Magic;

/**
 * The DRY Muggle class is magic free and is not repeating
itself.
 */
final class DryMuggle
{
    /**
     * We define our values in only one single place, ideally
```

```
in the whole codebase.
    * By using public constants we can provide safety,
clarity, self documentation
    * and trivially easy refactoring should these values need
to change.
    */
    public const CURRENCY_SYMBOL = '£';
    public const MIN_PRICE       = 20;
    public const NUM_DECIMALS    = 2;


    public function getCurrencySymbol(): string
    {
        return self::CURRENCY_SYMBOL;
    }


    public function formatPrice(int | float $price): string
    {
        return \number_format(num: $price, decimals: self::NUM_
DECIMALS);
    }


    public function getDisplayPrice(int | float $price): string
    {
        return self::CURRENCY_SYMBOL . \number_format(num:
$price, decimals: self::NUM_DECIMALS);
    }


    public function isValidPrice(int | float $price): bool
    {
        return $price > self::MIN_PRICE;
    }


    public function ensureValidPrice(int | float $price): int |
float
```

```
    {
        if ($this->isValidPrice($price)) {
            return $price;
        }

        return self::MIN_PRICE;
    }
}
```

As you can see, changing the currency or minimum price would require only a single code edit. When looking in detail at a specific method, you have the benefit of the const name to help you understand the purpose of the value, making the code self-documenting.

The general strategy to avoid magic values is to define them as consts that have a clear and descriptive name, and then ensure that you always use the single const everywhere you need that particular string.

In a nutshell, if you find yourself copying and pasting strings and numbers around in your code, or free typing them multiple times, you are almost certainly breaking this rule.

If you would like to read more about why this rule is important, this Stack Overflow thread is worth a read:

Anti-patterns – What is wrong with magic strings? – Software Engineering Stack Exchange

```
https://softwareengineering.stackexchange.com/questions/365339/
what-is-wrong-with-magic-strings
```

We've explored a few clean code concepts and I hope now that you understand what we are talking about when we refer to "clean code." The next step of your learning is to write your own code and then refactor it to try to make things as clean and clear as possible. You can use the previous clean code principles as a starting point and I would encourage you to continue to read up on clean code concepts and try to continually improve the clarity and "cleanliness" of your code.

Let's move on to discussing the standardized approaches to common coding scenarios: design patterns.

Design patterns

Now we have had a look at clean code, the next thing to learn about in this chapter is design patterns. As explained previously, these are tried and true code patterns that you can use to solve common problems. They provide well-used structure and nomenclature that makes your code clear in terms of what it does and also provides you with a scaffold to build upon when solving common problems.

Design patterns are generally grouped into four categories. The following sections detail the four categories, with some examples of each. Rather than trying to provide full code examples for each pattern (which would take up way too many pages), I am simply going to describe the pattern and then link to examples within open source code bases. For **Model, View, Controller (MVC)** and **Dependency Injection (DI)**, we have a chapter dedicated to each.

Creational patterns

Creational patterns are used when creating class instances. These make sense when the process of building or creating an instance is a little more complex than simply using a new `ClassName()`. Here are four example patterns that can each be used to solve different creational problems.

Factory

Quite possibly the most prevalent design pattern, a factory is a class whose sole purpose is to create instances of one or more classes:

symfony/AllMySmsTransportFactory.php at ffc2c1e1dacccf57848d1a63d92fc6fd48250bc1 · symfony/symfony · GitHub

```
https://git.io/JYxAa
```

As you can see in this example, factory classes often have a `create` method, which will return an instance of `TransportInterface`. In this instance, the specific instance is hinted at with a docblock due to legacy co/contravariance rules in PHP 7. In PHP 8, this could be changed to properly hint the correct type:

```php
<?php
//DateTime factory pattern example:
$instance = DateTime::createFromFormat('Y-m-d');
```

Builder

The **builder** is like a factory in the sense that it's about object creation, but where the process of creating a class has lots of moving parts, options, and conditional things going on.

Generally, the builder pattern will include multiple method calls before the actual creation method is called, whereas a factory is generally expected to do all the work with one method call.

A good example of this is the `QueryBuilder` in Doctrine:

The QueryBuilder – Doctrine Object Relational Mapper (ORM)

`https://www.doctrine-project.org/projects/doctrine-orm/en/2.8/reference/query-builder.html`

This is a utility that allows the developer to create an instance of a DQL query using an ergonomic set of methods to define various properties and then finally call `getQuery` to actually retrieve the configured instance. You might also notice that builders such as these also generally implement the Fluent pattern, which we will discuss shortly.

Notice the following code based on the Doctrine query builder and how it is used to ultimately create a `Query`:

```php
<?php
// $em instanceof EntityManager
// $instance is an instance of Query
$instance = $em->createQueryBuilder()
    ->select('u')
    ->from('User', 'u')
    ->where('u.id = ?1')
    ->orderBy('u.name', 'ASC')
    ->getQuery()
    ->getResult();
```

Prototype

In the prototype pattern, new instances are created via the use of `clone` as opposed to `new`. There exists a `prototype` instance, which is cloned when new instances are required.

Have a look at this example from Laminas (what used to be Zend Framework):

laminas-code/PrototypeClassFactory.php at ab0d54d8cb8b9ca1f6a8c3287e83724fbc61edbf · laminas/laminas-code · GitHub

```
https://git.io/JYxAM
```

As you can see, this takes a range of prototype instances and will return cloned instances on request.

The use case for the prototype pattern is when, for whatever reason, the process of creating a new object is very expensive and you need to have multiple unique instances of it. It could be a third-party library that performs slow API calls when it is instantiating itself, perhaps.

I will admit that this is not a pattern I can recall being used.

Singleton

The singleton pattern used to be very popular in PHP, however, this popularity has now waned due to serious issues around testability and coupling:

```php
class SingletonExample{
    /** Private static property that contains the one and only
instance */
    private static self $instance;


    /** Private constructor prevents normal instantiation */
    private function __construct(){}


    /**
     * Public static method to get the one and only instance.
     * Handles creation if the instance is not already active
     */
    public static function instance(): self
```

```
    {
        return self::$instance ??= new self();
    }
}
```

The point of a singleton is that it provides a very simple way to enforce that there is only ever one instance of a class. The downside is that it provides a static way to bring the class in as a dependency, which means that it can be coupled to your code all over the place, at any point or line, in any file.

With the advent of dependency injection containers that tend to default to maintaining single instance rules, the singleton's utility is no longer worth the cost of coupling and lack of testability.

The singleton is widely regarded as an anti-pattern, and I agree. By using a singleton, you build a hard dependency on that singleton object, which can make testing difficult. It also introduces global state, which PHP has done a great job of moving away from, and so you should avoid letting it in the back door by using singletons.

There are occasions where a singleton is a useful tool, especially when you need to enforce one and only one instance of a class as I did for the fake data, but for real production code, you are unlikely to want or need a classic singleton like this.

Back in the day, it was quite common to use a singleton to represent the database connection, with code that might look like this:

```
Database::instance()->query("select * from something");
```

With the advent of ORM and the strong advice against using singletons, this style has almost completely fallen out of favor, and I only wanted to illustrate it here so that you can recognize it. I am certainly not suggesting that it is a pattern you should look to use.

Structural patterns

Structural patterns are used as ways for classes to work together. These patterns, by definition, include a structure of classes rather than just a single class.

Facade

The facade pattern takes a complex or verbose operation that may require multiple objects and method calls and wraps it in a simple interface that takes the minimum number of arguments and requires the minimum number of method calls.

For example, you may create an email facade that provides a single method, `sendEmail`, but actually handles the following:

- The generation or conversion to HTML and text versions of the email
- The processing of attachments
- The connection to an email transport system
- The building and sending of a message
- Logging everything as it happens

You could easily expect the whole process to require multiple classes and many method calls. It could easily incorporate calls to entire modules of code, but your public interface is only a single method.

A real-world example of the Facade pattern might be the Spatie/Regex library, which attempts to wrap core regular expression functionality with an easier-to-use interface:

GitHub - spatie/regex: A sane interface for php's built in preg_* functions

```
https://github.com/spatie/regex
```

What about Laravel facades?

Try not to confuse the Facade pattern with Laravel facades, which are more of a magical way to access services statically as opposed to having explicit dependencies injected into class instances:

Facades – Laravel – The PHP Framework for Web Artisans

```
https://laravel.com/docs/8.x/facades
```

You might notice that Laravel facades look quite similar to the way that singleton classes were retrieved in days gone by. They are not as bad as the old singleton, but without proper handling, they can have a negative impact on the testability and modularization of your code.

Adapter

The adapter pattern is used when we need to make a class conform to an API that it does not naturally conform to. We do this using an adapter that implements the interface we need to implement and translates this into calls on the class we are adapting to.

A nice example of this can be seen in the PHP League Flysystem library:

GitHub – thephpleague/flysystem: Abstraction for local and remote filesystems

`https://github.com/thephpleague/flysystem/`

The Flysystem library provides a single sane API for filesystems and allows you to easily switch out the specific filesystem implementation. This allows you to do things such as develop against a local filesystem in local development, but use an Amazon S3 filesystem in production.

The Flysystem library defines a standardized interface for filesystems:

flysystem/FilesystemAdapter.php at 2.x · thephpleague/flysystem · GitHub

`https://git.io/JYxAh`

It then bundles various adapters such as AWS S3:

flysystem/AwsS3V3Adapter.php at 2.x · thephpleague/flysystem · GitHub

`https://git.io/JYxAj`

For example, take this implementation of the standard `delete` method defined in the interface, which translates or adapts this to S3-specific processes:

```php
    public function delete(string $path): void
    {
        $arguments = ['Bucket' => $this->bucket, 'Key' =>
$this->prefixer->prefixPath($path)];
        $command = $this->client->getCommand('DeleteObject',
$arguments);

        try {
            $this->client->execute($command);
        } catch (Throwable $exception) {
            throw UnableToDeleteFile::atLocation($path, '',
$exception);
        }
    }
```

The adapter pattern provides very high conformity to the LSP and is generally a great pattern to adopt.

Fluent

The Fluent pattern is used when we want to write code that is highly readable and perhaps defines a step-by-step process.

The crux of the Fluent pattern is that methods that do something return $this. This then allows client code to chain together multiple method calls against the same instance in one logical line of code.

Have a look at the following contrived example:

src/Part3/Chapter7/fluent.php

Repo: `https://git.io/JRw5l`

```php
<?php

declare(strict_types=1);

namespace Book\Part3\Chapter7;

$fluentClass = new class() {
    public function doSomething(): static
    {
        // do something
        return $this;
    }

    public function doSomethingElse(): static
    {
        //do something else
        return $this;
    }
};

//fluent usage
$fluentClass->doSomething()
    ->doSomethingElse()
    ->doSomething()
```

```
        ->doSomethingElse()
    ;
```

You have no doubt seen this technique being used all over the place, and now you also know that it is a design pattern.

Decorator

The decorator pattern is an alternative way to inherit and modify or extend functionality without using object inheritance. Instead, a class "decorates" the parent or wrapped class and acts as a simple proxy for methods that it does not want to change, but may modify the behavior of some methods and may add new methods.

Have a look at this example in Drupal:

drupal/MetadataBubblingUrlGenerator.php at 9.2.x · drupal/drupal · GitHub

```
https://git.io/JYxxe
```

You can see that `UrlGenerator` is taken as a dependency, and most methods are simple proxies that pass method calls straight through to `UrlGenerator`:

```
    public function getContext() {
        return $this->urlGenerator->getContext();
    }
```

However, there are some methods where behavior is modified and extended, for example:

```
  public function generateFromRoute($name, $parameters = [],
$options = [], $collect_bubbleable_metadata = FALSE) {
    $generated_url = $this->urlGenerator-
>generateFromRoute($name, $parameters, $options, TRUE);
    if (!$collect_bubbleable_metadata) {
      $this->bubble($generated_url, $options);
    }
    return $collect_bubbleable_metadata ? $generated_url :
$generated_url->getGeneratedUrl();
  }
```

This approach is quite similar conceptually to object inheritance. It is essentially the alternative strategy to use when you want to adopt composition instead of inheritance.

Behavioral patterns

Behavioral patterns define ways for classes to work. These patterns are generally focused on a single class, though they may define behaviors for working with other classes as properties.

Iterator

We have already had quite a good look at the Iterator pattern as it is a major part of the **Standard PHP Library** (**SPL**). To recap though, the Iterator pattern simply describes objects that are, well, iterable.

To see a real-world one, have a look at the Nette/Database `Selection` class that provides a mechanism to easily loop over database table data:

database/Selection.php at master · nette/database · GitHub

```
https://git.io/JYxxv
```

You can see that the class implements the all-important `\Iterator` interface and thus is iterable.

Strategy

The strategy pattern describes a scenario where there might be multiple ways or "strategies" to fulfill an interface. The actual choice of which strategy to use is not known until runtime. It allows you to create highly flexible code structures that can easily handle different scenarios.

The containing class will contain one or more instances of an interface that each represent different strategies for fulfilling the interface, and the choice of exactly which strategy to use can be determined at runtime.

Classic use cases for this pattern are things such as logging and caching. The class may need a `LoggerInterface` but doesn't need to know or care exactly what "strategy" the actual implementation is. Also, there may be runtime checks and calculations to determine exactly which strategy to use.

Observer

The observer pattern describes a scenario where a "subject" class actively informs one or more "observer" classes when certain events happen.

The The SPL (Standard PHP Library) defines a couple of built-in interfaces that you can use to give your observer-based code some structure.

First, the subject:

PHP Manual – SplSubject

`https://www.php.net/manual/en/class.splsubject.php`

```
SplSubject {
/* Methods */
abstract public attach ( SplObserver $observer ) : void
abstract public detach ( SplObserver $observer ) : void
abstract public notify ( ) : void
}
```

And then the observer:

PHP Manual – SplObserver

`https://www.php.net/manual/en/class.splobserver.php`

```
SplObserver {
/* Methods */
abstract public update ( SplSubject $subject ) : void
}
```

When the "subject" is updated, it will "notify" its observers.

The SPL interfaces are quite bare-bones though. For a fully-featured implementation of the observer pattern, I suggest you take a look at the Symfony `EventDispatcher` component:

GitHub – symfony/event-dispatcher: The EventDispatcher component provides tools that allow your application components to communicate with each other by dispatching events and listening to them:

`https://github.com/symfony/event-dispatcher`

The observer pattern is a great way to keep your classes decoupled but also allow changes in one piece of code to trigger actions in other pieces of code, without having to write any explicit method calls.

Chain of responsibilities

This pattern describes a situation where you want to basically play "pass the parcel" with an event or piece of data, passing it sequentially to a sequence of classes until one of them breaks the chain (for any reason) or all items in the chain have been visited.

The chain is composed of one or more classes that implement a standardized interface and includes a mechanism to register the next link in the chain as a property and to either break the chain or pass the data on to the next class in the chain.

One good example of the chain of responsibility pattern is with Laravel middleware:

Middleware – Laravel – The PHP Framework for Web Artisans

```
https://laravel.com/docs/8.x/middleware
```

In fact, any implementation of middleware is based on the principles of the chain of responsibility, if not an exact implementation of the pattern.

Middleware is a highly prevalent pattern in PHP. So much so, in fact, that PHP-FIG has created a PSR just to define a standardized HTTP middleware system (which is awesome, actually):

PSR-15: HTTP Server Request Handlers – PHP-FIG

```
https://www.php-fig.org/psr/psr-15/
```

Architectural patterns

As the name implies, architectural patterns are about the structure of your code on a more zoomed-out scale – the application or library as a whole.

MVC – Model-View-Controller

The MVC pattern is very widely used in modern PHP frameworks. The concept of this pattern is that your application is split into three sections or layers:

- Model – business logic, data, and persistence
- View – presentational logic, theming, and HTML
- Controller – request handling, routing, and generally pulling everything together to generate a response

We're going to do a much deeper dive into MVC in the next chapter, so I won't go into any more detail here.

Strangler

The Strangler pattern is not a description of what you would like to do when your client changes the requirements again, back to the way they were before you spent hours refactoring things to what they decided were the requirements last time you spoke to them.

The Strangler pattern defines a mechanism to allow you to gradually replace an old legacy system with a lovely modern system. Rather than throwing out the legacy system with all its battle-tested stability and feature-rich spaghetti code and replacing it with your shiny new system that has never served a real request, you instead wrap the legacy system in a thin layer of modern code and then gradually start to replace the legacy system with new code, doing this on a per-scenario or feature basis.

The eponymous article on this pattern is by Martin Fowler:

StranglerFigApplication

```
https://martinfowler.com/bliki/StranglerFigApplication.html
```

To implement this pattern with a legacy website system, you might first replace the view and/or routing layer with something modern but still use the legacy system to generate the data. Gradually, you might then start to replace sections of the website – perhaps the checkout in an e-commerce system – with new, modern, and beautiful code. In the meantime, there might be less important pages that are still served by the legacy system. Over time, you aim to gradually replace those as well, though the chances are there will always be some remnants of the legacy system in there, however, you will do your best to strangle most of them, smothering them in modern code.

Summary

As I previously mentioned, there are entire books written on design patterns, and so I have no expectations that you have managed to learn everything you need to know by reading this chapter only. What I do hope, though, is that you now have an understanding of what design patterns are, you have a good idea about the broad categories of design patterns, and I'd like to think that you might have got your head around a few of them. I suspect you recognize some of them from code that you are already used to working with. The best thing to do now is to continue writing code, but as you are architecting things, just take a moment to wonder whether it would be a good idea to use one of these established patterns, and then give it a go.

In the next chapter, we're going to do a deep dive into a design pattern I am almost certain you have already come across: MVC.

8
Model, View, Controller (MVC) Example

In this chapter, we're going to learn about the **Model, View, Controller** (**MVC**) pattern by building our own toy MVC system. We'll start off by revising what MVC actually means. With that understanding in place, we will then work through creating our own toy version – starting off with the Controller layer to handle requests, then the Model layer to work with data, and finally the View layer to render some **HTML**.

We will actually run the code and confirm that it all works with some test code to simulate a browser visit and the **PHPUnit** test class to confirm it really is all working.

This chapter will cover the following main topics:

- Model, View, Controller – MVC
- Controller
- Model
- View
- It lives

As usual, you can find all the code samples for this chapter in the main repo for the book available on GitHub at `https://github.com/PacktPublishing/The-Art-of-Modern-PHP-8`

Model, View, Controller – MVC

When working with modern **object-oriented programming** (**OOP**) frameworks in **PHP**, such as **Symfony** or **Laravel**, the first pattern you are going to see is called **MVC – Model, View, Controller** (`https://w.wiki/znd`).

In MVC, your application is split into three main areas. I think you can guess what the names are!

These three areas are as follows:

- **Model**: The *data* for your application – including **CRUD** (**create**, **retrieve**, **update**, **delete**).

- **View**: The *visual* – taking data and creating the output (usually HTML for PHP developers).

- **Controller**: The bit that handles requests. It uses the model to process data and prepare it for the View, then passes it to the View for rendering before finally serving back up as a response.

To assist with understanding MVC, I've put together a very simple *"toy"* MVC application. It is deliberately simple and lacks many features provided by full-blown frameworks, but I hope that by keeping it ultra-lean it will be easier to understand the MVC structure. As we go through this MVC app, we are also going to learn about other design patterns as they crop up. See if you can also see some clean code practices in play as well.

Rather than sticking to the MVC naming order, let's do this in a more logical order of responsibility when dealing with a request – Controller, Model, then View.

Controller

The first thing that a new request interacts with is the controller. As mentioned previously, the controller handles routing a request, coordinating the model to process the data, and then utilizing the view to get a response, which can then be returned. It acts as the outermost layer of your application.

Front controller

Within the MVC pattern there is another commonly used pattern called the Front Controller. This is the single point of entry for all web requests. Generally the Front Controller should be lean and delegate all actual work to specific controllers for specific requests.

The front controller's job is to take every single inbound request and decide what to do with it.

In some frameworks or applications, the front controller may handle all "Controller" level duties. However, in ToyMVC, we have decided to have discrete controllers for each section of the app. This keeps our classes small, allows us to stick to **SOLID** principles, and generally makes things nice and clear:

src/Part3/Chapter8/ToyMVC/FrontController.php

Repo: `https://git.io/JRw7A`

```php
<?php

declare(strict_types=1);

namespace Book\Part3\Chapter8\ToyMVC;

use Book\Part3\Chapter8\ToyMVC\Controller\ControllerInterface;
use Book\Part3\Chapter8\ToyMVC\Controller\Data\RequestData;
use Book\Part3\Chapter8\ToyMVC\Controller\Factory\
ControllerFactory;
use Book\Part3\Chapter8\ToyMVC\Controller\Factory\
RequestDataFactory;

final class FrontController
{
    public function __construct(
        private ControllerFactory $controllerFactory,
        private RequestDataFactory $requestDataFactory
    ) {
    }

    public function handleRequest(): void
```

```php
    {
        $requestData = $this->requestDataFactory::createFromGl
obals();
        $this->createController($requestData)
            ->getResponse($requestData)
            ->send()
        ;
    }


    private function createController(
        RequestData $requestData
    ): ControllerInterface {
        return $this->controllerFactory->createControllerForReq
uest($requestData);
    }
}
```

So what you can see here is that the front controller has two `__construct` dependencies – a factory for the request data, and a factory for building our actual controllers. That introduces us to our next design pattern – the **Factory**, which we will discuss soon.

It uses these factories to create the request data and the controller for the request, and then it uses those to do the work of handling the request.

Let's have a quick look at the `ControllerInterface`:

src/Part3/Chapter8/ToyMVC/Controller/ControllerInterface.php

Repo: `https://git.io/JRw7x`

```php
<?php

declare(strict_types=1);

namespace Book\Part3\Chapter8\ToyMVC\Controller;

use Book\Part3\Chapter8\ToyMVC\Controller\Data\RequestData;
use Book\Part3\Chapter8\ToyMVC\Controller\Data\Response;

interface ControllerInterface
```

```
{
    public function getResponse(RequestData $requestData):
Response;
}
```

So you can see that the controllers must implement one method, getResponse, which returns an instance of Response for a given RequestData instance.

Let's move on to our next pattern, which is the Factory.

Factory pattern

The Factory pattern is, as its name implies, used for manufacturing things – in this case, object instances. Factory methods are often static, though they do not have to be. The plain Factory pattern is by far the most common creational pattern you are likely to see in PHP.

Let's have a quick look at the factories utilized by the front controller.

First up is RequestDataFactory. In keeping with **KICK** naming conventions, it does exactly what it says on the tin: manufactures RequestData objects.

The RequestDataFactory has a single method that explains clearly what it does – which is access the PHP super global $_SERVER array and create a RequestData object, which can then be passed around.

This approach is nice as it keeps our meddling with super globals down to the barest minimum and makes it very clear when we do. Working directly with super globals throughout your code is definitely an anti-pattern.

src/Part3/Chapter8/ToyMVC/Controller/Factory/RequestDataFactory.php

Repo: https://git.io/JRw7p

```php
<?php

declare(strict_types=1);

namespace Book\Part3\Chapter8\ToyMVC\Controller\Factory;

use Book\Part3\Chapter8\ToyMVC\Controller\Data\RequestData;
use Book\Part3\Chapter8\ToyMVC\Controller\Data\RequestMethod;

final class RequestDataFactory
```

```
{
    public static function createFromGlobals(): RequestData
    {
        return new RequestData(
            $_SERVER['REQUEST_URI'],
            new RequestMethod($_SERVER['REQUEST_METHOD']),
            $_POST ?? null
        );
    }
}
```

Let's take a quick look at the RequestData and RequestMethod classes. First, we have RequestData:

src/Part3/Chapter8/ToyMVC/Controller/Data/RequestData.php

Repo: https://git.io/JRw7h

```php
<?php

declare(strict_types=1);

namespace Book\Part3\Chapter8\ToyMVC\Controller\Data;

final class RequestData
{
    /**
     * @param array<string,string> $postData
     */
    public function __construct(
        private string $uri,
        private RequestMethod $method,
        private ?array $postData = null,
    ) {
    }

    public function getMethod(): RequestMethod
    {
```

```php
        return $this->method;
    }

    public function getUri(): string
    {
        return $this->uri;
    }

    /** @return array<string, string>|null */
    public function getPostData(): ?array
    {
        return $this->postData;
    }
}
```

And then, RequestMethod:

src/Part3/Chapter8/ToyMVC/Controller/Data/RequestMethod.php

Repo: https://git.io/JRw7j

```php
<?php

declare(strict_types=1);

namespace Book\Part3\Chapter8\ToyMVC\Controller\Data;

use InvalidArgumentException;

/**
 * Note: We're deliberately only handling the most basic HTTP
 * verbs for the purposes of the Toy.
 * A real framework would handle other verbs such as PUT,
 * DELETE and maybe others.
 */
final class RequestMethod
{
    public const METHOD_GET  = 'GET';
    public const METHOD_POST = 'POST';
```

```php
    public const METHODS     = [
        self::METHOD_GET  => self::METHOD_GET,
        self::METHOD_POST => self::METHOD_POST,
    ];

    public function __construct(private string $name)
    {
        self::assertIsValidName($name);
        $this->name = \strtoupper($this->name);
    }

    public static function assertIsValidName(string $name):
void
    {
        if (isset(self::METHODS[$name])) {
            return;
        }
        throw new InvalidArgumentException(
            'Invalid method ' . $name . ', must be one of: ' .
\print_r(
                self::METHODS,
                true
            )
        );
    }

    public function getName(): string
    {
        return $this->name;
    }
}
```

As you can see, these are both simple, immutable, **DTO** objects.

The next factory is a little more complex. The ControllerFactory is responsible for making the correct instance of ControllerInterface for a given set of RequestData:

src/Part3/Chapter8/ToyMVC/Controller/Factory/ControllerFactory.php

Repo: `https://git.io/JRw5e`

```php
<?php

declare(strict_types=1);

namespace Book\Part3\Chapter8\ToyMVC\Controller\Factory;

use Book\Part3\Chapter8\ToyMVC\Controller\
CategoryPageController;
use Book\Part3\Chapter8\ToyMVC\Controller\ControllerInterface;
use Book\Part3\Chapter8\ToyMVC\Controller\Data\RequestData;
use Book\Part3\Chapter8\ToyMVC\Controller\Error\
NotFoundController;
use Book\Part3\Chapter8\ToyMVC\Controller\HomePageController;
use Book\Part3\Chapter8\ToyMVC\Controller\PostPageController;
use Book\Part3\Chapter8\ToyMVC\Meta\Route;
use Book\Part3\Chapter8\ToyMVC\Model\Repository\
CategoryRepository;
use Book\Part3\Chapter8\ToyMVC\Model\Repository\PostRepository;
use Book\Part3\Chapter8\ToyMVC\View\TemplateRenderer;
use InvalidArgumentException;
use ReflectionClass;
use ReflectionException;

final class ControllerFactory
{
    /**
     * Here we have an array of controller FQNs.
     * These represent the controllers that we will
     * check for matching a given set of RequestData.
     *
     * @see https://phpstan.org/writing-php-code/phpdoc-
types#class-string
     *
     * @var array<int, class-string<ControllerInterface>>
```

```
     */
    private const CONTROLLERS = [
        HomePageController::class,
        CategoryPageController::class,
        PostPageController::class,
    ];

    public function __construct(
        private CategoryRepository $categoryRepository,
        private PostRepository $postRepository,
        private TemplateRenderer $templateRenderer
    ) {

    }


    /**
     * This method will take a set of RequestData and will then
     * check all of the Controllers to see if one matches.
     *
     * To handle the matching, we are using a Route attribute
     * which includes a regex pattern to test against the
request URI.
     *
     * If we find a matching controller then we create that
controller
     *
     * @throws ReflectionException
     */
    public function createControllerForRequest(
        RequestData $requestData
    ): ControllerInterface {
        foreach (self::CONTROLLERS as $controllerFqn) {
            $route = $this->getRoute($controllerFqn);
            if ($route->isMatch($requestData)) {
                return match ($controllerFqn) {
                    HomePageController::class      => $this-
>createHomePageController(),
                    CategoryPageController::class => $this->cre
```

```
ateCategoryPageController(),
                    PostPageController::class      => $this-
>createPostPageController(),
                };
            }
        }


        return $this->createNotFoundController();
    }


    /**
     * @param class-string<ControllerInterface> $controllerFqn
     *
     * @throws ReflectionException
     */
    private function getRoute(string $controllerFqn): Route
    {
        $route =
            (new ReflectionClass($controllerFqn))-
>getAttributes(Route::class)[0]->newInstance();
        if ($route instanceof Route) {
            return $route;
        }
        throw new InvalidArgumentException(
            'Controller ' .
            $controllerFqn .
            ' does not have a Route attribute'
        );
    }


    private function createHomePageController():
HomePageController
    {
        return new HomePageController(
            $this->categoryRepository,
            $this->templateRenderer
        );
```

```
    }

    private function createCategoryPageController():
CategoryPageController
    {
        return new CategoryPageController(
            $this->categoryRepository,
            $this->templateRenderer
        );
    }

    private function createPostPageController():
PostPageController
    {
        return new PostPageController(
            $this->postRepository,
            $this->templateRenderer
        );
    }

    private function createNotFoundController():
NotFoundController
    {
        return new NotFoundController($this->templateRenderer);
    }
}
```

As you can see, we have some hard-coded, controller-class **fully qualified names** (FQNs) – as defined by accessing the ::class magic constant. These controllers are all checked to see if they match the request. If no matching controller is found, then we fall back to creating an instance of NotFoundController.

> **Note**
> This kind of hardcoding is bad and just a shortcut for the toy. We would normally keep functionality and configuration completely separate.

You might argue that the `ControllerFactory` is an example of the **Strategy** pattern due to the way it selects the correct strategy – in this case, a controller – based upon the specific request.

For the actual matching, we are using a special `Route` attribute that handles the actual matching logic.

> **Attributes reminder**
>
> A quick reminder on PHP attributes – an attribute is just a bog-standard PHP class with a couple of special rules:
>
> The class must be annotated with the special `#[Attribute]` attribute.
>
> The constructor parameters can only be scalar or simple expressions – the same as the rules for values that can be assigned to constants.

By moving the request matching logic into the standalone `Route` attribute, we help to keep the code a little more **DRY**. Let's take a look at the `Route` attribute:

src/Part3/Chapter8/ToyMVC/Meta/Route.php

Repo: `https://git.io/JRw5v`

```php
<?php

declare(strict_types=1);

namespace Book\Part3\Chapter8\ToyMVC\Meta;

use Attribute;
use Book\Part3\Chapter8\ToyMVC\Controller\Data\RequestData;
use Book\Part3\Chapter8\ToyMVC\Controller\Data\RequestMethod;

#[Attribute]
final class Route
{
    /** @var array<string, bool> */
    private array $methodNames;

    public function __construct(
        private string $routePattern,
```

```php
        string ...$methodNames
    ) {
        foreach ($methodNames as $methodName) {
            RequestMethod::assertIsValidName($methodName);

            $this->methodNames[$methodName] = true;
        }
    }


    public function isMatch(RequestData $requestData): bool
    {
        return $this->matchesMethodName($requestData)
            && $this->matchesRoutePattern($requestData);
    }


    private function matchesMethodName(RequestData
$requestData): bool
    {
        return isset($this->methodNames[$requestData-
>getMethod()
            ->getName()]);
    }


    private function matchesRoutePattern(RequestData
$requestData): bool
    {
        return \preg_match($this->routePattern, $requestData-
>getUri()) === 1;
    }
}
```

Cyclomatic complexity strategy – use key lookups

This class is a nice example of another cyclomatic-complexity-reducing strategy
– that of storing expected values as keys in an array so that the kind of checking
that might normally incur a `foreach`, `match`, or multiple `if` blocks can be
reduced to a single `isset` call.

First, we build an array in the constructor. This approach is interesting as we only actually care about the key. The value can be anything. A bool is nice here as it takes up the barest minimum of memory, and by using `true` we can use `isset` later on. When this is queried in the `matchesMethodName` call, it is as simple as checking if the key exists in the array. This is highly performant and also easy to read and comprehend.

So for our route-matching – an important piece of the Controller aspect of MVC – we are using this `Route` attribute. The first parameter it takes is a regular expression that is used to match against request-URIs, and the following parameters are one or more HTTP verbs such as `GET` or `POST`. As attributes can only take simple constructor parameters, we handle the conversion from a string to a `RequestMethod` instance within the constructor.

The `Route` class then handles the task of matching a given set of `RequestData`, first by checking if the route supports the `RequestMethod` of the request, and then checking if the request-URI matches the given regex.

For the last step in our exploration of the Controller aspect of MVC, let's look at a specific controller – the `CategoryPageController`.

src/Part3/Chapter8/ToyMVC/Controller/CategoryPageController.php

Repo: `https://git.io/JRw5f`

```php
<?php

declare(strict_types=1);

namespace Book\Part3\Chapter8\ToyMVC\Controller;

use Book\Part3\Chapter8\ToyMVC\Controller\Data\RequestData;
use Book\Part3\Chapter8\ToyMVC\Controller\Data\RequestMethod;
use Book\Part3\Chapter8\ToyMVC\Controller\Data\Response;
use Book\Part3\Chapter8\ToyMVC\Meta\Route;
use Book\Part3\Chapter8\ToyMVC\Model\Entity\Uuid;
use Book\Part3\Chapter8\ToyMVC\Model\Repository\
CategoryRepository;
use Book\Part3\Chapter8\ToyMVC\View\Data\CategoryPageData;
use Book\Part3\Chapter8\ToyMVC\View\TemplateRenderer;
```

```php
/** Note use of consts instead of magic strings for attribute
params */
#[Route(CategoryPageController::ROUTE_REGEX,
RequestMethod::METHOD_GET)]
final class CategoryPageController implements
ControllerInterface
{
    public const ROUTE_REGEX = '%^/c/(?<' .
                                Uuid::ROUTE_MATCH_KEY .
                                '>' .
                                Uuid::REGEXP_FRAGMENT .
                                ')$%m';

    public const TEMPLATE_NAME = 'CategoryPageTemplate.php';

    public function __construct(
        private CategoryRepository $categoryRepository,
        private TemplateRenderer $templateRenderer
    ) {
    }

    public function getResponse(RequestData $requestData):
Response
    {
        $uuid           =
            Uuid::createFromUri($requestData->getUri(),
self::ROUTE_REGEX);
        $categoryEntity = $this->categoryRepository-
>load($uuid);
        $templateData   = new
CategoryPageData($categoryEntity);
        $pageContent    =
            $this->templateRenderer->renderTemplate(
                self::TEMPLATE_NAME,
                $templateData
```

```
        );

        return new Response($pageContent);
    }
}
```

Notice that the `CategoryPageController` is annotated with the `Route` attribute placed above the class definition. The arguments passed into the `Route` attribute are class constants from the `CategoryPageController` itself and a class constant from the `RequestMethod`. By using class constants like this, we can ensure we keep things DRY.

You can see that the controller only currently implements one method, which is `getResponse`, as required by `ControllerInterface`. The Controller interacts with the Model and then the View layer in order to build its response. Let's now take a look at the Model.

Model

The Model represents the data and business logic for our app. In the toy MVC there is no real business logic, but in a full app, you would expect at least some form of CRUD functionality. In a real app, the Model is expected to be the most substantial aspect and certainly the bit that requires the most thorough testing, as in some regards it represents the true nature and purpose of the app itself.

In our toy, the Model is purely serving to retrieve data, but it is enough for us to introduce you to another design pattern, namely the **Repository**.

Entity pattern

An entity is a unit of data that represents a single thing. In the ubiquitous language of our application, the entity name will be meaningful and describe clearly what it represents.

For our toy MVC, we have two entity types:

- Category
- Post

The relationship between our entities is a **one-to-many** relation between `Categories` and `Posts` – meaning that `Categories` are related to zero or more `Posts`.

Let's take a quick look at `CategoryEntity`:

src/Part3/Chapter8/ToyMVC/Model/Entity/CategoryEntity.php

Repo: `https://git.io/JRw5J`

```php
<?php

declare(strict_types=1);

namespace Book\Part3\Chapter8\ToyMVC\Model\Entity;

use Book\Part3\Chapter8\ToyMVC\Model\Collection\PostCollection;

final class CategoryEntity implements EntityInterface
{
    public function __construct(
        private Uuid $uuid,
        private string $name,
        private PostCollection $postCollection
    ) {
    }

    public function getName(): string
    {
        return $this->name;
    }

    public function getPostCollection(): PostCollection
    {
        return $this->postCollection;
    }

    public function getUuid(): Uuid
    {
        return $this->uuid;
    }
}
```

What you can see is that the entity is currently an immutable **DTO**. It has three properties: a unique identifier, a name, and also a collection of `PostEntities`. We will look at collections a bit later.

The `CategoryEntity` implements the `EntityInterface`, which enforces that an entity must have a **universally unique identifier** (UUID):

src/Part3/Chapter8/ToyMVC/Model/Entity/EntityInterface.php

Repo: `https://git.io/JRw5U`

```php
<?php

declare(strict_types=1);

namespace Book\Part3\Chapter8\ToyMVC\Model\Entity;

interface EntityInterface
{
    public function getUuid(): Uuid;
}
```

Universally unique identifier (UUID)

Not a design pattern, but worth talking about while we are discussing the Model in MVC.

If you are not familiar with UUID, then in a nutshell I would describe it as a much, much better way of giving your entities unique IDs that is decoupled from your database autoincrement functionality. The UUID is generated in your own code, which means that you can create a whole graph of related entities and assign all the relation IDs between them, and finally persist the whole lot as a valid and cohesive whole. It is basically not possible to do that with autoincrement IDs.

For the toy, I have created a simple UUID implementation. Let's have a look:

src/Part3/Chapter8/ToyMVC/Model/Entity/Uuid.php

Repo: `https://git.io/JRw5T`

```php
<?php

declare(strict_types=1);
```

```php
namespace Book\Part3\Chapter8\ToyMVC\Model\Entity;

use InvalidArgumentException;
use RuntimeException;
use Stringable;

/**
 * This is a very simple UUID generator,
 * inspired by https://github.com/abmmhasan/UUID/blob/main/src/
Uuid.php
 * This is not suggested for production code!
 */
final class Uuid implements Stringable
{
    public const ROUTE_MATCH_KEY   = 'uuid';
    public const REGEXP_FRAGMENT   = '[0-9a-f]{8}(?:-[0-9a-f]
{4}){3}-[0-9a-f]{12}';
    private const VERSION          = 4;

    public function __construct(private string $uuid)
    {
        if ($this->isValid($this->uuid) === false) {
            throw new InvalidArgumentException('Invalid UUID '
. $this->uuid);
        }
    }

    public function __toString(): string
    {
        return $this->uuid;
    }

    public static function create(): self
    {
        $hex    = \bin2hex(\random_bytes(16));
        $chunks = \str_split($hex, 4);
```

```php
        $uuidString = \sprintf(
            '%08s-%04s-' . self::VERSION . '%03s-%04x-%012s',
            $chunks[0] . $chunks[1],
            $chunks[2],
            \substr($chunks[3], 1, 3),
            \hexdec($chunks[4]) & 0x3fff | 0x8000,
            $chunks[5] . $chunks[6] . $chunks[7]
        );

        return new self($uuidString);
    }

    public static function createFromUri(string $uri, string
$pattern): self
    {
        if (\preg_match($pattern, $uri, $matchGroups) !== 1) {
            throw new RuntimeException('Failed matching uri ' .
                                      $uri .
                                      ' with pattern ' .
                                      $pattern);
        }
        $id = $matchGroups[self::ROUTE_MATCH_KEY]
            ??
            throw new RuntimeException('matchGroups does not
include ' .
                                      self::ROUTE_MATCH_
KEY);

        return new self($id);
    }

    public function matches(self $uuid): bool
    {
        return (string)$this === (string)$uuid;
    }

    private function isValid(string $uuid): bool
```

```
    {
            return \preg_match('%^' . self::REGEXP_FRAGMENT .
'$%Di', $uuid) ===
                1;
    }
}
```

The actual implementation is naive and not production-ready, but is sufficient for the purposes of the toy. You might notice that there are two static factories bundled in to allow it to create instances of itself.

If you would like to use UUIDs in your own application, I would suggest you take a look at this library: `https://github.com/ramsey/uuid`.

Persistence and ORM

The persistence layer for almost all PHP applications is a relational database such as **MySQL**, **SQLite**, or **Postgres**. In modern PHP frameworks, you almost never work directly with the database or persistence layer. Instead, you interact with something called an **ORM**.

ORM stands for **object-relational mapper**. It does the job of translating object-oriented code and entities into classic relational database paradigms – tables, rows, and foreign keys.

An ORM is a beautiful thing in that it solves a very complex problem in a way that, with a little luck, you never have to worry about exactly how it does so. My favorite ORM layer is **Doctrine**. I suggest you check it out if you don't know it (`https://github.com/doctrine/orm`).

On the other hand, it is worth pointing out that an ORM is unlikely to fully protect you from needing to get down and dirty with the database at some point. As the database is almost always the first performance bottleneck in any application, then it is also the first place that code needs to be optimized, and that could involve reviewing the actual SQL queries being generated by your ORM, and maybe even overriding them.

In this regard, ORMs are often regarded as what is called a *"leaky abstraction"*: `https://w.wiki/3DQf`.

This simply means that the thing that has been abstracted away, in this case, the actual database, starts to leak through and perhaps requires direct interaction as soon as things get a little complex.

In a nutshell, using an ORM is unlikely to save you from having to properly learn your database, though they can be a great time-saver.

Singleton anti-pattern

For the toy, the persistence layer is being simulated with a hard-coded array of data which you can see in the `\Book\Part1\Chapter3\ToyMVC\FakeDataForToy` class.

I won't include the code as you don't need to see it, though I will point out that it implements the **Singleton** pattern, which we discussed in *Chapter 7, Design Patterns and Clean Code*. This is purely a shortcut for the toy.

Repository pattern

The Repository pattern solves the problem of how to retrieve entities from the persistence layer. The repository has the single task of, for a single entity, being responsible for the retrieval of specific entities. The retrieval can be by unique identifier or any other means. The repository can also be responsible for persisting any updated entities if you want, or you can opt to build a specific `EntitySaver` for this.

In our toy, we have two repositories, and they are both very similar. Let's take a look at the `CategoryRepository`:

src/Part3/Chapter8/ToyMVC/Model/Repository/CategoryRepository.php

Repo: `https://git.io/JRw5k`

```php
<?php

declare(strict_types=1);

namespace Book\Part3\Chapter8\ToyMVC\Model\Repository;

use Book\Part3\Chapter8\ToyMVC\FakeDataForToy;
use Book\Part3\Chapter8\ToyMVC\Model\Collection\
CategoryCollection;
use Book\Part3\Chapter8\ToyMVC\Model\Entity\CategoryEntity;
use Book\Part3\Chapter8\ToyMVC\Model\Entity\Uuid;
use RuntimeException;

final class CategoryRepository implements
CategoryRepositoryInterface
{
    public function loadAll(): CategoryCollection
    {
```

```php
        // Imagine that this method uses an ORM layer to build
entities from the DB
        return new CategoryCollection(...
FakeDataForToy::singleton()->getCategoryEntities());
    }


    public function load(Uuid $uuid): CategoryEntity
    {
        // Imagine that this method uses an ORM layer to query
for a specific Entity by ID
        foreach (FakeDataForToy::singleton()-
>getCategoryEntities() as $categoryEntity) {
            if ($categoryEntity->getUuid()->matches($uuid)) {
                return $categoryEntity;
            }
        }

        throw new RuntimeException('Failed finding category
with ID ' .
                                    $uuid);
    }
}
```

So the things you need to focus on in this code are the `load()` and `loadAll()` methods. This would be a bare minimum in a normal repository, and you may also have other methods to `loadByName()` and that kind of thing. The point is that the repository has the job of working with the persistence or ORM layer to retrieve entity instances as required.

You might notice that the `CategoryRepository` implements the `CategoryRepositoryInterface`:

src/Part3/Chapter8/ToyMVC/Model/Repository/CategoryRepositoryInterface.php

Repo: `https://git.io/JRw5I`

```php
<?php

declare(strict_types=1);
```

```php
namespace Book\Part3\Chapter8\ToyMVC\Model\Repository;

use Book\Part3\Chapter8\ToyMVC\Model\Collection\
CategoryCollection;
use Book\Part3\Chapter8\ToyMVC\Model\Entity\CategoryEntity;
use Book\Part3\Chapter8\ToyMVC\Model\Entity\Uuid;

interface CategoryRepositoryInterface
{
    public function loadAll(): CategoryCollection;

    public function load(Uuid $uuid): CategoryEntity;
}
```

This allows us to type hint for the interface instead of the actual repository. This in turn allows us to test classes that load categories (such as the `HomePageController`) and inject a stub repository that will not talk to the database at all, and will instead just return some test data. The point of a stub is that it will return exactly what we want, and it will do it really quickly so that tests are as fast as possible.

You already know what a single entity looks like, as returned by the `load()` method, but let's have a look at what you get when you call `loadAll()`, and our next pattern – Collection.

Collection pattern

A collection is a class that represents a collection of one or more instances of a specific class – in our case, entity classes. Collection classes generally implement the `Iterator` interface to allow simple `foreach` calls to iterate through the collection of entities.

If you work with ORMs, then you are certain to encounter collections, as they are used whenever there is a one-to-many relationship (where one entity is related to multiple instances of a related class). In our case, it is category entities that contain multiple posts.

The Collection pattern is a really common one, and thanks to more modern PHP features, you can achieve some nice type safety with a few simple tricks. Let's take a look at the `CategoryCollection`:

src/Part3/Chapter8/ToyMVC/Model/Collection/CategoryCollection.php

Repo: `https://git.io/JRw5L`

```php
<?php

declare(strict_types=1);

namespace Book\Part3\Chapter8\ToyMVC\Model\Collection;

use Book\Part3\Chapter8\ToyMVC\Model\Entity\CategoryEntity;
use Countable;
use Iterator;
use OutOfBoundsException;

/**
 * @implements Iterator<string, CategoryEntity>
 */
final class CategoryCollection implements Iterator, Countable
{
    /** @var CategoryEntity[] */
    private array $categoryEntities;

    public function __construct(CategoryEntity
...$categoryEntities)
    {
        $this->categoryEntities = $categoryEntities;
        $this->rewind();
    }

    public function next(): bool | CategoryEntity
    {
        return \next($this->categoryEntities);
    }

    /**
     * Careful here, you can return non scalar types, but
expect problems
```

```
    * later on that can be tricky to debug. Instead, return a
string or int
    * so that PHP gets an array type it expects.
    */
    public function key(): string
    {
        return (string)$this->current()->getUuid();
    }

    public function current(): CategoryEntity
    {
        $current = \current($this->categoryEntities);

        return $current instanceof CategoryEntity
            ? $current
            :
            throw new OutOfBoundsException('Failed getting
current CategoryEntity');
    }

    public function valid(): bool
    {
        return \key($this->categoryEntities) !== null;
    }

    public function rewind(): void
    {
        \reset($this->categoryEntities);
    }

    public function count(): int
    {
        return \count($this->categoryEntities);
    }
}
```

So the first thing to note is __construct which enforces that the collection is instantiated with one or more instances of CategoryEntity. PHP does not have typed arrays, but we do have the splat operator (. . .), which is close enough for our purposes. It allows the constructor to take multiple arguments, will type check them all, and then present them to the constructor body as an array. This means that by the time we are in our constructor, we can be assured that the $categoryEntities array contains only valid instances of CategoryEntity. This is perfect, as ultimately that is what we want our collection to represent.

This collection implements a few core interfaces that then allow the object to be iterated over in a simple foreach loop – namely the Iterator interface. It also implements the Countable interface, which is handy. I have chosen not to implement the ArrayAccess interface, as I want this collection to be immutable.

The primary goal of the collection is to provide type safety – that is, to allow any code working with the collection to be able to assume that every value retrieved from the collection is a valid CategoryEntity, or that an exception will be thrown if that is not the case for any reason. You can see this being implemented in the current() method. Internally, PHP calls this current() method when retrieving values in a foreach loop.

Hopefully, you can see how easy it is to make a type-safe iterable using the Collection pattern. You can choose to make it mutable if you wish, and you can also add other methods such as map and filter if they make sense.

This brings us to the end of the Model, and now we can move on to the final piece of MVC – the View.

View

The View represents the visual output that the application provides in response to a particular request. In most modern frameworks, the View layer includes a templating language that is designed to be frontend-developer-friendly, optimized for working on HTML and outputting safely escaped data. For the toy, we are sticking with plain PHP, though I have included a simple output escaping system.

The first thing that our app has to do is prepare the template data. I have kept the template data as a separate DTO, which is a pattern I encourage as it really helps to keep things organized. All template data implements a specific interface. Actually, the interface has no behavior in the toy – that is not an issue – but it does give us the option of enforcing standardized behavior later on, should we choose to.

> **What is a DTO again?**
>
> **DTO** stands for **Data Transfer Object**. It is simply an object that has no
> behavior and whose sole purpose is to be instantiated with data and then
> passed around. An immutable DTO is great as it is simple and predictable.

src/Part3/Chapter8/ToyMVC/View/Data/TemplateDataInterface.php

Repo: `https://git.io/JRw5t`

```php
<?php

declare(strict_types=1);

namespace Book\Part3\Chapter8\ToyMVC\View\Data;

interface TemplateDataInterface
{
}
```

The template data object represents the data dependencies for rendering a specific
template, and those dependencies are required as __construct parameters, for
example, on HomePageTemplateData:

src/Part3/Chapter8/ToyMVC/View/Data/HomePageData.php

Repo: `https://git.io/JRw5q`

```php
<?php

declare(strict_types=1);

namespace Book\Part3\Chapter8\ToyMVC\View\Data;

use Book\Part3\Chapter8\ToyMVC\Model\Collection\
CategoryCollection;

final class HomePageData implements TemplateDataInterface
{
    public function __construct(
        private CategoryCollection $categoryCollection
```

```
    ) {
    }

    public function getCategoryCollection(): CategoryCollection
    {
        return $this->categoryCollection;
    }
}
```

By using this single data object that contains everything in our templates, it allows us to get all the completion we need by type, hinting for only one thing in our template file.

Here is the corresponding HomePageTemplate file:

src/Part3/Chapter8/ToyMVC/View/Template/HomePageTemplate.php

Repo: https://git.io/JRw5m

```php
<?php

declare(strict_types=1);

namespace Book\Part3\Chapter8\ToyMVC\View\Template;

use Book\Part3\Chapter8\ToyMVC\View\Data\HomePageData;
use Book\Part3\Chapter8\ToyMVC\View\Esc;

// Note this one line of DocBlock allows all of the code in
this template to be statically analysed
// and allows our IDE to autocomplete all method calls etc for
us
/* @var $templateData HomePageData */

?>
<!DOCTYPE html>
<html>
<head>
    <title>Home Page</title>
</head>
```

```
<body>
<h1>Categories</h1>
<ul>
    <?php foreach ($templateData->getCategoryCollection() as
$catId => $category) { ?>
        <li>
            <a href="/c/<?php echo $catId; ?>"><?php echo
Esc::_($category->getName()); ?></a>
            <ol>
                <?php foreach ($category->getPostCollection()
as $postId => $post) { ?>
                    <li>
                        <a href="/p/<?php echo $postId;
?>"><?php echo Esc::_($post->getTitle()); ?></a>
                    </li>
                <?php } ?>
            </ol>
        </li>
    <?php } ?>
</ul>
</body>
</html>
```

You can see that there is just one docblock line to hint for the $templateData variable and assigning it a type. This allows IDEs to autocomplete easily with the minimum of boilerplate. All of the rest of the code completion in the template can be worked out by my IDE, which gives a really convenient developer experience.

Notice how we can just use foreach on the collections, and we retrieve the UUID as a string and PostEntity. Thanks to our type hinting, my IDE gives this completion on PostEntity:

Figure 8.1 – IDE-completion.png

You might also notice the `Esc::_()` calls. I have put this in here just to remind you never to output unescaped data. Most framework templating languages will handle this escaping for you automatically, but it is worth checking. Have a quick look at what it is doing to escape output:

src/Part3/Chapter8/ToyMVC/View/Esc.php

Repo: `https://git.io/JRw5Y`

```php
<?php

declare(strict_types=1);

namespace Book\Part3\Chapter8\ToyMVC\View;

final class Esc
{
    public static function _(string $input): string
    {
        return \htmlspecialchars(string: $input, flags: ENT_QUOTES);
    }
}
```

As you can see, it's just a wrapper around `htmlspecialchars`. The short `_` naming convention for this method is just to try to make it unobtrusive in your template code. If you ever do roll your own framework or templating system, you must make sure you are properly handling escaping output.

OWASP Top Ten Web Application Security Risks | OWASP

`https://owasp.org/www-project-top-ten/`

So we have looked at the template data and the template itself. Now let's take a look at `TemplateRenderer` that does the work of putting these two things together to get the actual HTML output:

src/Part3/Chapter8/ToyMVC/View/TemplateRenderer.php

Repo: `https://git.io/JRw5O`

```php
<?php
```

```php
declare(strict_types=1);


namespace Book\Part3\Chapter8\ToyMVC\View;


use Book\Part3\Chapter8\ToyMVC\View\Data\TemplateDataInterface;
use RuntimeException;
use tidy;


final class TemplateRenderer
{
    /**
     * This method does the work of using the template to
render some actual
     * HTML.
     *
     * The data variable is available to the template which is
simple PHP
     * that is then required. The ob_ functions use output
buffering to
     * capture the output of the template and then allow us to
return it as a
     * string
     */
    public function renderTemplate(
        string $templateName,
        TemplateDataInterface $templateData
    ): string {
        \ob_start();
        require __DIR__ . '/Template/' . \
basename($templateName);

        $html = \ob_get_clean();
        if ($html === false) {
            throw new RuntimeException('failed getting
output');
        }
```

```
            return $this->pretty($html);
    }


    /**
     * This method uses tidy to prettify the HTML from the
template
     * You would not do this in production, purely doing here
for the book.
     */
    private function pretty(string $html): string
    {
        $config = [
            'indent' => true,
            'wrap'   => 200,
        ];
        $tidy    = new tidy();
        $tidy->parseString($html, $config, 'utf8');
        $tidy->cleanRepair();

        return (string)$tidy;
    }
}
```

So what you can see here is that we have one public method that takes the name of a template file and an instance of `TemplateDataInterface`. Within the scope of the render method, we actually require the template file. As this is just a plain PHP file, it is included, and the code within the file runs within the scope of the method. That means that it has access to the variables within this scope of which we have only one, the `$templateData` variable. Hopefully, you can see why this means that we can type-hint for and access that `$templateData` variable in our template file.

To capture the output, the `require` statement is wrapped in an output buffer, which is started with `ob_start`. This is something that allows code to echo out content, or even include raw HTML as we do in the template files. Instead of being output, it is caught in the buffer. We can then retrieve the contents of the buffer and turn it off with `ob_get_clean`.

Finally, for the purposes of the toy, we are prettifying the HTML, though for a real app you should not care about pretty HTML. If anything, you should be minifying it as much as possible to reduce response sizes.

It lives

Just to show that the toy MVC is fully functional, here is the bit of code that simulates a single hit to the home page:

src/Part3/Chapter8/toy_mvc.php

Repo: `https://git.io/JRw53`

```php
<?php

declare(strict_types=1);

namespace Book\Part3\Chapter8;

use Book\Part3\Chapter8\ToyMVC\BrowserVisit;

require __DIR__ . '/../../../vendor/autoload.php';

$homePage = (new BrowserVisit())->visit('/');

echo $homePage;
```

Output:

```
joseph@php-book: ~

joseph@php-book:~$ php toy_mvc.php
<!DOCTYPE html>
<html>
  <head>
    <title>
      Home Page
    </title>
  </head>
  <body>
    <h1>
      Categories
    </h1>
    <ul>
      <li>
        <a href="/c/b5794dc7-5c6b-4b51-aa68-bf32be610f93">Category
1</a>
        <ol>
          <li>
            <a href="/p/81020de4-9545-4e6b-a962-1c427a6438a4">Post
1</a>
          </li>
          <li>
            <a href="/p/99e5174d-0bac-4096-9dd1-ef5b6db8c5bb">Post
2</a>
          </li>
        </ol>
      </li>
      <li>
        <a href="/c/9364bece-ab6b-4906-8b55-62cf17b415c2">Category
2</a>
        <ol>
          <li>
            <a href="/p/40c0924c-9d1b-4e78-8cf7-7e752b5937db">Post
3</a>
          </li>
          <li>
            <a href="/p/a1232f10-5311-42f2-b4c4-45857d94fef4">Post
4</a>
          </li>
        </ol>
      </li>
    </ul>
  </body>
</html>
```

To simulate the browser, we have a simple class called `BrowserVisit`:

src/Part3/Chapter8/ToyMVC/BrowserVisit.php

Repo: `https://git.io/JRw5s`

```php
<?php
```

```php
declare(strict_types=1);


namespace Book\Part3\Chapter8\ToyMVC;


/**
 * This class lets us very simply simulate a browser visiting
our toy MVC app.
 */
final class BrowserVisit
{
    private FrontController $frontController;

    public function __construct()
    {
        $this->frontController =
AppFactory::createFrontController();
    }


    public function visit(string $uri): string
    {
        $this->setSuperGlobals($uri);
        \ob_start();

        $this->frontController->handleRequest();

        return (string)\ob_get_clean();
    }


    private function setSuperGlobals(string $uri): void
    {
        $_SERVER['REQUEST_URI']    = $uri;
        $_SERVER['REQUEST_METHOD'] = 'GET';
    }
}
```

Which in turn uses a factory to build the front controller and all the dependencies:

src/Part3/Chapter8/ToyMVC/AppFactory.php

Repo: `https://git.io/JRw5G`

```php
<?php

declare(strict_types=1);

namespace Book\Part3\Chapter8\ToyMVC;

use Book\Part3\Chapter8\ToyMVC\Controller\Factory\
ControllerFactory;
use Book\Part3\Chapter8\ToyMVC\Controller\Factory\
RequestDataFactory;
use Book\Part3\Chapter8\ToyMVC\Model\Repository\
CategoryRepository;
use Book\Part3\Chapter8\ToyMVC\Model\Repository\PostRepository;
use Book\Part3\Chapter8\ToyMVC\View\TemplateRenderer;

final class AppFactory
{
    public static function createFrontController():
FrontController
    {
        return new FrontController(
            new ControllerFactory(
                new CategoryRepository(),
                new PostRepository(),
                new TemplateRenderer()
            ),
            new RequestDataFactory()
        );
    }
}
```

You may also want to have a look at this test, which does a basic smoke test of the home page and of every page linked to from there. We will cover testing in much more detail in another book, but hopefully this test is relatively clear:

tests/Medium/Part3/Chapter8/ToyMVC/VisitEverythingTest.php

Repo: `https://git.io/JRw5Z`

```php
<?php

declare(strict_types=1);

namespace Book\Tests\Medium\Part3\Chapter8\ToyMVC;

use Book\Part3\Chapter8\ToyMVC\BrowserVisit;
use PHPUnit\Framework\TestCase;

/**
 * @medium
 * @coversNothing
 *
 * @internal
 */
final class VisitEverythingTest extends TestCase
{
    private const EXPECTED_VISITS = 8;
    private int $visits;
    private BrowserVisit $browserVisit;

    public function setUp(): void
    {
        parent::setUp();
        $this->browserVisit = new BrowserVisit();
        $this->visits       = 0;
    }

    /** @test */
    public function itCanVisitAllPages(): void
```

```
    {
        $homePage = $this->visit('/');

        \preg_match_all('%href="(?<uri>[^"]+)"%', $homePage,
$matches);

        foreach ($matches['uri'] as $uri) {
            $this->visit($uri);
        }
        $this->visit('not exists');
        self::assertSame(self::EXPECTED_VISITS, $this->visits);
    }

    private function assertLoaded(string $page): void
    {
        self::assertStringEndsWith('</html>', \trim($page));
    }

    private function visit(string $uri): string
    {
        $page = $this->browserVisit->visit($uri);
        $this->assertLoaded($page);
        ++$this->visits;

        return $page;
    }
}
```

What this test does is hits the home page by calling $this->visit('/'). The visit method uses the same BrowserVisit class we looked at just a moment ago, and it also does a basic check to confirm the page loaded and increments a visits counter, so we can assert that we visited the expected number of pages.

Summary

In this chapter, we created an entire toy MVC system and proved that it works through the use of some automated testing. Rather than follow the order of naming in MVC, we started by looking at the Controller layer, and we implemented a front controller that handles dispatching requests to the correct controller.

Next, we built our Model layer. For the purposes of the toy, we are using hard-coded data and not using any kind of persistence layer. In real life, you would never do this and instead would expect to be interacting with some form of persistence (most usually a database). We looked at the Entity, Repository, and Collection patterns. We were using a UUID for IDs, which is definitely something I would encourage you to consider as a much better ID than simple integer IDs and relying on database autoincrement values.

Next, we built our View layer. We used a DTO to handle storing and sharing template data – this keeps our View layer nicely decoupled from the other layers, and really aids with testing and generally keeping things tidy.

Finally, we confirmed that it all works by simulating a real browser visit. We included a PHPUnit test, which will actually spider and visit every link on the page to confirm it is all basically working (a smoke test).

I hope this has helped you understand the concepts behind MVC. They say that every PHP developer has an MVC framework in them, just waiting to be set free. The world doesn't really need so many half-assed MVC frameworks, but I do encourage you to have a go at building your own, just for fun. For real projects, you almost certainly want to use one of the existing and battle-tested frameworks.

In the next chapter, we're going to do a similar exercise, but this time we're going to look at **Dependency Injection (DI)**.

9
Dependency Injection Example

In this chapter, we are going to look at a very popular pattern in modern PHP – the **dependency injection** (**DI**) container. This is a system that acts as a global application-level factory and combines configuration and instance management.

You could have a read through Fabien Potencier's article from way back in 2009, which tried to educate the PHP masses about what a DI container is and why we should be using one:

```
http://fabien.potencier.org/do-you-need-a-dependency-
injection-container.html.
```

Bear in mind that this is a vintage article, but the basic points are all there, and it is worth a read through. It's also an interesting bit of PHP history.

We're going to learn all about what a DI container does by building our own toy DI container. Hopefully, this will help clarify how simple the concept is, something that is not always easy when you try to delve into the code of real DI containers.

This chapter will cover the following main topics:

- Inversion of control container
- Dependency injection and the service locator
- The service locator anti-pattern

As usual, you can find all the code samples for this chapter in the main repo for the book available on GitHub at `https://github.com/PacktPublishing/The-Art-of-Modern-PHP-8`.

Inversion of control container

Martin Fowler referred to DI containers as "inversion of control containers."

Inversion of Control Containers and the Dependency Injection Pattern:

`https://martinfowler.com/articles/injection.html`.

Inversion of control is another design pattern where the "flow of control" is inverted from the standard procedural paradigm, where control is generally in the hands of the main program you are writing. Instead, the primary control is in the hands of the framework you are using, and you, as a developer, inject your custom logic into the standard flow of the framework.

Instead of our custom code-calling library functions, we have a framework that calls our custom code as part of its process.

Inversion of control – Wikipedia:

`https://w.wiki/iH5`

Dependency injection containers provide a powerful mechanism for this, whereby we can replace specific pieces of a framework-based application with our custom implementations of standard interfaces that are used by the framework.

If we come back to the loggers that we discussed previously, we can configure our framework-based application to use a specific custom logger by telling the DI container to inject our custom logger when any service requests to `LoggerInterface`.

This may all seem a bit theoretical and abstract, but keep this in mind as we look at what a DI container is by building a very simple DI container and service locator.

Dependency injection and the service locator

Something you may have realized when looking at ToyMVC is the fact that there is quite a lot of work going on to build instances of objects. Also, you could imagine that if the app grew to real-world sizes, then the amount of work that would need to be done in `AppFactory` could become quite substantial.

Furthermore, due to the complexity of building up a large graph of object instances, there is also the issue that this is generally going to be very wasteful. PHP's requests are not stateful and when instantiating an MVC app, it is almost certain to serve one – and only one – request. There is no need to fire up instances of every single piece of the application when we may not need them all.

Thankfully, there is now a widely accepted best practice solution for this that is incredibly developer-friendly – dependency injection, or DI for short.

Now, I say this is developer-friendly, but that does not mean to say that building your own dependency injection system is simple – far from it! The good news, though, is that there are now multiple well-built and battle-tested free open source DI libraries that you can use.

I suggest taking a look at these:

- `https://symfony.com/doc/current/components/dependency_injection.html`
- `https://php-di.org/`

If you are working with a modern PHP framework or platform, then chances are DI is already being implemented, and you should probably go with the flow in terms of how that particular framework operates DI. There are multiple ways to approach DI, and the question of which approach to take is subjective; different frameworks and apps handle this differently.

In the spirit of learning how things work by building them, let's have a go at creating our own Toy DI container.

Note

The code you are about to read is just for educational purposes and not something you should use in a real project. It has been kept deliberately very simple and nowhere near ready for proper production use. The intention is to illustrate the concept of a DI container in the minimum amount of readable and comprehensible code.

The first thing we should do is implement the accepted PSR container interface.

src/ContainerInterface.php

Repo: `https://git.io/JqfD2`

```php
<?php
```

```php
declare(strict_types=1);

namespace Psr\Container;

/**
 * Describes the interface of a container that exposes methods
to read its entries.
 */
interface ContainerInterface
{
    /**
     * Finds an entry of the container by its identifier and
returns it.
     *
     * @param string $id Identifier of the entry to look for.
     *
     * @throws NotFoundExceptionInterface  No entry was found
for **this** identifier.
     * @throws ContainerExceptionInterface Error while
retrieving the entry.
     *
     * @return mixed Entry.
     */
    public function get(string $id);

    /**
     * Returns true if the container can return an entry for
the given identifier.
     * Returns false otherwise.
     *
     * `has($id)` returning true does not mean that `get($id)`
will not throw an exception.
     * It does however mean that `get($id)` will not throw a
`NotFoundExceptionInterface`.
     *
     * @param string $id Identifier of the entry to look for.
     *
```

```php
 * @return bool
 */
public function has(string $id);
}
```

First up, we have our ServiceLocator. This object has the job of fulfilling the contract defined in `ContainerInterface`. The ServiceLocator is storing information about what service IDs map to what classes and allows us to retrieve class instances by service ID.

src/Part3/Chapter9/ToyDI/ServiceLocator.php

Repo: `https://git.io/JRw75`

```php
<?php

declare(strict_types=1);

namespace Book\Part3\Chapter9\ToyDI;

use Psr\Container\ContainerInterface;

final class ServiceLocator implements ContainerInterface
{
    /**
     * This is an array of service IDs to the class name
     * configured for the service.
     *
     * @var array<string, class-string>
     */
    private array $idsToClassNames;

    private ServiceFactory $serviceFactory;

    public function __construct(
        ServiceDefinitionInterface ...$serviceDefinitions
    ) {
        foreach ($serviceDefinitions as $serviceDefinition) {
            $this->storeDefinition($serviceDefinition);
```

```
        }
        $this->serviceFactory = new ServiceFactory($this);
    }


    /**
     * This is the first of the two methods defined in the PSR
ContainerInterface.
     * The interface does not define a param type and so we are
not able to either
     * due to the contravariance (remember that) rules that say
parameter types are only able to become looser
     * thanks to covariance rules, we are able to add return
type hints though.
     *
     * @throws NotFoundException
     */
    public function get($id): object
    {
        // first determine which class to use for the service
ID
        $className = $this->getClassFullyQualifiedNameForId($
id);


        // then we use the service factory to get or create the
instance
        return $this->serviceFactory->getInstance($className);
    }


    /**
     * This is the second of the two methods defined in the PSR
ContainerInterface.
     */
    public function has($id): bool
    {
        return isset($this->idsToClassNames[$id]);
    }
```

```
    /** @return array<string,class-string> */
    public function getIdsToClassNames(): array
    {
        return $this->idsToClassNames;
    }


    private function storeDefinition(
        ServiceDefinitionInterface $serviceDefinition
    ): void {
        foreach ($serviceDefinition->getIds() as $id) {
            // First we build a lookup between IDs to class
names
            $this->idsToClassNames[$id] =
                $serviceDefinition-
>getClassFullyQualifiedName();
        }
    }


    /**
     * @throws NotFoundException
     *
     * @return class-string
     */
    private function getClassFullyQualifiedNameForId(string
$id): string
    {
        return $this->idsToClassNames[$id]
            ?? throw new NotFoundException(
                'Failed finding service class for ' . $id
            );
    }
}
```

Hopefully, you can see how we use the serviceDefinitions that are passed in to build up the internal array so that they are ready to be queried once the container is used to retrieve services. We implement the two PSR interfaces and add whatever type of safety we can, though due to contravariance rules, we are not able to add parameter types.

The actual work of instantiating services, including parsing their dependencies, has been delegated to a special `ServiceFactory`. The `ServiceFactory` is responsible for building and storing an instance of a service, including parsing the service dependencies from the constructor and instantiating those. This is the real "dependency injection" bit.

src/Part3/Chapter9/ToyDI/ServiceFactory.php

Repo: `https://git.io/JRw7d`

```php
<?php

declare(strict_types=1);

namespace Book\Part3\Chapter9\ToyDI;

use InvalidArgumentException;
use ReflectionClass;
use ReflectionException;
use ReflectionParameter;
use RuntimeException;

final class ServiceFactory
{
    /**
     * This is an array of class names to actual instances of
     that class.
     * This allows us to ensure we keep only one instance of a
     given class.
     *
     * @var array <class-string, object|null>
     */
    private array $classNamesToInstances;

    public function __construct(private ServiceLocator
$serviceLocator)
    {
        $this->buildClassNamesToInstances();
    }
```

```
    /** @param class-string $className */
    public function getInstance(string $className): object
    {

        $this->assertServiceClassName($className);


        // if we already have an instance stored, we just
return that
        return $this->classNamesToInstances[$className]
            // otherwise we create an instance and store the
result
            // note, the ??= null coalesce assignment operator,
assigns the value of
            // the right hand side to the left when the left is
null
            ??= new $className(...$this->getDependencyInstances
($className));
    }


    private function buildClassNamesToInstances(): void
    {

        foreach ($this->serviceLocator->getIdsToClassNames() as
$className) {
            // We build an array with the key as class name and
value as null,
            // ready to be replaced with an instance of the
class on demand.
            // Note that this implicitly de-duplicates classes
that are defined with multiple IDs
            $this->classNamesToInstances[$className] = null;
        }

    }


    private function assertServiceClassName(string $className):
void
    {

        if (
        \array_key_exists(
            key: $className,
```

```
            array: $this->classNamesToInstances
        )
    ) {
        return;
    }
    throw new NotFoundException('Class ' . $className . '
is not defined as a service');
}


/**
 * @param class-string $className
 *
 * @throws ReflectionException
 *
 * @return array<int,object>
 */
private function getDependencyInstances(string $className):
array
{
    $return = [];
    // use reflection to retrieve an instance of
ReflectionMethod for the constructor
    $constructor = (new ReflectionClass($className))-
>getConstructor();
    if ($constructor === null) {
        throw new InvalidArgumentException("{$className}
does not have a constructor");
    }
    // now we loop over all the parameters of the
constructor and build an array of dependencies in the correct
order
    // note that we have no safety here at all - a real
implementation would need to do a lot more sanity checking
    foreach ($constructor->getParameters() as
$reflectionParameter) {
        $return[] =
            $this->getInstance($this->getServiceClassString
($reflectionParameter));
```

```php
        }

        return $return;
    }


    /** @return class-string */
    private function getServiceClassString(
        ReflectionParameter $reflectionParameter
    ): string {
        return (string) (
            $reflectionParameter->getType()
            ??
            throw new RuntimeException('failed getting class
string for type')
        );
    }
}
```

So, as you can see, the ServiceFactory queries the ServiceLocator to pull out all the class names so that it can build an internal array, ready to store class instances. The list of classes is implicitly deduplicated by using the class name as the key. When asked to get an instance, it ensures that it is a valid service class. Then, it checks if we already have an instance. If not, it creates a new instance. It uses reflection to parse the constructor parameters to get the types. For each type, it will go and create an instance and can recursively instantiate a dependency tree this way.

To demonstrate how the container is used, we have a ContainerFactory that handles building the service definitions and then uses those to create an instance of the ServiceLocator. You might have noticed a large number of imports for the various dummy services I created to test this. For the Toy DI, we have simply hardcoded the map of class names to service IDs.

src/Part3/Chapter9/ToyDI/ContainerFactory.php

Repo: https://git.io/JRw7F

```php
<?php

declare(strict_types=1);
```

```php
namespace Book\Part3\Chapter9\ToyDI;

use Book\Part3\Chapter9\ToyDI\Service\DepTree\LevelOneDep;
use Book\Part3\Chapter9\ToyDI\Service\DepTree\LevelOneService;
use Book\Part3\Chapter9\ToyDI\Service\DepTree\LevelThreeDep;
use Book\Part3\Chapter9\ToyDI\Service\DepTree\
LevelThreeService;
use Book\Part3\Chapter9\ToyDI\Service\DepTree\LevelTwoDep;
use Book\Part3\Chapter9\ToyDI\Service\DepTree\LevelTwoService;
use Book\Part3\Chapter9\ToyDI\Service\DepTree\
UbiquitousService;
use Book\Part3\Chapter9\ToyDI\Service\EchoStuff\EchoBarService;
use Book\Part3\Chapter9\ToyDI\Service\EchoStuff\
EchoStuffInterface;
use Book\Part3\Chapter9\ToyDI\Service\MathsStuff\
AdditionService;
use Book\Part3\Chapter9\ToyDI\Service\MathsStuff\
MathsInterface;

final class ContainerFactory
{
    public const SHORTHAND_NAME_FOR_MATHS = 'maths';

    /**
     * This is an array with the configured service class as
the key and an array of one or more service IDs as the
     * value.
     *
     * These IDs can just be the class FQN, or they can be any
other arbitrary string.
     *
     * This configurability is fundamental to the inversion of
control principle.
     *
     * This allows us to handle mapping interfaces to
concretions and also have services available with arbitrary
     * string IDs such as the shorthand name for maths
     *
```

```php
 * @var array<class-string,array<int,string>>
 */
private const SERVICE_CLASSES_TO_IDS = [
    AdditionService::class    => [
        MathsInterface::class,
        AdditionService::class,
        self::SHORTHAND_NAME_FOR_MATHS,
    ],
    EchoBarService::class     => [
        EchoStuffInterface::class,
        EchoBarService::class,
    ],
    LevelOneService::class    => [LevelOneService::class],
    LevelOneDep::class        => [LevelOneDep::class],
    LevelTwoService::class    => [LevelTwoService::class],
    LevelTwoDep::class        => [LevelTwoDep::class],
    LevelThreeService::class  => [LevelThreeService::class],
    LevelThreeDep::class      => [LevelThreeDep::class],
    UbiquitousService::class  => [UbiquitousService::class],
];

public function buildAppContainer(): ServiceLocator
{
    return new ServiceLocator(...$this-
>getSimpleDefinitions());
}

/** @return ServiceDefinitionInterface[] */
private function getSimpleDefinitions(): array
{
    $definitions = [];
    foreach (self::SERVICE_CLASSES_TO_IDS as $className =>
$ids) {
        $definitions[] = $this->getSimpleDefinition($ids,
$className);
    }
```

```php
        return $definitions;
    }


    /**
     * @param array<int,string> $ids
     * @param class-string        $className
     */
    private function getSimpleDefinition(
        array $ids,
        string $className
    ): SimpleServiceDefinition {
        return new SimpleServiceDefinition($ids, $className);
    }
}
```

So, what you can see here is that there is some hard-coded configuration that is mapping IDs – in this case, it is mapping the class and interface names to the actual service class. These service IDs can be anything, but it is usual for them to be interface or class names predominantly. What you might notice is that we are implementing the same class for an interface and then itself. This is a fairly standard thing to do so that any class requiring the interface will be given the concretion and of course, anything depending on the specific concretion will also get what it expects.

To illustrate this arbitrary service name, a service has been defined with an ID of "maths."

The app factory takes the array of IDs to class names and for each, it builds a SimpleServiceDefinition that contains that data. This array is then unpacked with the splat operator and placed in the constructor for the ServiceLocator.

src/Part3/Chapter9/ToyDI/SimpleServiceDefinition.php

Repo: https://git.io/JRw7b

```php
<?php

declare(strict_types=1);

namespace Book\Part3\Chapter9\ToyDI;
```

```php
final class SimpleServiceDefinition implements
ServiceDefinitionInterface
{
    /**
     * @param array<int,string> $ids
     * @param class-string       $className
     */
    public function __construct(
        private array $ids,
        private string $className
    ) {
    }

    /** @return array<int,string> */
    public function getIds(): array
    {
        return $this->ids;
    }

    /** @return class-string */
    public function getClassFullyQualifiedName(): string
    {
        return $this->className;
    }
}
```

The resulting container is ready to be used to provide instances of service classes, complete with any dependencies. This ensures that only a single instance of any specific class is instantiated and calculates and resolves service class dependencies. Hopefully, you can see how much of a time and hassle saver this concept is.

Next up, I would like to show you the test that has been created to ensure that the ToyDI container works as expected.

Don't worry if this test code is brand new to you; we will explore this kind of testing in much more detail later.

tests/Small/Part3/Chapter9/ToyDI/ContainerTest.php

Repo: `https://git.io/JRw7N`

```php
<?php

declare(strict_types=1);

namespace Book\Tests\Small\Part3\Chapter9\ToyDI;

use Book\Part3\Chapter9\ToyDI\ContainerFactory;
use Book\Part3\Chapter9\ToyDI\Service\DepTree\LevelOneService;
use Book\Part3\Chapter9\ToyDI\Service\DepTree\LevelThreeDep;
use Book\Part3\Chapter9\ToyDI\Service\DepTree\
LevelThreeService;
use Book\Part3\Chapter9\ToyDI\Service\DepTree\LevelTwoService;
use Book\Part3\Chapter9\ToyDI\Service\DepTree\
UbiquitousService;
use Book\Part3\Chapter9\ToyDI\Service\EchoStuff\EchoBarService;
use Book\Part3\Chapter9\ToyDI\Service\EchoStuff\EchoFooService;
use Book\Part3\Chapter9\ToyDI\Service\EchoStuff\
EchoStuffInterface;
use Book\Part3\Chapter9\ToyDI\Service\MathsStuff\
AdditionService;
use Book\Part3\Chapter9\ToyDI\Service\MathsStuff\
MathsInterface;
use Book\Part3\Chapter9\ToyDI\Service\MathsStuff\
MultiplicationService;
use Book\Part3\Chapter9\ToyDI\ServiceLocator;
use Generator;
use PHPUnit\Framework\TestCase;

/**
 * @small
 *
 * @internal
```

```
 * @covers \Book\Part3\Chapter9\ToyDI\ContainerFactory
 * @covers \Book\Part3\Chapter9\ToyDI\ServiceFactory
 * @covers \Book\Part3\Chapter9\ToyDI\ServiceLocator
 */
final class ContainerTest extends TestCase
{
    private ServiceLocator $container;

    /**
     * This setup method is called before each and every test.
     * That means that each test gets a pristine new instance
of the container ready to play with.
     */
    public function setUp(): void
    {
        $this->container = (new ContainerFactory())-
>buildAppContainer();
    }

    /**
     * A simple test to ensure we can retrieve the echo service
     * with both the interface and class name as service ID.
     *
     * @test
     */
    public function itCanGetEchoService(): void
    {
        self::assertInstanceOf(
            expected: EchoBarService::class,
            actual: $this->container-
>get(EchoStuffInterface::class)
        );
        self::assertInstanceOf(
            expected: EchoBarService::class,
            actual: $this->container-
>get(EchoBarService::class)
        );
```

```php
    }

    /**
     * Another test to ensure we can retrieve the service.
     * for this service we also have a "short" service ID which
is just an arbitrary string
     * Note that this test returns an array.
     * This resulting array is used as input on the
itReturnsTheSameInstance test
     * which has defined this test as a dependency.
     *
     * @test
     *
     * @return MathsInterface[]
     */
    public function itCanGetMathsService(): array
    {
        $byInterfaceId = $this->container-
>get(MathsInterface::class);
        self::assertInstanceOf(
            expected: AdditionService::class,
            actual: $byInterfaceId
        );
        $byClassId = $this->container-
>get(AdditionService::class);
        self::assertInstanceOf(
            expected: AdditionService::class,
            actual: $byClassId
        );
        $byShortName = $this->container->get(ContainerFactory::
SHORTHAND_NAME_FOR_MATHS);
        self::assertInstanceOf(
            expected: AdditionService::class,
            actual: $byShortName
        );

        return [$byInterfaceId, $byClassId, $byShortName];
```

```
    }


    /**
     * Here we have a test that uses values returned from other
tests in order to do further checks
     * This is a nice way of keeping tests DRY and also
splitting test concerns for extra clarity.
     *
     * @test
     * @depends itCanGetMathsService
     * @depends itCanBuildServicesWithDependencies
     *
     * @param object[] $services
     */
    public function itReturnsTheSameInstance(
        array $services
    ): void {
        [$serviceOne, $serviceTwo, $serviceThree] = $services;
        $actual                                   = (
            ($serviceOne === $serviceTwo) && ($serviceOne ===
$serviceThree)
        );
        self::assertTrue($actual);
    }


    /**
     * Here we have another test retrieving services.
     * This time we are testing a deliberately multi
dimensional dependency graph
     * that also includes a "Ubiquitous Service" that is
required at every level.
     * We return all instances of the Ubiquitous service so
that
     * it can be checked in the itReturnsTheSameInstance test.
     *
     * @test
     *
```

```php
     * @return UbiquitousService[]
     */
    public function itCanBuildServicesWithDependencies(): array
    {
        /** @var LevelOneService $levelOneService */
        $levelOneService = $this->container-
>get(LevelOneService::class);
        self::assertInstanceOf(
            expected: LevelOneService::class,
            actual: $levelOneService
        );
        $levelThreeDep = $levelOneService->levelTwoService-
>levelThreeService->levelThreeDep;
        self::assertInstanceOf(
            expected: LevelThreeDep::class,
            actual: $levelThreeDep
        );

        return [
            $levelOneService->ubiquitousService,
            $levelOneService->levelTwoService-
>ubiquitousService,
            $levelOneService->levelTwoService-
>levelThreeService->ubiquitousService,
        ];
    }


    /**
     * this is a data provider, providing values to be used
     * in the hasReturnsTrueForValidServiceIds test.
     *
     * @dataProvider
     *
     * @return Generator<string, array<int,string>>
     */
    public function provideValidServiceIds(): Generator
    {
```

```php
        yield EchoStuffInterface::class =>
[EchoStuffInterface::class];

        yield MathsInterface::class => [MathsInterface::class];

        yield LevelOneService::class =>
[LevelOneService::class];

        yield LevelTwoService::class =>
[LevelTwoService::class];

        yield LevelThreeService::class =>
[LevelThreeService::class];
    }


    /**
     * this tests that the call to `has` returns true. We test
multiple values
     * by utilising the dataProvider method
provideValidServiceIds.
     *
     * @dataProvider provideValidServiceIds
     * @test
     */
    public function hasReturnsTrueForValidServiceIds(
        string $service
    ): void {
        self::assertTrue($this->container->has($service));
    }


    /**
     * this is a another data provider, providing values to be
used
     * in the hasReturnsFalseForInvalidServiceIds test.
     *
     * @dataProvider
     *
     * @return Generator<string, array<int,string>>
     */
    public function provideInvalidServiceIds(): Generator
    {
```

```php
        yield EchoFooService::class => [EchoFooService::class];
        yield MultiplicationService::class =>
[MultiplicationService::class];
        yield static::class => [static::class];
    }


    /**
     * this tests that the call to `has` returns false. We test
multiple values
     * by utilising the dataProvider method
provideInvalidServiceIds.
     *
     * @dataProvider provideInvalidServiceIds
     * @test
     */
    public function hasReturnsFalseForInvalidServiceIds(
        string $service
    ): void {
        self::assertFalse($this->container->has($service));
    }
}
```

What the test is doing, as I hope you can understand by reading it, is checking that we can get instances of two simple services, where we have an interface and configured the container to return a concretion of that interface. Then, we tested a more complex service that has a three-tier dependency graph. We tested this to ensure that when a service is retrieved multiple times, we always get the same instance. Finally, we have two tests, along with their data providers, to confirm that the has method is working correctly.

To underline the fact that this Toy DI container is not production-ready, here are some features that a real DI container should allow but are not currently covered:

- Defining factories for services.
- Closures for factories.
- Allowing multiple instances of a single class.
- Private services – these can not be retrieved directly from the service locator and can only be injected as dependencies.

- Autowiring – parsing folders of PHP classes and configuring them as services automatically.

Some other features that DI containers may choose to support are as follows:

- Setter injection; that is, allowing dependencies to be injected via `setService(ServiceClass $service)` methods instead of the constructor.

- Annotation/attribute injection; that is, parsing metadata for properties and setting them directly using reflection.

- Wrapping other containers.

You could try implementing some of these features in the Toy DI container as an exercise – it's a great way to get your head around a concept.

Hopefully, you now understand what a DI container does and what the ServiceLocator is. Let's have a look at one of the ways a service locator can become a foot gun. We're going to look at the anti-pattern of using the DI container directly in your code, thereby breaking inversion of control and generally shooting yourself in the foot.

The service locator anti-pattern

One aspect of using a container that I must caution you against is using it directly as a service locator. What I mean by this is that your code should almost exclusively have no idea or requirement to be loaded via the DI container. You should not be using the DI container directly in your code.

Your classes should simply define dependencies and then use those dependencies. There are very, very few circumstances where anything other than your front controller or outermost layer should know about the container.

Remember the rules of *Fight Club*? Well, it's the same here. Your objects don't know about the container, and no one talks about the container. We pretend that you spent hours carefully hand wiring and instantiating all the objects required for your app to serve a particular request.

If you do write code that uses the container directly to retrieve services, then you have built a huge amount of coupling into your container and framework, significantly reduced the ease of testing, obfuscated class dependencies, and generally shot yourself in the foot.

What you should do instead is feel free to break your big classes up into smaller classes and share functionality by sharing class instances as dependencies. The convenience of DI means that there is generally very little cost or hassle in taking this approach, something that is not true if you find yourself having to wire up a complex dependency graph by hand.

Summary

That brings us to the end of Part 3 of this book. We've covered a lot of ground in these three chapters and, of course, that means that we have not been able to have a really deep dive into some topics. However, I hope you have learned enough to understand some basic concepts and now know how to research and learn more about these topics.

We started by looking at technical debt and how you can avoid this by adopting clean code practices. We briefly touched upon some major topic areas of clean code and particularly the popular acronyms SOLID and DRY, as well KICK, which was purposely created for this book! We talked about naming things clearly and trying to write self-documenting code. We learned about the perils of cyclomatic complexity and the wonders of early returns as a proven method to reduce this. Immutability was the next topic, and we explored some of the perils of mutable classes when working with PHP's "by reference" object variables. The last thing we mentioned in the clean code section was trying to keep your types as meaningful as possible and avoiding overly broad return types in particular, since these can lead to developer confusion and bugs. PHP 8 brings sane co/contravariance rules that allow you to return meaningful types while still conforming to an interface, and this is something you should take advantage of.

We wrapped up *Chapter 7, Design Patterns and Clean Code,* by looking at design patterns. We learned a bit about design patterns as a concept and had a look at the basic categories of design patterns; that is, creational, structural, behavioral, and architectural. For each category, we had a look at a few specific patterns, and also provided links to places you can see these patterns being used in the wild. Design patterns is quite a big topic; there are whole books dedicated to it, so there is no expectation that this half chapter is all you need, but it should provide a useful starting point.

Next, we took a detailed look at MVC and built up our own toy implementation of the MVC pattern. While working through this, we explored other design patterns, such as the Front Controller, Factory, Repository, and even the Singleton pattern, though you have been warned strongly away from that one! I hope you agree that the toy also features some clean code principles, though compromises were made to keep the code brief and book-friendly.

Finally, we explored dependency injection and worked through a toy implementation of a DI container. Hopefully, you understand that the toy is by no means feature-complete or designed for production use, but you can see the problem that it solves and the way it allows you to configure a service locator. With a little reflection, it can automatically build a whole graph of objects with dependencies on each other.

We confirmed that the whole point of DI is that you don't use the container. Instead, you stick to **plain old PHP objects** (**POPO**) with clearly defined dependencies. Those POPOs shouldn't know or care about the container or how the dependencies got there. You should feel free to write highly modular code and create arbitrarily complex dependency graphs, safe in the knowledge that the DI container will take care of instantiation.

In the next and final part of this book, we're going to learn about Composer. Modern PHP is built around this tool, making it an essential part of your toolset. We're also going to have a sneak preview of some up-and-coming PHP features that haven't been released at the time of writing.

Section 4 –
PHP 8 Composer Package Management (and PHP 8.1)

This section includes two chapters that are all about Composer and working with and publishing libraries of PHP code that allow the modern PHP developer to quickly and efficiently utilize high-quality reusable libraries of code to provide functionality and features to your projects.

This section contains the following chapters:

- *Chapter 10, Composer For Dependencies*
- *Chapter 11, Creating Your Own Composer Package*

10
Composer For Dependencies

In this chapter, we are going to look at something that really changed the whole ecosystem in PHP. It was perhaps the most significant development in the history of PHP since the introduction of proper OOP back in PHP 5 days.

That development was the release of Composer and the advent of proper dependency management in PHP.

In this chapter, we're going to start by reviewing exactly what Composer and dependency management are all about.

Then, we are going to make sure we understand what autoloading is and how Composer provides us with a fully-featured autoloader that solves class loading once and for all.

Next, we will get into the real reason for using Composer, which is to acquire third-party packages and libraries so that we can easily bring functionality and features into our application, as provided by high-quality third-party libraries.

Once we've looked at how to bring in dependencies, we are going to go over the mechanism for ensuring we get the correct version of those dependencies by using version constraints, as well as the special syntax that Composer provides to manage this.

Finally, we will review the difference between dev and prod dependencies, as well as the mechanism that allows you to require all kinds of special tooling for your development environment but keep your production environment lean and mean.

This chapter will cover the following main topics:

- What is Composer?

- Composer autoloader

- Using Composer to require packages

- Version constraints

- Dev and prod dependencies

As usual, you can find all the code samples for this chapter in the main repo for the book available on GitHub at `https://github.com/PacktPublishing/The-Art-of-Modern-PHP-8`

So, without further ado, let's dive in!

What is Composer?

Composer is a dependency manager. The introduction to Composer from the official website sums this up quite nicely:

> *"Composer is a tool for dependency management in PHP. It allows you to declare the libraries your project depends on and it will manage (install/ update) them for you."*

It is definitely worth having a read through the official Composer documentation, which is clear and comprehensive.

Introduction – Composer

`https://getcomposer.org/doc/00-intro.md`

What are dependencies?

So, we know that Composer is for dependency management, but what are dependencies? Well, simply put, they are modules of code that your main application depends on. Those modules can be third party, or they can be your own first-party modules that you share between your applications.

Let's say that your application needs to send emails. You could roll your own email sending system in pure PHP and use the mail function for this.

PHP: mail – Manual

`https://www.php.net/manual/en/function.mail.php`

A much more sensible option would be to use a robust, well-tested, and fully featured library such as Swiftmailer.

Swiftmailer: A feature-rich PHP Mailer – Documentation – Swift Mailer

`https://swiftmailer.symfony.com/docs/introduction.html`

If you choose to use Swiftmailer, then you have now decided that your application has a dependency that it needs to function.

"Ah, no problem," you might say to yourself as you head to the Releases page of the library and download a compressed archive of all the code ready to be dropped into your application manually. However, I suspect that you might quickly find that the code you've downloaded does not work, and the reason may well be that it does not include all the code that Swiftmailer needs to run.

Dependency resolution

Swiftmailer itself has its own dependencies. At the time of writing, these are:

```
{
    "php": ">=7.0.0",
    "egulias/email-validator": "^2.0|^3.1",
    "symfony/polyfill-iconv": "^1.0",
    "symfony/polyfill-mbstring": "^1.0",
    "symfony/polyfill-intl-idn": "^1.10"
}
```

PHP itself is a given and hopefully, if you are reading this book, you are at the very least using PHP 7. But what is this `egulias/email-validator` thing?

Well, that is another package. The authors of Swiftmailer have decided that rather than rolling out their own email validation system, it would be much more sensible to use a robust, well tested, and fully featured email validation library, and they have chosen this one:

GitHub - egulias/EmailValidator: PHP Email address validator

`https://git.io/J3fda`

So, now, if you want to get Swiftmailer to work, you are going to have to install this library as well. This is already getting quite complex, and I haven't even mentioned autoloading yet.

Instead, we can use Composer as a dependency management system. It will allow us to define our dependencies – in this case, Swiftmailer – and it will install not only Swiftmailer itself, but also all the packages and libraries that Swiftmailer depends upon, as well as those dependent packages; well, it will install their dependencies as well, all the way down…

Our workflow for adding Swiftmailer to our project is as simple as running the following command:

```
composer require "swiftmailer/swiftmailer"
```

But wait, there's more

In a months' time, you realize that there was a bug with Swiftmailer. You check the GitHub issues page for Swiftmailer and realize that someone else has already had this issue and reported it. The Swiftmailer developers have seen this bug and fixed it, and a new version has been released.

Included in this new release is also some new functionality and to provide that functionality, the Swiftmailer devs have added a new dependency that must be installed. If you were to try to resolve this manually, then you might expect having to do a full days' work getting all this code manually updated.

Instead, with a composer managed dependency, upgrading to the new version with the bug fixed is as simple as using this command:

```
composer update "swiftmailer/swiftmailer"
```

In a nutshell, it's awesome

Hopefully, you can see why Composer has been such a brilliant addition to the PHP ecosystem. It has made the task of reusing shared libraries of PHP code almost too easy. This, in turn, has triggered a seismic shift in the way that PHP code is created and shared. Excellent libraries exist that can be freely reused among all different kinds of projects. Installation and updating is an absolute breeze.

The problem that dependency management solves is that of using disparate modules of code, possibly with multiple dependencies, and resolving all of these in a set of modules of a specific version that should work together and provide you with the functionality you need.

Get it installed!

Rather than wasting trees on some pages reproducing the already excellent installation docs, I'll just let you know where to find them:

Introduction – Composer

`https://getcomposer.org/doc/00-intro.md#installation-linux-unix-macos`

Now, let's move on and look at another one of Composer's superpowers – autoloading. (Don't worry if you don't know what that is; it will all become clear!)

Composer autoloader

Not only does Composer handle dependency management, which is already no mean feat, it also provides us with a simple developer experience when writing code that uses our dependencies, or even our application code.

The problem that it solves is that it will automatically require the PHP files for any classes that are needed by any other classes. Loading PHP files on demand saves us a huge amount of boilerplate code and general pain. The term for automatically loading PHP files is known as "autoloading."

Old-fashioned versus autoloaded

To illustrate what autoloading is all about, let's have a look at some old-fashioned PHP code and compare it with some modern autoloader-based code.

First, let's define two classes that we will require/autoload.

First, we have two simple classes:

src/Part4/Chapter10/Dependencies/ClassOne.php

Repo: `https://git.io/JRw5H`

```php
<?php

declare(strict_types=1);

namespace Book\Part4\Chapter10\Dependencies;

final class ClassOne
```

```php
{
}
```

src/Part4/Chapter10/Dependencies/ClassTwo.php

Repo: `https://git.io/JRw5Q`

```php
<?php

declare(strict_types=1);

namespace Book\Part4\Chapter10\Dependencies;

final class ClassTwo
{
    public function __construct(private ClassOne $classOne)
    {
    }

    public function getClassOne(): ClassOne
    {
        return $this->classOne;
    }
}
```

Old-fashioned

Here is some old-fashioned code that has to manually `require_once` the relevant PHP files so that the classes are defined. Then, we can write code that uses them.

src/Part4/Chapter10/oldFashioned.php

Repo: `https://git.io/JRw57`

```php
<?php

declare(strict_types=1);

namespace Book\Part4\Chapter10;
```

```
/**
 * Old fashioned PHP code where we have to manually bring in
the PHP files for any classes we want to use.
 *
 * We use `require_once` because there was always a risk that
the same file might be used in a standard `require` more
 * than once. Declaring the same class twice causes a fatal
error.
 *
 * Imagine something real-world rather than this contrived
example
 */
require_once __DIR__ . '/Dependencies/ClassOne.php';
require_once __DIR__ . '/Dependencies/ClassTwo.php';

use Book\Part4\Chapter10\Dependencies\ClassOne;
use Book\Part4\Chapter10\Dependencies\ClassTwo;

$class = new ClassTwo(new ClassOne());
```

Modern autoloaded

In contrast, we have this modern code, which uses the autoloading capabilities provided by Composer.

src/Part4/Chapter10/autoloadedBliss.php

Repo: `https://git.io/JRw55`

```php
<?php

declare(strict_types=1);

namespace Book\Part4\Chapter10;

use Book\Part4\Chapter10\Dependencies\ClassOne;
use Book\Part4\Chapter10\Dependencies\ClassTwo;

/**
```

```
    * This line brings in the Composer autoloader which just takes
  care of everything for us.
    */
  require __DIR__ . '/../../../vendor/autoload.php';


  /**
    * And we can then freely refer to classes without any messy
  work to locate and require PHP files.
    */
  $class = new ClassTwo(new ClassOne());
```

A real-world, old-fashioned example

To see a real-world example of require bloat, just have a look at this file from the popular WordPress plugin Ninja Forms.

ninja-forms/ninja-forms.php at master – jayharle/ninja-forms – GitHub

```
https://git.io/J3Jch
```

Here is a preview:

```
#line 68
require_once( NINJA_FORMS_DIR . "/includes/database.php" );


# ... lots of lines


#line 234
require_once( NINJA_FORMS_DIR . "/includes/admin/save.php" );
```

This is not the fault of the plugin developer. Unfortunately, WordPress remains free of Composer and autoloading and is one of the few modern PHP projects to do so. Although there are some community solutions trying to bring Composer goodness into the WordPress ecosystem, a plugin developer must assume that no autoloading is available.

Extra points

Those of you who have been paying attention might have noticed that generally, a lot of the code samples so far in this book have been using the Composer autoloader. I chose to do this without explanation as it allowed me to cut down on boilerplate code, and I knew that I would be explaining it soon. Have a look back through the previous files, such as `toy_mvc.php`, to spot the autoloader in use.

src/Part3/Chapter8/toy_mvc.php

Repo: `https://git.io/JRw53`

```php
<?php

declare(strict_types=1);

namespace Book\Part3\Chapter8;

use Book\Part3\Chapter8\ToyMVC\BrowserVisit;

require __DIR__ . '/../../../vendor/autoload.php';

$homePage = (new BrowserVisit())->visit('/');

echo $homePage;
```

Autoloading in PHP

Let's take a quick look at what autoloading is and how it works in PHP.

There is a special function provided by the SPL, `spl_autoload_register`:

PHP: spl_autoload_register – Manual

`https://www.php.net/manual/en/function.spl-autoload-register.php`

The argument that you pass into `spl_autoload_register` is a `callable` – an anonymous function, or the name of a function – that will handle autoloading duties and return a boolean.

Whenever the PHP engine hits a class that it has not loaded yet, it will trigger the autoloading process.

The `spl_autoload_register` function can be called one or more times to create a queue of functions that will be called when PHP hits a reference to a class that it has not loaded yet. When this occurs, the engine will work through this queue of functions until one successfully loads the correct PHP file.

To see a very simple example, have a look at this file:

src/Part4/Chapter10/bespokeAutoloader.php

Repo: `https://git.io/JRw5d`

```php
<?php


declare(strict_types=1);


namespace Book\Part4\Chapter10;


use Book\Part4\Chapter10\Dependencies\ClassOne;
use Book\Part4\Chapter10\Dependencies\ClassTwo;
use RuntimeException;


/*
 * We call spl_autoload_register and pass in our bespoke
closure which handles autoloading.
 *
 * This autoloader has been crafted to load classes from the
`Dependencies` sub folder of the Chapter10 directory.
 * This means this is not a good example for general purpose
autoloading!
 */
\spl_autoload_register(static function (string $classFqn): void
{
    // find the position of the last / character
    $offset = \strrchr($classFqn, '\\');
    if ($offset === false) {
        throw new RuntimeException('Failed finding \\ in
$classFqn ' . $classFqn);
```

```php
    }
    // get all the text after the last / character
    $className = \substr($offset, 1);


    // now check for the class filename in the Dependencies sub
directory based on this text
    $path = __DIR__ . '/Dependencies/' . $className . '.php';
    if (!\file_exists($path)) {
        // return on failure allows the next autoloader in the
chain to have a go at loading this class
        return;
    }
    require $path;
});


/**
 * And we can then freely refer to classes without any messy
work to locate and require PHP files.
 */
$class = new ClassTwo(new ClassOne());
```

I would regard writing your own autoloader as something *quite unusual* these days, so I have decided not to go into any further detail on it; instead, I suggest that you simply use Composer for autoloading duties.

You can take a look at the class loader that Composer uses here:

composer/ClassLoader.php at master – composer/composer – GitHub

`https://git.io/J3UIn`

If you don't want to look at it, suffice to say that it includes a lot of functionality that provides a comprehensive solution to autoloading.

If you would like to create your own for educational purposes, then I can only encourage you to do so, but I don't advise it for any real projects.

Another interesting point for those familiar with autoloading in PHP 5 or 7 is that the classical `__autoload` function has been completely removed from PHP 8.

Now that you have a grasp of dependencies and autoloading, let's move on and start using Composer.

Configuring Composer autoloader

For the Composer autoloader to be able to load your project classes, you need to add some configuration to the `composer.json` file.

Generally, you will configure this twice – once for production code, often stored in a folder called `src`, and then another.

The modern standard is to configure this with PSR4, which we discussed back in *Chapter 1, Object-Oriented PHP*, but for reference, here is a link:

PSR-4: Autoloader – PHP-FIG

`https://www.php-fig.org/psr/psr-4/`

PSR4 allows us to define a root namespace for a specific folder, and then from that root folder and namespace combination, it is expected that each folder corresponds to an equivalent and identically named namespace level:

```
    "autoload": {
  "PhpBook\\MyFirstProject": "src"
  },
```

For our project, we chose the `PhpBook\MyFirstProject` root namespace and assigned this to the `src` folder in our project root. With this configuration, Composer will autoload our code, so long as we create classes in the correct namespace; for example:

src/Part4/Chapter10/MyFirstProject/src/Foo/Bar.php

Repo: `https://git.io/JRw5F`

```php
<?php

declare(strict_types=1);

namespace PhpBook\MyFirstProject\Foo;

final class Bar
{
}
```

You can (and should) also configure a dev autoloader, which is generally used to autoload your test classes. This is exactly the same, but the JSON key is `autoload-dev` instead of `autoload`.

So, now that you understand what autoloading is and how Composer makes this easy for us, let's look at the main reason we should use Composer – to manage the process of bringing third-party packages into your application.

Using Composer to require packages

So, now that you have an idea of what dependencies are, what dependency management and resolution are all about, and have also understood the benefits of autoloading, it's time to start using Composer.

I assume you have already installed Composer, but if not, here is the link again:

Introduction – Composer

```
https://getcomposer.org/doc/00-intro.md#installation-linux-
unix-macos
```

Finding dependencies

The primary source of packages for Composer-based projects is a website called Packagist:

Packagist

```
https://packagist.org/
```

This is the default "repository" that Composer searches when looking for packages that are defined as dependencies.

At the time of writing, Packagist contains over 300,000 packages, with 2.8 million versions available. Chances are, if you need something, then there is a package for it.

The initial mechanism for discovering packages is to simply search on Packagist; for example:

Packagist

```
https://packagist.org/?query=logging
```

Here, we can look at a specific package; for example:

monolog/monolog – Packagist

```
https://packagist.org/packages/monolog/monolog
```

And from this page, we can see a wide range of basic information and can also find links to the home page and GitHub (or other VCS) for the package; for example:

GitHub – Seldaek/monolog: Sends your logs to files, sockets, inboxes, databases, and various web services

`https://git.io/v7gJh`

Once we have decided on a package that we would like to install as a dependency, then it is time to create a `composer.json` file so that we can instruct Composer to install it for us.

Let's do that now and bring in Monolog:

Initialization of composer.json

The first thing we need to do is initialize our `composer.json` file. This is a special file that Composer reads when you run `composer` commands. It contains all the information it needs in order to understand and control what dependencies to install, as well as a load of other useful information for other features.

You can write the `composer.json` file manually, and I do generally do this, but when you are just getting started, there is an easier way:

```
cd /my/project/root/directory
composer init
```

Here, you can run the `composer init` command. After, you will be given an interactive text-based user interface that will take you through setting up your `composer.json` file.

I'm going to initialize a project in the `src/Part4/Chapter10/MyFirstProject` directory of the code repository.

When I run the `composer init` command, I am presented with this first:

```
   Welcome to the Composer config generator



 This command will guide you through creating your composer.json
 config.

 Package name (<vendor>/<name>) [book_ops/my-first-project]:
```

This forms a question (what is the package name?) with a default answer in square brackets; that is, [book_ops/my-first-project]. To accept the default answer, you can just hit *Enter*. Alternatively, you can type in your own answer before hitting *Enter*.

What is a vendor?

In Composer, packages have two main attributes:

- Vendor name
- Package name

The vendor name is your own personal name. Ideally, this should be something unique and not already registered, so a quick search on https://packagist.org is suggested so that you can choose a unique vendor name.

If we never intend to publish this project on Packagist, then we don't need to worry too much about the vendor or package name as it won't be used for anything. For the purposes of this book, I'm going to go with the default answer: book_ops/my-first-project.

Once you accept this, you will be asked other questions. You can choose to leave some of these blank for now, while others are somewhat important.

Minimum stability

The composer.json schema – Composer

https://getcomposer.org/doc/04-schema.md#minimum-stability

This question is asking how "unstable" we are happy for packages to be. This is an important consideration as it can dramatically affect the stability of our application. The default is for the minimum stability to be stable, so you can either just leave this blank or answer stable if you prefer to be explicit.

If you choose another minimum stability, then you can expect to install pre-release versions of packages that are prone to change and being broken. That's not something I would advise.

Package type

The composer.json schema – Composer

https://getcomposer.org/doc/04-schema.md#type

This will default to `library`, which, again, is the one you are going to want to use, so either leave this blank or explicitly put `library`.

License

This is only something you need to worry about if you ever intend to release the code. If you do not intend to release the code publicly, then you can choose to put `proprietary` as the license, which says "hands off" to anyone who might come across a copy of your project.

So far, so good

At this point, we've set the basic metadata that Composer has asked for, which means we can start to specify our dependencies:

```
  Welcome to the Composer config generator



  This command will guide you through creating your composer.json
  config.

  Package name (<vendor>/<name>) [book_ops/my-first-project]:
  Description []:
  Author [Joseph Edmonds <php-book@php-book.local>, n to skip]:
  Minimum Stability []: stable
  Package Type (e.g. library, project, metapackage, composer-plugin)
  []: library
  License []: proprietary


  Define your dependencies.

  Would you like to define your dependencies (require) interactively
  [yes]?
```

If we answer `yes` (just hit *Enter* as it is the default answer), then we will go into a round of dependency installation. You can choose to skip this and just edit the `composer.json` file if you prefer.

Installing monolog

We want to install monolog, so hit *Enter* and then search for `monolog`:

```
Would you like to define your dependencies (require) interactively
[yes]?
Search for a package: monolog


Found 15 packages matching monolog

   [0] monolog/monolog
   [1] symfony/monolog-bundle
   [2] symfony/monolog-bridge
   [3] maxbanton/cwh
   [4] easycorp/easy-log-handler Abandoned. Use  instead.
   [5] theorchard/monolog-cascade
   [6] bramus/monolog-colored-line-formatter
   [7] wazaari/monolog-mysql
   [8] flynsarmy/slim-monolog
   [9] tylercd100/lern
  [10] inpsyde/wonolog
  [11] amphp/log
  [12] rahimi/monolog-telegram
  [13] nikolaposa/monolog-factory
  [14] neeckeloo/monolog-module


Enter package # to add, or the complete package name if it is not
listed:
```

This has given us a list of matches. We want to choose the first one here, so put in 0 and hit *Enter*:

```
Enter the version constraint to require (or leave blank to use the
latest version):
```

At this point, Composer is giving us the option to require a specific version of the package. There could be reasons why we need to use an old version, but in general, you will always want the latest version that can be installed, so just leave this blank and hit *Enter*:

```
Enter package # to add, or the complete package name if it is not
listed: 0
Enter the version constraint to require (or leave blank to use the
latest version):
Using version ^2.2 for monolog/monolog
Search for a package:
```

We are now back at the search prompt. If you do not want to install any more packages, you can just hit *Enter* and it will move you on. Of course, if you do want to install more packages, you can do that by repeating this process as many times as required:

```
Search for a package:
Would you like to define your dev dependencies (require-dev)
interactively [yes]?
```

Now, it is asking us if we would like to install any dev dependencies. These are dependencies that are only of use when we're doing development work and are not for production use. Let's enter no for now:

```
Search for a package:
Would you like to define your dev dependencies (require-dev)
interactively [yes]? no

{
    "name": "book_ops/my-first-project",
    "type": "library",
    "require": {
        "monolog/monolog": "^2.2"
    },
    "license": "proprietary",
    "authors": [
        {
            "name": "Joseph Edmonds",
            "email": "php-book@php-book.local"
        }
    ],
```

```
        "minimum-stability": "stable"
}


Do you confirm generation [yes]?
```

At this point, Composer is giving us a preview of the composer.json structure that is to be created based upon our answers to the various questions. Assuming it is all good, just hit *Enter* to accept the default of yes:

```
Would you like to install dependencies now [yes]?
```

Now that we have a composer.json file, we can install the defined dependencies. Of course, this is our primary goal, so let's hit *Enter*:

```
Do you confirm generation [yes]?
Would you like to install dependencies now [yes]?
No lock file found. Updating dependencies instead of installing from
lock file. Use composer update over composer install if you do not
have a lock file.
Loading composer repositories with package information
Updating dependencies
Lock file operations: 2 installs, 0 updates, 0 removals
  - Locking monolog/monolog (2.2.0)
  - Locking psr/log (1.1.3)
Writing lock file
Installing dependencies from lock file (including require-dev)
Package operations: 2 installs, 0 updates, 0 removals
  - Downloading monolog/monolog (2.2.0)
  - Installing psr/log (1.1.3): Extracting archive
  - Installing monolog/monolog (2.2.0): Extracting archive
11 package suggestions were added by new dependencies, use `composer
suggest` to see details.
Generating autoload files
1 package you are using is looking for funding.
Use the `composer fund` command to find out more!
```

With that, the packages have been installed. We have Monolog, which is the package we explicitly required, and we also have psr/log, which is a dependency of Monolog.

Ignore the vendor directory in your VCS

If you look in the filesystem, you will notice a `vendor` subdirectory in your project root. This is where dependencies are installed by Composer. You should notice that it now contains lots of folders and files.

It is a generally accepted best practice to make sure you instruct your VCS (for example, Git) to ignore the contents of this directory by adding `vendor` to your project's `.gitignore` file.

src/Part4/Chapter10/MyFirstProject/.gitignore

Repo: `https://git.io/Jn5Hk`

```
vendor
```

This means that your project history only contains your code. You can rely on Composer to bring in the right versions for all your third-party requirements. It does this using a lock file. We'll look at that next.

The composer.lock file

Once Composer does its dependency resolution work to figure out exactly which version of each package should be installed, it creates a `composer.lock` file to store this information.

This file is not one you should ever edit or even look at, to be honest. It is highly verbose and acts as a cache for Composer so that it knows exactly what versions of the packages to install. When it completes its dependency resolution task, it determines a set of package versions that are mutually compatible and also compatible with your environment – your PHP version and PHP extensions, for example. To save having to do this job every time, and also to ensure that the correct package versions have been installed, the lock file "locks" versions down to the specific Git commit or tag that should be installed for each package.

With this lock file, you or anyone else can quickly and easily install the same versions. This is a very good thing. It is this mechanism that allows you to work on your code locally, push it to production, and then install the same versions of your dependencies in production so that you can be sure that everything will work as it does for you in your local development environment.

I strongly suggest that you track your `composer.lock` file in your VCS, and I also strongly suggest that you only ever run Composer updates in your development environment. In any other environments – staging, CI, testing, and production – you should only ever run `composer install --no-dev`.

The extra `--no-dev` flag instructs Composer to only install your production dependencies, which is exactly what you should be doing for production.

Adding extra dependencies

Now that we have a `composer.json` file, we can edit it manually, or we can use Composer commands to add extra dependencies.

For example, we have decided that we would like to bring in a DI container, so we search Packagist and we find this library:

php-di/php-di – Packagist

`https://packagist.org/packages/php-di/php-di`

Just below the title of the package, Packagist gives us the command we need to run – it even highlights it on click, ready to copy and paste:

```
composer require php-di/php-di
```

When we run this command, we instruct Composer to bring in this new dependency, along with any of its dependencies. This is the output:

```
$ composer require php-di/php-di


Using version ^6.3 for php-di/php-di
./composer.json has been updated
Running composer update php-di/php-di
Loading composer repositories with package information
Updating dependencies
Lock file operations: 5 installs, 0 updates, 0 removals
  - Locking opis/closure (3.6.2)
  - Locking php-di/invoker (2.3.0)
  - Locking php-di/php-di (6.3.2)
  - Locking php-di/phpdoc-reader (2.2.1)
  - Locking psr/container (1.1.1)
Writing lock file
Installing dependencies from lock file (including require-dev)
Package operations: 5 installs, 0 updates, 0 removals
  - Downloading psr/container (1.1.1)
  - Downloading php-di/phpdoc-reader (2.2.1)
```

```
  - Downloading php-di/invoker (2.3.0)
  - Downloading opis/closure (3.6.2)
  - Downloading php-di/php-di (6.3.2)
  - Installing psr/container (1.1.1): Extracting archive
  - Installing php-di/phpdoc-reader (2.2.1): Extracting archive
  - Installing php-di/invoker (2.3.0): Extracting archive
  - Installing opis/closure (3.6.2): Extracting archive
  - Installing php-di/php-di (6.3.2): Extracting archive
2 package suggestions were added by new dependencies, use `composer
suggest` to see details.
Generating autoload files
3 packages you are using are looking for funding.
Use the `composer fund` command to find out more!
```

At this point, the Composer file in our project now looks like this:

```json
{
    "name": "book_ops/my-first-project",
    "type": "library",
    "require": {
        "monolog/monolog": "^2.2",
        "php-di/php-di": "^6.3"
    },
    "license": "proprietary",
    "authors": [
        {
            "name": "Joseph Edmonds",
            "email": "php-book@php-book.local"
        }
    ],
    "minimum-stability": "stable"
}
```

If you look in the vendor subdirectory, you will notice that we now have lots more files and folders in there. Composer has also updated the composer.lock file; this is a change you probably want to commit to your VCS history.

Let's move on and look at version constraints in more detail, as well as how you can configure your composer.json file so that you only get the versions you want.

Version constraints

When we `require` a package in our `composer.json` file, we also have to define a "version constraint." This instructs Composer on exactly what versions are acceptable to be installed.

The most flexible option is to specify * as the version constraint, which means "anything." It will still respect the configured minimum stability but beyond that, anything goes. This is generally a terrible idea as things could change wildly from one version to the next when you update packages, breaking your application in weird and wonderful ways.

Instead, we always want to specify some kind of constraint. When we call `composer require`, Composer will calculate a constraint for us. You can see these in the `composer.json` file we created in MyFirstProject:

```
    "monolog/monolog": "^2.2",
    "php-di/php-di": "^6.3"
```

What Composer has used here is what is called the "Caret Version Range."

Versions and constraints – Composer

`https://getcomposer.org/doc/articles/versions.md#caret-version-range-.`

This is a sensible default option for version constraints. Focusing on Monolog in particular, it means the following:

- The version must be 2.2.0 or greater.
- The version must be 2.x.y, never 3.x.y.

SemVer in a nutshell

If you are not familiar with this "three numbers" version system, then it's time for a quick primer. **SemVer** is short for **Semantic Versioning**."

Semantic Versioning 2.0.0 | Semantic Versioning

`https://semver.org/`

As stated on the official SemVer website, the three numbers correspond to the following:

- The MAJOR version, when you make incompatible API changes.
- The MINOR version, when you add functionality in a backward-compatible manner.
- and PATCH version, when you make backward-compatible bug fixes.

What this means is that each time one of your dependencies is updated and they release a new version, they will create a release with a specific version number corresponding to the level of change that the new release brings.

Minor bug fixes are PATCH. New functionality that doesn't affect existing functionality is MINOR. Changes to existing functionality are generally MAJOR unless they do not risk breaking anything.

When we require packages, we can define which versions we will accept when updating the package.

Generally, we would **never want** MAJOR version changes to come in as these are almost certain to break our application. The process of updating a MAJOR version of a dependency is highly likely to require code changes to our core application code.

We also generally **want** to accept MINOR changes as these are likely to benefit our application and should not, in theory, bring any issues.

We almost certainly **want** to accept PATCH releases as these should only be bug fixes/improvements that are completely safe to install.

Let's learn how we can configure our `composer.json` file to allow only those updates we want on a per-package basis using Composer's version range syntax.

Caret (^) Version Range

The Caret Version Range is the most usual syntax and includes a version number prefix with a caret; for example:

```
^2.2.12
```

In general, we would be happy to accept MINOR changes, and we almost certainly want PATCH changes that may simply fix bugs, security issues, and more, regardless of whether we are aware of them.

This set of standard acceptable version changes is neatly taken care of with the Caret Version Range. We simply set out the minimum acceptable version – for example, `^2.2.12` – and Composer will install the most up-to-date version of the package that it can, up to but *not* including `3.0.0`.

Tilde (~) Version Range

If we want more control and, for example, want to restrict MINOR updates, then we can use the Tilde Version Range, like so:

```
~2.2.12
```

The Tilde Version Range only allows changes to be made to the outermost version. So, when we define a full three-section SemVer version, then this means the first two sections are not allowed to change.

In our example of ~`2.2.12`, this means that we will accept `2.2.20` but will not accept `2.3.0` as the `3` is not the last section included in our range.

Exact version

If we want to specify an exact version to include with no option to update it, then we can simply specify that version with no extra operators:

```
2.2.12
```

This will only ever install `2.2.12` and will never update it without us explicitly changing the version constraint in `composer.json`. This kind of very strict constraint is unusual, but you may find you need it to, for example, avoid bugs in recent package versions.

Version range

The most verbose option but also perhaps the clearest is to explicitly declare the acceptable version range. Standard operators can be used here, like so:

```
>, >=, <, <=, !=
```

By using these operators, you can craft a custom and explicit version range; for example:

```
>=2.2.12 <2.2.18
```

This would ensure `2.2.12` as a minimum, but never `2.2.18` or higher. It is unusual to need this kind of constraint, but it's good to know you can do this.

Multiple acceptable versions

If you are creating library code that is designed to work, for example, with multiple PHP versions, then you can specify this explicitly.

You can do this using the "OR" operator, `||`. (The single pipe is also acceptable as an "OR" operator, `|`).

For example, if you are writing some code to work with different PHP versions, you can specify this as follows:

```
"php": "^7.4 || ^8.0",
```

Full documentation

I believe that the previous sections have covered most of the scenarios you are likely to come across, but this is not the full range of possibilities that Composer supports. To read about these possibilities and to further understand the version constraints system, I suggest that you have a good read through this page of the official docs:

Versions and constraints – Composer

```
https://getcomposer.org/doc/articles/versions.md
```

Now, let's move on and discuss how you can keep a set of dependencies you need for your production functionality, as well as how to keep a list of extra tools to install to assist with your development, QA, and testing requirements.

Dev and prod dependencies

Composer splits dependencies into two types: dev and prod.

The concept here is quite simple – prod dependencies are those that are needed for your application to run. This might include emailing, logging, framework components, and so on. This is the default when requiring new dependencies.

The other dependency type is dev and is used when we want to bring in tooling that assists with development. There are all kinds of development tools in the PHP ecosystem to power things, such as unit testing, static analysis, coding standards, and more. When we install these kinds of tools, they can often bring in large numbers of their own dependencies as well, creating a very large PHP code base.

Requiring dev dependencies

When we require a new dependency that we want to be a dev dependency, we can simply add a --dev flag to the command; for example:

```
composer require phpunit/phpunit --dev
```

This command will update the composer.json file and add a new require-dev section if it does not already exist. In that section, we list our dev dependencies in the same way that prod dependencies are listed in the require section:

```
"require-dev": {
"phpunit/phpunit": "^9.5"
}
```

Installing without dev dependencies

When dev dependencies are defined, these will always be installed alongside the standard (production) dependencies.

When we are installing our project in a production environment, though, it is generally quite important that we don't install the dev dependencies. These dev dependencies can bring security issues and simply add bloat, which will slow things down.

To only install our production dependencies, we can simply pass the `--no-dev` flag; for example:

```
#install

composer install --no-dev
```

Summary

That brings us to the end of this chapter. If you are new to Composer, then I hope that you now understand what it is all about and are eagerly planning to utilize it in your new and existing projects. You will never look back!

If you already knew of Composer, then perhaps you just skipped this whole chapter, but if not, then I hope you found some useful clarifications and maybe a renewed appreciation of just how awesome it is.

In the next chapter, we're going to have a look at how we can create a Composer package that is designed to be reused across multiple projects, and maybe even released as open source on Packagist for the benefit of the community at large – an excellent choice!

11
Creating Your Own Composer Package

In this chapter, we are going to continue looking at Composer. This time, we are going to try to create a small but useful package that we can reuse across all of our projects.

The first thing, of course, is to create the actual library that you want to publish. I would encourage you to think twice before publishing an empty "hello world" type package, as Packagist is a real system and there is no benefit in clogging it up with useless libraries.

That being said, let's just make a "hello world" Composer package and try to show some common scenarios. If you decide to upload your version to Packagist, *please make sure to remove it once you are done!*

You can see the simple "hello world" project that has been created here:

**The-Art-of-Modern-PHP-8/composer-module-hello-world at main · PacktPublishing/
The-Art-of-Modern-PHP-8 · GitHub**

```
https://git.io/JRwFX
```

This chapter will cover the following main topics:

- Writing `composer.json`
- Using source folders and namespaces

- Executable Binaries Configured under bin

- Using versions and tagging

- Private Git repos as Composer dependencies

- Publishing on Packagist

First, we're going to look at getting the `composer.json` metadata in good order.

As usual, you can find all the code samples for this chapter in the main repo for the book available on GitHub at `https://github.com/PacktPublishing/The-Art-of-Modern-PHP-8`.

Writing composer.json

You have already been introduced to the `composer.json` file in the previous chapter. The `composer.json` file includes all the crucial information that controls what dependencies and requirements your project has. However, it also includes lots of meta-information. This metadata is used when your package is published on Packagist.

You don't need to worry about this too much while you are developing, but when you want to publish on Packagist, it is beneficial to ensure that your metadata is in good order.

Let's take a look at the `composer.json` file for this project:

composer-module-hello-world/composer.json

Repo: `https://git.io/JRw58`

```
{
    "name": "yourname/hello-world",
    "description": "A hello world package",
    "keywords": [
      "hello world"
    ],
    "license": "GPL-3.0-or-later",
    "authors": [
      {
        "name": "Joseph Edmonds",
        "email": "info@ltscommerce.dev"
      }
```

```
    ],
    "require": {
        "php": ">= 8.0.1"
    },
    "autoload": {
        "psr-4": {
            "YourName\\HelloWorld\\": "src/"
        }
    },
    "autoload-dev": {
        "psr-4": {
            "YourName\\HelloWorld\\Test\\": "tests/"
        }
    },
    "require-dev": {
        "roave/security-advisories": "dev-master",
        "phpunit/phpunit": "^9.5"
    },
    "minimum-stability": "stable",
    "config": {
        "bin-dir": "bin"
    },
    "bin": [
        "bin/hello"
    ]
}
```

The main aspects of meta information that we want to ensure we are happy with when publishing to Packagist.org are:

- Name
- Description
- Keywords
- License

Name

This is simply the name of the package, presented in the `vendor/package-name` style. This needs to be unique, and you need to have already registered the vendor name. The convention is that the vendor name and package name are the same as the GitHub user and repo name. This is not required, but it does make sense.

For example:

Packagist URL	GitHub URL
https://packagist.org/packages/swiftmailer/swiftmailer	https://github.com/swiftmailer/swiftmailer
https://packagist.org/packages/craftcms/commerce	https://github.com/craftcms/commerce
https://packagist.org/packages/yii-extension/asset-bootstrap5	https://github.com/yii-extension/asset-bootstrap5

Description

The description is the text that is displayed within the search results on Packagist. It is also prominently displayed at the top of the actual package page. This should be concise, meaningful, and clearly describe what the package does, or is for, in a sentence or two.

Keywords

This is an array of keywords and phrases that people might use to search for your package. Don't go mad here, but do throw at least two or three keywords in there to help people discover your package.

License

There are many licenses that you can choose from, and the differences between the licenses vary in some restrictions that are in place.

MIT

If you would like your package to be freely used without any real restrictions, then the MIT license is the best choice.

GNU GPLv3

If you feel that the package should not be included in money-making code bases, then you might choose to use the GNU GPLv3 license instead. This obliges anyone using your package to also release their code openly. For this "hello world" package, I have opted to use GPL so that if anyone else decides to make loads of money out of the ability to echo "hello world" on the command line, then they need to at least share their code. `</sarcasm>`

Choosing a license

A great website for reading about and comparing the various licenses is the following:

Choose an open source license | Choose a License

`https://choosealicense.com/`

Now that your metadata is in order, let's recap the PSR-12 autoloading configuration so that you can have your module code nicely namespaced and autoloaded by Composer.

Using source folders and namespaces

You might have noticed the two configurations `autoload` and `autoload-dev` These allow us to configure folders of source code in our module and map them to specific base namespaces. You hopefully recall that we discussed this topic in *Chapter 10, Composer For Dependencies*. However, it is worth mentioning again, because you need to get these autoload sections configured correctly with the namespace for your code.

For example, this file is located in the `src` folder and so has the namespace defined as `YourName\HelloWorld`:

composer-module-hello-world/src/MessageProviderInterface.php

Repo: `https://git.io/JRw54`

```php
<?php

declare(strict_types=1);

namespace YourName\HelloWorld;

interface MessageProviderInterface
{
```

```php
    /**
     * Get the hello world message in the configured Language
     */
    public function getMessage(): string;
}
```

This test file is located in the tests/Cli folder, and so has the namespace defined as YourName\HelloWorld\Tests\Cli:

composer-module-hello-world/tests/Cli/ArgsTest.php

Repo: https://git.io/JRw5B

```php
<?php

declare(strict_types=1);

namespace YourName\HelloWorld\Tests\Cli;

use PHPUnit\Framework\TestCase;
use YourName\HelloWorld\Cli\Args;
use YourName\HelloWorld\Language;

class ArgsTest extends TestCase
{
    /** @test */
    public function itCanParseLanguageArg(): void
    {
        $testArgv = [Args::ARG_LANG => Language::LANG_ENGLISH];
        $expected = Language::LANG_ENGLISH;
        $actual   = (new Args($testArgv))->getLanguageCode();
        self::assertSame($expected, $actual);
    }

    /** @test */
    public function itExceptsOnInvalidArg(): void
    {
        $this->expectException(\
InvalidArgumentException::class);
```

```
        $this->expectExceptionMessage('Invalid argument foo');
        new Args(['foo=bar']);
    }
}
```

Hopefully, this simple configuration is now clear. Let's look at another important piece of configuration that can make for a smooth developer experience on the command line – executables.

Executable Binaries Configured under bin

It is quite common for a person to want to provide some kind of executable with their Composer package.

You will probably have noticed that, when installing some packages, Composer not only creates the source folders and files under vendor but also creates a `bin` or `vendor/bin` directory (depending on how you have things configured) that contains all the executable files that your dependencies provide.

It is definitely worth reading the official documentation on this:

`https://getcomposer.org/doc/articles/vendor-binaries.md`

For our `HelloWorld` package, we have an executable defined that provides the mission-critical functionality of our package:

composer-module-hello-world/bin/hello

Repo: `https://git.io/JRw5R`

```php
#!/usr/bin/env php
<?php

declare(strict_types=1);

/**
 * Handle the fact that you may be executing this from your own
package,
 * or as an installed dependency
 */
$autoloaderPath = (static function (): string {
    foreach ([__DIR__ . '/../../../autoload.php', __DIR__ .
```

```
'/../vendor/autoload.php'] as $file) {
        if (file_exists($file)) {
            return $file;
        }
    }
    throw new \RuntimeException('Failed finding composer
autoloader');
})();

/** Load the found autoloader */
require $autoloaderPath;

/**  Parse CLI args */
$args = new \YourName\HelloWorld\Cli\Args($argv);

/** Create language based on language code args */
$language = new \YourName\HelloWorld\Language($args-
>getLanguageCode());

/** Create message provider with configured language */
$messageProvider = new \YourName\HelloWorld\
MessageProvider($language);

/** Create output instance and use to send output */
$output = new \YourName\HelloWorld\Cli\CliOutput();
$output->sendOutput($messageProvider);
```

Output:

There are a few things to note about binaries like this.

Extensionless files

It is a convention to remove the `.php` extension from these files, though you do not have to.

You can instruct a CLI shell, such as Bash, to execute the file using PHP by using what is called a "shebang" at the top of your file:

```
#!/usr/bin/env php
```

Incorporating this line also generally instructs your IDE to regard the file as a PHP file so that you still get all the PHP IDE goodness you expect.

Executable permissions

It may seem obvious, but you probably want to mark your executable file as executable in terms of file permissions. This permission is tracked by Git. To make your `bin` file executable (in Linux), simply run:

```
chmod +x bin/hello
```

Finding an autoloader

Your `bin` file might be executed by you when you are working on the package, or it might be executed by someone who has installed your package. These two scenarios mean that the paths to the `vendor/autoload.php` file are different and you need to account for this.

You can see this at the top of the `bin/hello` file where we use an anonymous function to find the autoloader or throw an exception if that fails. This code snippet might be one you want to keep in your copypasta arsenal as it, or something like it, is essential.

So, now that you have your package with your executable all nicely configured, you need to make sure you understand how you can safely and productively release new versions of your library, while allowing projects that use your library to be safe from any breaking changes that they don't want. This is done by using versions and tagging.

Using versions and tagging

It is fully expected that your package will not be perfect the moment you publish. Even if you did somehow manage to achieve perfection, the world keeps changing, and you might find that the latest PHP version that has just come out requires some tweaks to your code. You need to provide a mechanism for projects that are using your package to make sure they only get the known, safe versions that they want.

When you update your library and hit a stable point that you would like to release as a new version that is ready to be used in production projects, all you need to do is create a Git tag with a semantic version (to be explained soon) and push this up to the VCS that Packagist is connected to – for example, GitHub:

Resources to learn Git

```
https://try.github.io/
```

Creating a Git tag

Before you can create a tag, you must have created at least one commit. In general, there will be a whole sequence of commits leading up to the point where you feel it is worth creating a tag. The tag represents a meaningful point and one that you would like other users of your package to be able to check out easily.

To create a tag, you can use the Git tag command:

```
#There must be at least one commit
git commit -m 'at least one commit needs to exist'


# X.Y.Z are digits representing the version you are creating
git tag -a 'X.Y.Z' -m 'Tag textual title'


# Tags must be explicitly pushed, by default
git push --tags
```

The preceding commands create a commit, then a tag, and finally push that tag to the default remote repository, for example, GitHub.

> **What is a Git tag?**
>
> When working with Git, we are continuously creating and pushing "commits." Each commit represents a single snapshot of the entire tracked code base. Generally, we work in "branches," where the most up-to-date commit represents the current state of that branch. Tags allow us to be very specific in saying that we want an exact commit. Tags are basically a shorthand way of checking out a specific commit without having to reference it by its commit hash, which is an unwieldy 32-character string.

The three-number format for versioning is important, and you need to take care to ensure that you are updating this numbering correctly between versions. The name for this three-number style is "semantic versioning" or "SemVer" for short. Let's learn about that now.

SemVer

It is important that you correctly version your releases with SemVer. This is crucial so that consumers of your package can safely update their version without getting any nasty surprises.

The three numbers correspond to three levels of change in the package, and they include major, minor, and patch.

Let's discuss these three levels of change now.

Major

The first number represents the major version. Any change in the major version implies that there are "breaking changes" or "BCs" for short.

> **What are breaking changes?**
>
> Breaking changes are exactly what they describe. They are changes that are likely to break your code. They might be minor breakages that are not too tricky to fix, or they could be nuke-from-orbit-and-start-over levels of breakage. You cannot know what level of breakage will occur, but breakages of at least some form are generally on the cards.

Minor

Minor changes are changes that can be quite significant, but they should never bring in any breaking changes. This means that minor-level changes are generally only going to bring in new features and functionality, or maybe tidy up existing functionality, without changing the interface or output of anything. This means that anyone using your library should be able to upgrade to your latest minor version, and should not incur any new bugs or breakages in their own application code.

Patch

Patch changes are the lightest levels of change. These changes do not bring in any new functionality and are generally reserved for smaller bug, security, and performance fixes to existing functionality. These must never bring in any breaking changes – they should only really be fixing things, never breaking them. This level of change should be safe (even for paranoid users of your library) to update to without any fear of breaking things in an application.

Hopefully, you are now clear on what the three numbers mean in SemVer and will ensure that, as you release new versions, you carefully update your latest tag to ensure that people only get the updates they want without any risk of breaking their projects. The next thing to discuss is how you can work on development versions of your package and even release development and pre-release tagged versions.

Stable and development versions

If you are working on a project that you do not yet regard as properly finished, but would like to release some SemVer protected versions, then you should version this with 0 as the major version. The following is stated in the SemVer specification:

> *"Major version zero (0.y.z) is for initial development. Anything MAY change at any time. The public API SHOULD NOT be considered stable."*

If you are working on your next release, but it is not yet done, you can suffix it with an extra bit of text to signify that this is a "work in progress" release of some form. For example, if you are working on version 2.0.0 and have a release candidate that you would like to share with your testing team, you might create a 2.0.0-RC1 tag to signify that this is "Release Candidate 1 of version 2.0.0."

Composer recognizes the following suffixes:

Suffix	Description
dev	Pure development work in progress, not stable at all
alpha	Not necessarily work in progress, but not tested at all and expected to be buggy
beta	Less expectation of bugs, but nowhere near ready for production
RC	Fingers crossed it is bug-free, not recommended for production use
stable	Bug-free and good for use in production

Users of your library can declare exactly what stability they are prepared to accept. For example, someone who is desperate for a bug fix or feature in your latest release candidate might be willing to risk bugs and can instruct Composer to allow release candidates by updating their composer.json file so that the require section looks like this:

```
{
    "require": {
        "yourname/yourpackage": "^2.0.0@RC"
    }
}
```

By suffixing the @RC on the end, you are letting Composer know that while your minimum stability might be set to stable (the default value) for this particular package, the minimum stability is overridden to allow @RC-suffixed versions to be acceptable.

Hopefully, you are now clear on how you can release more than just stable versions of your package. With this information around suffixes and zero versions, you are also able to release development and pre-release versions without any risk of these finding their way into projects that are expecting production-quality stable code from your package.

The next thing we are going to discuss is how you can share your packages among your own projects without making them public or publishing them on Packagist.

Private Git repos as Composer dependencies

You would be forgiven for thinking that you must release a package on Packagist if you want to be able to use it as a Composer package with your other projects. This is definitely not the case, and for those little packages that you would prefer to keep completely private, you should definitely use this trick.

You can share your Composer package privately among your own projects by simply having it accessible on a **version control system** (**VCS**), such as Git. The most popular publicly accessible implementation of Git is undoubtedly GitHub, though there are many other choices, including hosting your own private repositories on your own server.

In the projects where you want to use this shared library, you must add a little extra JSON config to instruct Composer that it needs to go and query this specific repository.

The best place to learn about this technique is on the official docs page:

Repositories - Composer

```
https://getcomposer.org/doc/05-repositories.md
```

In a nutshell, we tell Composer that it must go and read a specific Git repo by defining it as a custom repository. Let's imagine that, for some reason, you have decided to bring in the repo containing the code for this book into a Composer-based project. The first thing you would need to do is add the repo as a repository:

```
{
    "repositories": {
        "type": "vcs",
        "url": "https://github.com/YourName/HelloWorld"
    }
}
```

The one thing that we must have in the repository we are bringing in is a `composer.json` file. With this `require` statement, we are bringing in the **master** branch. This is achieved by simply putting the branch name prefixed with `dev-`. We are also explicitly overriding the minimum stability to `dev` so that Composer will bring this in, even though we have the minimum stability set to `stable`.

There are other things you can do with custom repositories, and I suggest you have a thorough read of the documentation. However, I suspect that the previous trick to bring in private repositories is probably the one you are most likely to use.

If you are planning to release a package on Packagist, it might make sense to first test it out as a private package, so that you can ensure everything works the way you want.

If you don't imagine anyone else in the world would ever need or want your package, then you might question if it should ever be published on Packagist.

If you are sure that your package is going to make the world a better place and would like to share it with your fellow developers, then let's move on to looking at how to get your package published on Packagist.

Publishing on Packagist

Once you have completed creating your package, and you deem it worthy of bearing your name in the ever-critical eyes of the internet, then you might decide it is time to publish it on Packagist.

First of all, you need to create an account. This is fairly straightforward. You also need to confirm that your project `composer.json` file is in good order, and you have updated GitHub or another repository with all the latest changes.

If you are publishing a literal "hello world," please remove it once you are done experimenting!

Things to check before you publish

Before you publish your package, you might want to check a few things (assuming that the code itself all works correctly).

The first one is that you have a decent README.md file. This file should sit at the root of your repository and should contain clear, concise instructions on how to use your package. The contents of this file will form the bulk of the content on the page for your package on Packagist. If you have verbose, multi-page documentation for your package (or even a full-blown documentation site), then the nice thing to do is simply provide high-level installation and summary documentation in the README.md file, and then provide clear links to your full documentation.

The next thing to check is that you are correctly specifying the PHP version you support. If you have created your package in PHP 8 and have not tested it in anything lower, then you should specify PHP 8 as a minimum. If your package requires other optional PHP extensions, such as curl or bcmath, then you should specify these as requirements as well.

You can read the full documentation about how to require specific "platform packages" here:

Basic usage - Composer

```
https://getcomposer.org/doc/01-basic-usage.md#platform-
packages
```

Submitting your package to Packagist

We are ready to submit, so click the big green **Check** button. This will confirm the package name and ask you to submit it again to confirm the name:

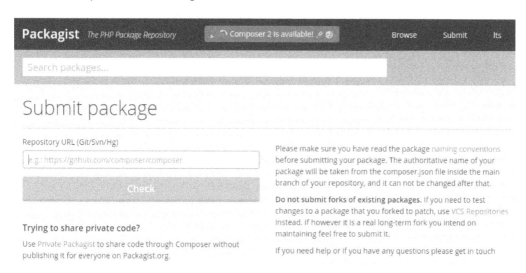

Please perform a double-check at this point to avoid having to delete it and start over.

Created

Your package has now been created on Packagist and you should see a screen that looks a bit like this:

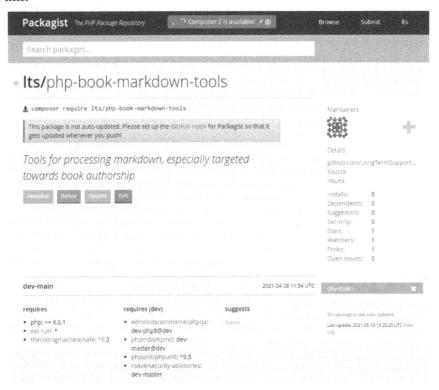

Depending on how you created your Packagist account, you might notice the big red warning saying that the package is not being auto-updated. This means that you will need to remember to manually trigger an update in Packagist every time you update your library. Of course, that would be a huge pain, and so the best thing to do is configure auto-updates.

Configuring auto-updates

For this section, we are going to assume that your package is on GitHub. The first thing we need to do when configuring auto-updates is to confirm that our Packagist account and GitHub account are hooked up, and for that, we need to head to the profile edit section of Packagist:

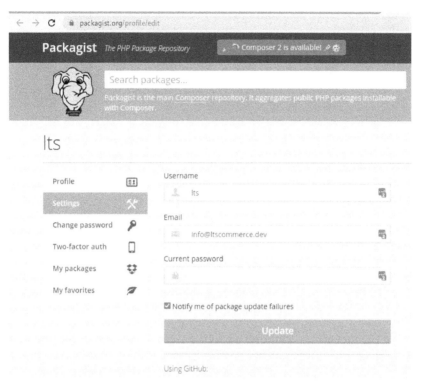

If your account is properly hooked up with GitHub and the correct permissions have been granted, then Packagist will automatically configure your repo to update Packagist. You can double-check the permissions in GitHub by visiting the link that GitHub emailed to you with the subject: *[GitHub] A third-party OAuth application has been added to your account.*

If you have chosen not to use GitHub, then you will need to configure webhooks to notify Packagist of new versions. Of course, the method for this depends entirely on the system hosting the repo.

If you were just testing, delete it

If what you uploaded to Packagist is just a test project, a "hello world" or something similar that has no actual value to the community, then it is best if you just remove it. Now that you have a Packagist library up there and have learned how this works, be a nice user and clean up after yourself.

I got in touch with Jordi and asked him how he felt about people pushing "hello world" type packages:

I'd say the nice thing to do/teach at the end of a tutorial is to learn to use the delete button to clean up after yourself ;)

9:40 AM

It's very easy to remove a package from Packagist. Simply click the red **Delete** button. It's the same as taking your litter home after a picnic. It's just the polite and socially conscientious thing to do.

Summary

In this chapter, we worked on the tasks you will need to handle if you want to create your own Composer-based package or library that can be shared with your other projects, or even with the wider world of PHP developers via Packagist.

First, we covered the metadata configuration in the composer.json file that needs to be sorted so that Packagist or other systems can work correctly. Then we had a quick review of namespaces and source folders and the relevant configuration in composer.json. After this, we looked at how you can configure your package to offer an executable file that will be set up as a symlink when your package is installed. Then we looked again at SemVer and how you should carefully create new releases following a SemVer versioning system so that users of your package (including your own projects) can safely require the versions that they need without getting any unwanted or unexpected breaking changes. With the package complete, we then looked at ways you can require this package in your own projects while keeping the repository private. Finally, we looked at how you can publicly release your package on Packagist so that you and anyone else in the world can freely and easily incorporate it into their projects. Finally, I encouraged you to delete any "hello world" packages you might have deployed onto Packagist, in order to avoid cluttering it.

While all of this should be enough to allow you to create and release your own package, it does not replace a good read of the official Composer documentation. I definitely encourage you to do this.

In the next and final chapter, we're going to have a look at some of the exciting new features being included with the upcoming (at time of writing) PHP 8.1 release. This includes such awesomeness as Enums, Readonly Properties, and more.

Section 5 – Bonus Section - PHP 8.1

The final section of the book is all about PHP 8.1 and the excellent new features that are included in this new release. It is not an exhaustive list but instead focuses on a selection of features that are most likely to matter to you day to day.

This section contains the following chapter:

12
The Awesomeness
That Is 8.1

I've been eagerly waiting to write this chapter until the feature freeze date for the upcoming (at the time of writing) **PHP 8.1**. The features that have made it into this release are amazing. For a lowly point release, it seriously packs a punch. PHP releases have a habit of being like that these days.

I only have one chapter, so I don't have an opportunity to do a deep dive into all of the new features, and I have the difficult task of deciding which features to cover and in how much depth. By the time you're reading this, the chances are that PHP 8.1 has been released, and I would definitely encourage you to use it.

If you want to read the full list of features and changes, you can take a look at this file:

php-src/UPGRADING at master · php/php-src · GitHub

```
https://git.io/JBE7t
```

This UPGRADING document is the most up-to-date authoritative list of changes at the time of writing.

There are a number of changes, many of which make PHP more sane to work with (such as static method variables working the way you would expect them to when inherited), and there are brand-new headline features that will potentially make a big difference to the way you write your code. As these big changes are the most exciting, I'm going to focus on them, and I'll leave it as an exercise for you to thoroughly read through the UPGRADING document to get a complete understanding of this version.

This chapter will cover the following main topics:

- Enumerations
- Readonly properties
- Intersection types
- Never return type
- Final constants

As usual, you can find all the code samples for this chapter in the main repo for the book available on GitHub at https://github.com/PacktPublishing/The-Art-of-Modern-PHP-8.

Enumerations

An **enumerated type** – **enum** for short – is a special type that has a constrained list of possible values, or enumerators.

If you would like to learn more background on this topic, you can read the lengthy **Wikipedia** article at https://w.wiki/3i7Z. However, the sentence at the start of this section does pretty much sum it up.

To understand the PHP implementation of enums, the best place to look at the time of writing is the **RFC** page:

PHP: rfc:enumerations

https://wiki.php.net/rfc/enumerations

Basic and backed enums

One way to think of enums is a bit like a constant array. Something that is hardcoded and can never change when the code is running. There are two kinds of enums – basic (or pure) and backed. These two types of enums correlate conceptually somewhat with indexed and associative arrays, in that a basic enum has just the value, and backed enums have a key and a value associated with that key.

Like associative array keys, **backed enums** can be either strings or ints. However, unlike arrays, these cannot be mixed, as all cases must be backed with the same type. The type of backing is declared after the enum name in the following style:

```
enum EnumName: string
```

Here is a simple basic enum with a trait. Note that enums are like classes in that they can contain methods, traits, and implement interfaces. Also, note that basic enum cases have a single property, name, which can be accessed in the usual way with the -> symbol.

src/Part4/Chapter12/Enums/BasicEnum.php

Repo: https://git.io/JRw5u

```php
<?php

declare(strict_types=1);

namespace Book\Part4\Chapter12\Enums;

enum BasicEnum implements ProvidesRandomCaseInterface
{
    /** Enums define one or more cases that they can possibly
exist as */
    case Foo;
    case Bar;

    /** Enums can use traits as long as they don't have
properties */
    use RandomCaseTrait;
}
```

For reference, here is the trait that is being used:

src/Part4/Chapter12/Enums/RandomCaseTrait.php

Repo: https://git.io/JRw5z

```php
<?php

declare(strict_types=1);
```

```php
namespace Book\Part4\Chapter12\Enums;

trait RandomCaseTrait
{
    public function getRandomCaseName(): string
    {
        $cases     = self::cases();
        $randomKey = \array_rand($cases);

        return $cases[$randomKey]->name;
    }
}
```

Notice the use of the `cases` method that is implemented by all enums, which gives you a simple array of all the cases.

Up next is a **backed enum**. Note that the backed type must be defined with the following style:

```php
enum BackedEnum: string
```

This is to define that this `enum` has string values backing the cases.

Note that backed enum cases have not only the `name` property but also a `value` property as well:

src/Part4/Chapter12/Enums/BackedEnum.php

Repo: `https://git.io/JRw5g`

```php
<?php

declare(strict_types=1);

namespace Book\Part4\Chapter12\Enums;

/**
```

```php
 * Notice the backed enum has to declare its backing type
 */
enum BackedEnum: string implements ProvidesRandomCaseInterface
{
    /** Backed enum cases define the name and the value */
    case Baz = 'Baz';
    case Taz = 'Taz';

    /** Enums can also define constants and methods, like a
class */
    public const DEFAULT = self::Taz;

    /** Enums can use traits */
    use RandomCaseTrait;

    /** And define methods */
    public function getRandomCaseAsArray(): array
    {
        $caseName = $this->getRandomCaseName();
        $case     = self::from($caseName);

        return [$case->name, $case->value];
    }
}
```

Creating enum instances

For a basic enum, you must create it explicitly in code by assigning the case to a variable. For backed enums, you can create an instance using scalar data, and you have two methods to assist with this:

- From – to be used with trusted data that is guaranteed to correspond to one of the expected cases.

- tryFrom – to be used with untrusted data. It will return a null if the scalar value doesn't match.

Have a look at this code snippet, which illustrates these three creation styles:

src/Part4/Chapter12/enums.php

Repo: `https://git.io/JRw52`

```php
<?php

declare(strict_types=1);

namespace Book\Part4\Chapter12;

require __DIR__ . '/autoload.php';

use Book\Part4\Chapter12\Enums\BackedEnum;
use Book\Part4\Chapter12\Enums\BasicEnum;

/** Create explicitly */
$basic  = BasicEnum::Bar;
$backed = BackedEnum::Taz;
echo "\nbasic is $basic->name and backed is $backed->name";

/** Create from a scalar value (eg a DB record) - only with
backed enums */
$fromDb = BackedEnum::from('Baz');
echo "\nfrom DB is $fromDb->value";

/** Create from untrusted data, eg user input - only with
backed enums */
// let's just imagine this is a user submitted form:
$_POST['BackedEnum'] = 'Baaaz';
// there's clearly a typo and it doesn't match, so it will use
the default instead
$fromPost = BackedEnum::tryFrom($_POST['BackedEnum']) ??
BackedEnum::DEFAULT;
echo "\nfrom POST is $fromPost->value";
```

```
/** Call Methods */
echo "\nA random BasicEnum case is {$basic-
>getRandomCaseName()}";
echo "\nA random BackedEnum case is {$backed-
>getRandomCaseName()} and a random array is: " .
     print_r($backed->getRandomCaseAsArray(), true);
```

Output:

```
joseph@php-book: ~

joseph@php-book:~$ php enums.php

basic is Bar and backed is Taz
from DB is Baz
from POST is Taz
A random BasicEnum case is Foo
A random BackedEnum case is Baz and a random array is: Array
(
    [0] => Taz
    [1] => Taz
)
```

Not just classes with cases

Enums might look a lot like classes – and it's true, they are similar in appearance. They can not only contain the case that makes them special, but they can also define constants and methods, implement interfaces, and even use traits (as long as those traits don't define properties).

However, there are some things that enums cannot do, and these make them distinct from classes:

- **No inheritance**

    Enums cannot be part of any inheritance chain. You can think of them as being automatically declared final. This means that there is no difference between private and protected access modifiers for enum constants and methods.

- **No properties**

    Enums cannot have state and so cannot contain any properties. This makes them a very pure datatype, which is definitely a *good thing*.

- **No construct/destruct**

  You don't create an instance of an enum like you do a class. This is because enums have no state – they simply represent a single `case` from the possible cases that are defined.

Hopefully, you now have a good grasp of how enums work and can probably already imagine some ways that you might refactor existing code to use enums instead. Let's move on to looking at another major new feature in PHP – **readonly properties**.

Readonly properties

Readonly properties are an awesome new feature for modern PHP code that is embracing patterns such as immutable data objects. Immutable objects are inherently extremely safe and predictable as they simply cannot change. This makes for reliable and easy-to-comprehend code.

The feature is deceptively simple. There is a new `readonly` keyword that you can prefix a class property with (including in constructor promotion) and that denotes that property as, well, read-only.

What this really means is that it is write-once, and read-only from that point on. The value can be set in the constructor or anywhere else within the class methods. It cannot be set from outside the class. Once that value has been set, it's locked.

The classic way to create an immutable DTO would be something like this:

src/Part4/Chapter12/ReadOnly/ClassicImmutable.php

Repo: `https://git.io/JRw5a`

```php
<?php

declare(strict_types=1);

namespace Book\Part4\Chapter12\ReadOnly;

class ClassicImmutable
{
    public function __construct(private int $num, private int
$numWithDefault = 2)
    {
```

```php
    }

    public function getNum(): int
    {
        return $this->num;
    }

    public function getNumWithDefault(): int
    {
        return $this->numWithDefault;
    }


}
```

As you can see, properties are defined with private visibility, and then we have explicit getter methods for each property. This means that the values are only readable.

With `readonly` properties, this becomes the following:

src/Part4/Chapter12/ReadOnly/ReadOnlyDTO.php

Repo: `https://git.io/JRw5V`

```php
<?php

declare(strict_types=1);

namespace Book\Part4\Chapter12\ReadOnly;

class ReadOnlyDTO
{
    public function __construct(public readonly int $num,
    public readonly int $numWithDefault=2)
    {


    }
}
```

You can see how these are equivalent in the following code:

src/Part4/Chapter12/read-only.php

Repo: `https://git.io/JRw5w`

```php
<?php

declare(strict_types=1);

namespace Book\Part4\Chapter12;

use Book\Part4\Chapter12\ReadOnly\ClassicImmutable;
use Book\Part4\Chapter12\ReadOnly\ReadOnlyDTO;

require __DIR__ . '/autoload.php';

$immutable = new ClassicImmutable(1);

echo "\nJust created, the Immutable required param num
is {$immutable->getNum()} and the param with default is
{$immutable->getNumWithDefault()}";

$readonly = new ReadOnlyDTO(1);

echo "\nJust created, the Readonly required param num is
{$readonly->num} and the param with default is {$readonly-
>numWithDefault}";
```

Output:

```
joseph@php-book: ~

joseph@php-book:~$ php read-only.php
Just created, the Immutable required param num is 1 and the param with
default is 2
Just created, the Readonly required param num is 1 and the param with
default is 2
```

Great, fewer characters and boilerplate to type – always nice – but is it particularly exciting? you might ask. It's a good question, so let's explore how it differs.

Have a look at this class:

src/Part4/Chapter12/ReadOnly/InitOnce.php

Repo: https://git.io/JRw5o

```php
<?php

declare(strict_types=1);

namespace Book\Part4\Chapter12\ReadOnly;

class InitOnce
{
    public readonly int $foo;

    /**
     * It is only possible to call this method once. Any
subsequent call will fail with a fatal error
     */
    public function setFoo(int $bar): void
    {
        $this->foo = $bar;
    }
}
```

Notice that we have a public set method. We are not setting the value in __construct, in fact, we are leaving it hanging out there in an uninitialized state until something external calls the setter. However, once that setter is called, it cannot be called again, otherwise, you'll end up triggering a fatal error:

src/Part4/Chapter12/readonly-init-once.php

Repo: https://git.io/JRw5K

```php
<?php
```

```php
declare(strict_types=1);

namespace Book\Part4\Chapter12;

use Book\Part4\Chapter12\ReadOnly\InitOnce;

require __DIR__ . '/autoload.php';

$initOnce = new InitOnce();

$initOnce->setFoo(1);
echo "\nfoo is now {$initOnce->foo}";

echo "\nthe next call will fail..\n\n";
$initOnce->setFoo(2);
```

Output:

```
joseph@php-book:~

joseph@php-book:~$ php readonly-init-once.php

foo is now 1
the next call will fail..

PHP Fatal error:  Uncaught Error: Cannot modify readonly property
Book\Part4\Chapter12\ReadOnly\InitOnce::$foo in
/home/book_ops/php-book-code/src/Part4/Chapter12/ReadOnly/InitOnce.php:16
Stack trace:
#0
/home/book_ops/php-book-code/src/Part4/Chapter12/readonly-init-once.php(17):
Book\Part4\Chapter12\ReadOnly\InitOnce->setFoo()
#1 {main}
  thrown in
/home/book_ops/php-book-code/src/Part4/Chapter12/ReadOnly/InitOnce.php
on line 16
```

Now you might be saying to yourself, *I can still do that without this readonly stuff, it just requires a bit more boilerplate.* You probably intend to do something like this:

src/Part4/Chapter12/ReadOnly/ClassicImmutableInitOnce.php

Repo: `https://git.io/JRw56`

```php
<?php

declare(strict_types=1);

namespace Book\Part4\Chapter12\ReadOnly;

class ClassicImmutableInitOnce
{
    private int $foo;

    public function setFoo(int $bar): void
    {
        if (isset($this->foo)) {
            throw new \RuntimeException('You can not set foo
more than once');
        }
        $this->foo = $bar;
    }
}
```

The preceding code will work, but once you need to accept nulls then you are getting into a tricky situation, for example:

src/Part4/Chapter12/ReadOnly/ClassicImmutableInitOnceNullable.php

Repo: `https://git.io/JRw5i`

```php
<?php

declare(strict_types=1);

namespace Book\Part4\Chapter12\ReadOnly;

class ClassicImmutableInitOnceNullable
{
```

```php
    private ?int $foo;

    public function getFoo(): ?int
    {
        return $this->foo;
    }

    public function setFoo(?int $bar): void
    {
        if (isset($this->foo)) {
            throw new \RuntimeException('You can not set foo
more than once');
        }
        $this->foo = $bar;
    }
}
```

As you can see by running the following code, when null is a valid value, then `isset` checks will not help you in preventing multiple writes if the first write was a null.

src/Part4/Chapter12/classic-readonly-init-once.php

Repo: `https://git.io/JRw5P`

```php
<?php

declare(strict_types=1);

namespace Book\Part4\Chapter12;

use Book\Part4\Chapter12\ReadOnly\
ClassicImmutableInitOnceNullable;

require __DIR__ . '/autoload.php';

$dto = new ClassicImmutableInitOnceNullable();
$dto->setFoo(null);
```

```php
echo "\n Foo is " . var_export($dto->getFoo(), true);
$dto->setFoo(1);
echo "\n Foo is " . var_export($dto->getFoo(), true);
```

Output:

```
joseph@php-book: ~

joseph@php-book:~$ php classic-readonly-init-once.php

Foo is NULL
 Foo is 1
```

Now, of course, the real clever clogs among you will probably have figured out another solution to handle the null situation – gold star! For those of you that haven't got a solution up your sleeve, consider it a side quest.

The point is, though, that we're needing to add more and more boilerplate code to make a proper readonly property, and I'll bet for every way that you can think of to enforce a property as read-only, I can find a way around it, probably using **Reflection**.

Can we use Reflection to beat readonly*?*

src/Part4/Chapter12/readonly-reflection.php

Repo: https://git.io/JRw5X

```php
<?php

declare(strict_types=1);

namespace Book\Part4\Chapter12;

use Book\Part4\Chapter12\ReadOnly\ReadOnlyDTO;

require __DIR__ . '/autoload.php';

$readonly = new ReadOnlyDTO(1);
```

```
echo "\nJust created, the Readonly required param num is
{$readonly->num} and the param with default is {$readonly-
>numWithDefault}";
```

```
echo "\nSo what happens if we get clever and try to defeat the
readonly restriction..?\n\n";
$reflection = new \ReflectionClass($readonly);
$property   = $reflection->getProperty('num');
$property->setValue($readonly, 10);
```

Output:

```
joseph@php-book: ~

joseph@php-book:~$ php readonly-reflection.php

Just created, the Readonly required param num is 1 and the param with
default is 2
So what happens if we get clever and try to defeat the readonly
restriction..?

PHP Fatal error:  Uncaught Error: Cannot modify readonly property
Book\Part4\Chapter12\ReadOnly\ReadOnlyDTO::$num in
/home/book_ops/php-book-code/src/Part4/Chapter12/readonly-reflection.php:18
Stack trace:
#0
/home/book_ops/php-book-code/src/Part4/Chapter12/readonly-reflection.php(18):
ReflectionProperty->setValue()
#1 {main}
  thrown in
/home/book_ops/php-book-code/src/Part4/Chapter12/readonly-reflection.php
on line 18
```

That's a no then.

So, as you can see, `readonly` properties are a simple, powerful addition to the language that allows you to create robust, immutable DTO objects with the absolute minimum amount of code.

There are a couple of gotchas that you are likely to hit though, so let's explore those now.

Readonly gotchas

There are a couple of gotchas. The first is that the readonly-ness does not propagate into properties that are objects. The second is that there are issues with the classic use of `clone`. Let's explore these now.

Mutable readonly properties

Yes, it sounds like an oxymoron, but it can happen… to you! So, take care out there kids…

Here is a simple (but, I suspect, common) gotcha – using the standard mutable `DateTime` object:

src/Part4/Chapter12/ReadOnly/ReadonlyMutableProperty.php

Repo: `https://git.io/JRw51`

```php
<?php

declare(strict_types=1);

namespace Book\Part4\Chapter12\ReadOnly;

class ReadonlyMutableProperty
{
    public function __construct(public readonly \DateTime $dateTime)
    {
    }

}
```

When we play with this object, we can see that while the property is readonly, we can mutate the *date* freely:

src/Part4/Chapter12/readonly-mutable-property.php

Repo: `https://git.io/JRw5M`

```php
<?php

declare(strict_types=1);
```

```
namespace Book\Part4\Chapter12;

use Book\Part4\Chapter12\ReadOnly\ReadonlyMutableProperty;

require __DIR__ . '/autoload.php';

$dto = new ReadonlyMutableProperty(\
DateTime::createFromFormat(format: 'Y/m/d', datetime:
'2021/08/02'));
echo "\nDate is currently: {$dto->dateTime->format('Y/m/d')}";

$dto->dateTime->setDate(2022, 1, 1);
echo "\nDate is now: {$dto->dateTime->format('Y/m/d')}";
```

Output:

```
joseph@php-book: ~

joseph@php-book:~$ php readonly-mutable-property.php

Date is currently: 2021/08/02
Date is now: 2022/01/01
```

What is actually happening is that the readonly property is enforcing that we can only have one object instance, and we can't replace it with another object instance. There is nothing in there that also says that the object itself cannot change state.

The `DateTime` one is a classic example of accidental mutability, and fortunately it's very easy to fix by simply using `DateTimeImmutable` instead. However, when you are working with other objects, you are going to need to take care to ensure that objects that are intended to be readonly have readonly properties themselves and are generally immutable.

To defend against this, consider only using immutable objects as readonly properties. This neatly brings us into our next point, which relates to a gotcha when working with immutable objects that implement `createWith` type methods, and issues with `clone`.

Clone

A common pattern when working with immutable objects is to provide an easy way to create a new instance with updated properties.

Take a look at this contrived class:

src/Part4/Chapter12/ReadOnly/ReadonlyCreateWithClone.php

Repo: `https://git.io/JRw5D`

```php
<?php

declare(strict_types=1);

namespace Book\Part4\Chapter12\ReadOnly;

class ReadonlyCreateWithClone
{
    private readonly mixed $expensiveThing;

    public function __construct(public readonly int $foo){
        // do something to generate the expensive thing
        $this->expensiveThing='ooh that was hard work';
    }

    public function with(int $foo):self{
        // to avoid having to recreate the expensive thing and
to generally make this easy, a common pattern is to use clone
        $clone = clone $this;
        $clone->foo = $foo;

        return $clone;
    }
}
```

Note that the clone approach causes a fatal error. The issue is that, simply enough, the clone copies the already initialized value across and so it continues to be read-only:

src/Part4/Chapter12/readonly-create-with-clone.php

Repo: `https://git.io/JRw5y`

```php
<?php
```

```php
declare(strict_types=1);

namespace Book\Part4\Chapter12;

use Book\Part4\Chapter12\ReadOnly\ReadonlyCreateWithClone;

require __DIR__ . '/autoload.php';

$dto = new ReadonlyCreateWithClone(1);
$new = $dto->with(2);
```

Output:

```
joseph@php-book: ~

joseph@php-book:~$ php readonly-create-with-clone.php

PHP Fatal error:  Uncaught Error: Cannot modify readonly property
Book\Part4\Chapter12\ReadOnly\ReadonlyCreateWithClone::$foo in
/home/book_ops/php-book-
code/src/Part4/Chapter12/ReadOnly/ReadonlyCreateWithClone.php:19
Stack trace:
#0
/home/book_ops/php-book-code/src/Part4/Chapter12/readonly-create-with-clone.php(12):
Book\Part4\Chapter12\ReadOnly\ReadonlyCreateWithClone->with()
#1 {main}
  thrown in
/home/book_ops/php-book-code/src/Part4/Chapter12/ReadOnly/ReadonlyCreateWithClone.php
on line 19
```

Instead, you need to craft a more manual approach to creating new instances with updated values. The approach in the following code allows you to create a new instance, overriding values as required. Combined with named parameters, it becomes a nicely ergonomic approach:

src/Part4/Chapter12/ReadOnly/ReadonlyCreateManually.php

Repo: https://git.io/JRw5S

```php
<?php

declare(strict_types=1);
```

```php
namespace Book\Part4\Chapter12\ReadOnly;

class ReadonlyCreateManually
{
    private readonly mixed $expensiveThing;

    public function __construct(
        public readonly int $foo,
        public readonly string $bar,
        public readonly \stdClass $object,
        mixed $expensiveThing = null
    )
    {
        $this->expensiveThing = $expensiveThing ?? $this->createExpensiveThing();
    }

    private function createExpensiveThing(): mixed
    {
        // imagine something that takes a long time or lots of resources to create
        return 'that was hard work - created at ' . time();
    }

    /**
     * This is our immutable new instance creation method.
     *
     * All constructor params are replicated but are all optional with null default.
     *
     * If any parameter is desired to be overridden it can be passed in,
     * otherwise the current value will be assigned to the new instance.
     *
     * Note that object instances should be cloned for better immutability
```

```
     *
     * Combined with named parameters, this approach becomes a
very ergonomic way
     * to create new instances with updated values
     */
    public function with(int $foo=null, string $bar=null, \
stdClass $object=null): self
    {
        return new self(
            foo: $foo ?? $this->foo,
            bar: $bar ?? $this->bar,
            object: clone ($object ?? $this->object),
            expensiveThing: $this->expensiveThing
        );
    }
}
```

Here you can see this in action, and hopefully you agree that the combination of these PHP 8 and 8.1 features provides a really nice developer experience:

src/Part4/Chapter12/readonly-create-manually.php

Repo: `https://git.io/JRw59`

```php
<?php

declare(strict_types=1);

namespace Book\Part4\Chapter12;

use Book\Part4\Chapter12\ReadOnly\ReadonlyCreateManually;

require __DIR__ . '/autoload.php';

$object      = new \stdClass();
$object->num = 100;
$dto         = new ReadonlyCreateManually(foo: 1, bar: 'lorem
ipsum', object: $object);
```

```
echo "\nOriginal DTO: " . var_export($dto, true);


$newObject              = new \stdClass();
$newObject->string = 'abc123';


$new = $dto->with(bar: 'updated string', object: $newObject);
echo "\nNew DTO created with overridden properties: " . var_
export($new, true);
```

As you can see, the new instance was created and only select parameters were overridden, with the previous values being copied across where they were not set. Do note, this approach won't work where the properties themselves are nullable, as you will not be able to override a set value with a null because the coalesce (??) will always fail. I can't think of a neat solution for that off the top of my head, and so I leave it to you to try as an exercise – have fun!

Let's now look at our next sweet addition to the language – **intersection types**.

Intersection types

PHP 8 brought us **union types**, which is a feature where a parameter or return type can be one of a list of types, separated by the pipe (|) symbol. This is a hugely useful addition to the language and allows us to loosen the type strictness while being able to avoid using mixed as the type, or omit type hinting altogether. You can read all about union types in the RFC that was accepted into PHP 8:

PHP: rfc:union_types_v2

```
https://wiki.php.net/rfc/union_types_v2
```

There is another scenario where we might want to list multiple types, and rather than allowing things to be looser, it is a scenario where we want things to be stricter.

An intersection type is one where the parameter, variable, or return must be all of the listed types. This is opposed to union types, where it can be any of the listed types. The syntax is very similar to a union type, however, the joining character is & instead of |. This corresponds neatly with the standard logical meaning of these characters as representing AND and OR respectively.

You can read the intersection types RFC here:

PHP: rfc:pure-intersection-types

```
https://wiki.php.net/rfc/pure-intersection-types
```

Imagine a situation where you have a comprehensive set of interfaces that each define a particular behavior and there is the expectation that a single class will implement multiple interfaces. PHP 8.1 allows us to handle this scenario much more elegantly and flexibly by using intersection types.

To illustrate this, look at the following scenario where we have a method that requires that our parameter implements two methods that are defined in two separate interfaces:

First, a `Hello` interface that defines a `hello` method:

src/Part4/Chapter12/IntersectionType/HelloInterface.php

Repo: `https://git.io/J0kW2`

```php
<?php

declare(strict_types=1);

namespace Book\Part4\Chapter12\IntersectionType;

interface HelloInterface
{
    public function hello(): string;
}
```

And secondly, a `World` interface that defines a `world` method.

src/Part4/Chapter12/IntersectionType/WorldInterface.php

Repo: `https://git.io/J0kWa`

```php
<?php

declare(strict_types=1);

namespace Book\Part4\Chapter12\IntersectionType;

interface WorldInterface
```

```php
{
    public function world(): string;
}
```

Now, clearly this is totally contrived, but I hope that you can imagine a scenario where there are methods defined in two separate interfaces, and you need both of them.

Before PHP 8.1, if we wanted to keep things flexible and only type hint for an interface, we would have to create a new compound interface that simply extended the two required interfaces:

src/Part4/Chapter12/IntersectionType/HelloWorldInterface.php

Repo: `https://git.io/J0kWV`

```php
<?php

declare(strict_types=1);

namespace Book\Part4\Chapter12\IntersectionType;

/**
 * This interface has no value other than combining the two
interfaces.
 * This adds bloat and obfuscation to our code.
 */
interface HelloWorldInterface extends HelloInterface,
WorldInterface
{

}
```

And then for any class that we need to be able to pass into our method, we need to make sure that this compound interface is implemented:

src/Part4/Chapter12/IntersectionType/IntersectionPhp80.php

Repo: `https://git.io/J0kWw`

```php
<?php
```

```php
declare(strict_types=1);

namespace Book\Part4\Chapter12\IntersectionType;

class IntersectionPhp80 implements HelloWorldInterface
{

    public function hello(): string
    {
        return 'hello';
    }

    public function world(): string
    {
        return 'world';
    }
}
```

Our method or function would then look like this:

src/Part4/Chapter12/intersection-type-php80.php

Repo: `https://git.io/J0kWr`

```php
<?php

declare(strict_types=1);

namespace Book\Part4\Chapter12;

use Book\Part4\Chapter12\IntersectionType\HelloWorldInterface;
use Book\Part4\Chapter12\IntersectionType\IntersectionPhp80;

require __DIR__ . '/autoload.php';
```

```php
/**
 * Before intersection types, any scenario where we need
multiple interfaces, we have to create a new special interface
 * that extends the interfaces we require, and then of course
we need to make sure whatever class we are using
 * implements our special interface. This can all lead to a lot
of code bloat
 */
function acceptsHelloWorld(HelloWorldInterface $helloWorld):
void
{
    echo $helloWorld->hello() . ' ' . $helloWorld->world();
}

acceptsHelloWorld(new IntersectionPhp80());
```

Output:

```
joseph@php-book: ~
joseph@php-book:~$ php intersection-type-php80.php
hello world
```

In PHP 8.1, we can remove the requirement for this extra compound interface and keep things much simpler by listing the real interfaces that we implement:

src/Part4/Chapter12/IntersectionType/IntersectionPhp81.php

Repo: https://git.io/J0kWo

```php
<?php

declare(strict_types=1);

namespace Book\Part4\Chapter12\IntersectionType;
```

```php
class IntersectionPhp81 implements HelloInterface,
WorldInterface
{

    public function hello(): string
    {
        return 'hello';
    }

    public function world(): string
    {
        return 'world';
    }
}
```

Correspondingly, our method or function can simply list the required interfaces:

src/Part4/Chapter12/intersection-type-php81.php

Repo: https://git.io/J0kWK

```php
<?php

declare(strict_types=1);

namespace Book\Part4\Chapter12;

use Book\Part4\Chapter12\IntersectionType\HelloInterface;
use Book\Part4\Chapter12\IntersectionType\WorldInterface;
use Book\Part4\Chapter12\IntersectionType\IntersectionPhp81;

require __DIR__ . '/autoload.php';

/**
 * Instead, with an Intersection Type, we can simply list the
 * interfaces required to be implemented for the given
```

```
 * method/function to work, and we do not need to enforce
anything further.
 */
function acceptsHelloWorld(HelloInterface&WorldInterface
$helloWorld): void
{
    echo $helloWorld->hello() . ' ' . $helloWorld->world();
}


acceptsHelloWorld(new IntersectionPhp81());
```

Output:

```
joseph@php-book: ~
joseph@php-book:~$ php intersection-type-php80.php
hello world
```

So, as you can see, intersection types allow us to create methods and properties that can be pseudotyped to just the combination of required interfaces. This allows us to be explicit in our type requirements and avoid excessive bloat in creating compound interfaces. It's a very welcome addition that can lead to much cleaner, more flexible, and easier-to-test code.

Our next feature is a new return type – the **never return type**.

Never return type

Some functions or methods will never return anything because they do things that will halt execution. Examples of this type of function or method could be methods or functions that throw an `exception`, or maybe they literally call `die` or `exit` to fully halt all execution.

It is worth having a read through the RFC, which is based on the original **noreturn type** nomenclature:

PHP: rfc:noreturn_type

```
https://wiki.php.net/rfc/noreturn_type
```

While these kinds of methods are probably quite rare, it is nice to know that we can now properly assign a return type and that can also be enforced by interfaces and inheritance rules to ensure a consistent API and behavior.

Some scenarios where you might use a never return type are as follows:

- A `throwException` method that simply throws an exception and so can never return.

- An `httpRedirect` method that issues a 301 HTTP header and then ends execution with exit.

- A `loop` method that will loop continuously until execution stops for some reason, for example, a server daemon.

Inheritance and covariance

The never type is what's called a **bottom type**. This means that there is no type that is able to be under the `never` type. This is important when we remember our co/contravariance rules.

To recap *Chapter 6, Parameter, Property, and Return Types* quickly:

When extending classes or implementing interfaces, we are only allowed to make parameters less specific or make return types more specific.

So, the "bottom" type in this sense means that it is at maximum specificity. You cannot have a type more specific than `never`, and this means that any interface or class method with `never` as a `return` type cannot be overridden in a child class with any other `return` type.

Really no return, ever

One thing to bear in mind is that `never` really means *never*. Your method with a `never` `return` type can't have any kind of `return` statement. Having a `return` will throw a **TypeError**, and if uncaught, will become a fatal error.

This means that you can't have conditional logic that stops execution only sometimes. Nor can you do anything like **yield**. This strictness is what makes the type so useful – it provides certainty for developers, IDEs, and static analysis tools that execution will stop when this method is called.

Return type only

Similar to **void**, the never type can only be used as a standalone return type. It cannot be a parameter type, nor can it be used in any union or intersection type.

So that concludes our look at the never return type. The next and final feature we're going to look at is **final constants**. Do you see what I did there?

Final constants

I am a huge fan of using constants in PHP as I believe they are an excellent solution to avoid *"magic strings"* and *"magic numbers"* creeping into your code base and making them brittle, hard to refactor, and making typo related bugs an infuriatingly likely issue.

Constants provide a nice solution in that they are solid and predictable, and they cannot be accidentally or deliberately updated with new values – they are hardcoded.

One feature of PHP constants is that they can be overridden in child classes. This can be quite useful where you desire it, but it would also be quite common to desire that your constants are, well... constant.

For class properties and methods, we have had the ability to mark them as `final` for quite some time. This means that it cannot be overridden in a child class and is a very useful way to ensure things remain robust and predictable.

Before PHP 8, the one place where constants could not be overridden was where the constant was defined in an interface. I'll admit I was not aware of this one, and perhaps you weren't either. If you were, please forget it because it is no longer the case in 8.1!

Instead, in PHP 8.1, constants can be overridden at every level unless they are marked as `final`. That's it – simple.

Have a look at the following code to see how this all works. First, here's an interface that defines some constants:

src/Part4/Chapter12/FinalConst/ConstInterface.php

Repo: `https://git.io/J0kW6`

```php
<?php

declare(strict_types=1);
```

```php
namespace Book\Part4\Chapter12\FinalConst;

interface ConstInterface
{
    const FOO   = 'bar';
    const THING = 'interface thing';
}
```

Now, we add a parent class that is implementing the interface, overriding the constants, and making one of them final. In the parent class, we are illustrating the difference between accessing constants using `self` and `static`:

src/Part4/Chapter12/FinalConst/ParentClass.php

Repo: `https://git.io/J0kWi`

```php
<?php

declare(strict_types=1);

namespace Book\Part4\Chapter12\FinalConst;

class ParentClass implements ConstInterface
{
    /**
     * this would not be allowed in less than PHP 8.1 as
interface constants were basically final,
     * however in 8.1 it is now allowed
     */
    public const THING = 'parent thing';
    /**
     * We're overriding the interface const and then making it
final
     */
    final public const FOO = 'baz';

    /**
```

```
     * This will always return the value of ParentClass::FOO as
the method is defined in ParentClass and it is
     * accessing the const using `self`
     */
    public static function getSelfThing(): string
    {
        return self::THING;
    }


    /**
     * This will return the value of FOO in the context of
whichever class it was called from, thanks to late static
     * binding
     */
    public static function getStaticThing(): string
    {
        return static::THING;
    }

}
```

We then have a child class that extends the parent and simply overrides one of the constants:

src/Part4/Chapter12/FinalConst/ChildClass.php

Repo: https://git.io/J0kWP

```php
<?php

declare(strict_types=1);

namespace Book\Part4\Chapter12\FinalConst;

class ChildClass extends ParentClass
{
    public const THING = 'child thing';
}
```

Then, let's look at the following code, which runs through how these are working, and finally illustrates how trying to override a final constant is a fatal error:

src/Part4/Chapter12/final-const.php

Repo: `https://git.io/J0kWX`

```php
<?php

declare(strict_types=1);

namespace Book\Part4\Chapter12;

use Book\Part4\Chapter12\FinalConst\ChildClass;
use Book\Part4\Chapter12\FinalConst\ConstInterface;
use Book\Part4\Chapter12\FinalConst\ParentClass;

require __DIR__ . '/autoload.php';

/**
 * Constants are accessible down the inheritance chain like any
other class property. The visibility is controlled with
 * standard private/protected/public controls. We can make it
final at any level in the chain
 */
printf('
interfaceFoo = %s
parentFoo    = %s
childFoo     = %s

',
                ConstInterface::FOO,
                ParentClass::FOO,
                ChildClass::FOO);
/**
```

```
 * Constants can be overridden at every step of the inheritance
chain, unless marked as final
 */
printf('
interfaceThing = %s
parentThing    = %s
childThing     = %s


',
            ConstInterface::THING,
            ParentClass::THING,
            ChildClass::THING);

/**
 * We can see the difference between the self and static
versions of these with this code:
 */
printf('
ChildClass::getSelfFoo = %s
ChildClass::getStaticFoo = %s


',
            ChildClass::getSelfThing(),
            ChildClass::getStaticThing()
);

/**
 * Trying to override a final const is a fatal error
 */
class OhNoYouDont extends ParentClass
{
    public const FOO = 'this wont work';
}
```

Output:

```
joseph@php-book: ~

joseph@php-book:~$ php final-const.php

interfaceFoo = bar
parentFoo    = baz
childFoo     = baz


interfaceThing = interface thing
parentThing    = parent thing
childThing     = child thing


ChildClass::getSelfFoo = parent thing
ChildClass::getStaticFoo = child thing

PHP Fatal error:  Book\Part4\Chapter12\OhNoYouDont::FOO cannot
override final constant
Book\Part4\Chapter12\FinalConst\ParentClass::FOO in
/home/book_ops/php-book-code/src/Part4/Chapter12/final-const.php on
line 54
```

So, as you can see in PHP 8.1, constants become very similar to class properties in that they can be overridden at every level unless they are marked as final. You should definitely consider marking your constants `final` by default, and only exceptionally allow them to be overridden. This will increase the robustness and predictability of your code.

Summary – end of the book

It's come to the end of the book. I really hope you have enjoyed reading this book and have learned at least a couple of things. I've certainly enjoyed writing it!

It's been a long journey, and we've covered a huge amount of content. However, I'll do my best to summarize the whole book in only a few paragraphs.

In *Part 1*, we looked at **object-oriented PHP**. *Chapter 1, Object-Oriented PHP* was a quick introduction to object-oriented PHP and a lifeline for anyone who doesn't already know it – hopefully if you didn't, then you took a bit of time to learn it before tackling the rest of the book. *Chapter 2, Inheritance and Composition, Encapsulation and Visibility, Interfaces and Concretions,* looked at inheritance in particular and contrasted this with the more modern *"composition"* style, which results in neater, easier-to-test code. *Chapter 3, Advanced OOP Features,* involved checking out some of the more advanced **object-oriented programming** (**OOP**) features in PHP, including fun stuff such as iterators and metaprogramming.

In *Part 2*, we worked on types, with *Chapter 4, Scalar, Arrays, and Special Types,* being an introduction to the concept of types and a closer look at scalar, arrays/iterables, the *"nothing"* types null/void/uninitialized, and finally, resources. In *Chapter 5, Object Types, Interfaces, and Unions,* we jumped right back into OOP with a look at object types and how these work with inheritance. We looked at a comparison of objects and how this works when checking for equality or identity. Then we looked at references, and finally at different ways of creating objects. *Chapter 6, Parameter, Property, and Return Types,* was where we really learned the utility of types, in their use as parameter and return types. The big thing to learn in this chapter was the contravariance and covariance rules – repeated here one last time… when extending classes or implementing interfaces, we can only:

- Make parameters less specific.
- Make return types more specific.

Part 3 saw us move away from learning about the language and into the fun stuff – actually writing code. We tried to lay some good foundations in *Chapter 7, Design Patterns and Clean Code,* by compressing around two books' worth of **design patterns** and **clean code** concepts into a single chapter. My brain was pretty fried by the end of that one. In *Chapter 8, Model, View, Controller (MVC) Example,* we had a look at the **Model, View, Controller** (**MVC**) pattern, and tried to learn it by building a very simple MVC app. We applied the same technique in an effort to explain and demonstrate how dependency injection works. We did this by building a minimalist DI container in *Chapter 9, Dependency Injection Example.* There was a lot of code to read in this part of the book, and it was definitely a point where visiting the GitHub repo would be an excellent idea.

Part 4 saw us spend a couple of chapters learning about **Composer** – probably the single biggest thing to happen to PHP. The whole ecosystem (apart from **WordPress**) has embraced Composer, and it would be fair to say that it has had a fundamental impact on the way PHP projects are built. For this reason, it was worth spending two whole chapters on it. *Chapter 10, Composer For Dependencies,* was more focused on you using Composer to bring in dependencies, and *Chapter 11, Creating Your Own Composer Package,* was about you packaging up your own code so that it could be used in other projects.

This final chapter was the most challenging to write, as I had to leave the comfortable reassurance of my IDE telling me I'm not being stupid, and I had to really double-check my code was accurate. I hope I didn't mess that up! We looked at PHP 8.1, and as I type this, PHP 8.1 is in beta and due to be released later this year. There are some excellent new features, though unfortunately I was not able to look at all of them. Instead, I focused on the ones that I thought were most relevant to you, and hope that I illustrated how they are going to impact the code you read and write on a daily basis.

And that's it – I really hope you enjoyed reading the book! I also hope that, at some future date, I can provide you with some more written education and entertainment about this, or maybe another topic.

Cheers,

Joseph :)

`Packt.com`

Subscribe to our online digital library for full access to over 7,000 books and videos, as well as industry leading tools to help you plan your personal development and advance your career. For more information, please visit our website.

Why subscribe?

- Spend less time learning and more time coding with practical eBooks and Videos from over 4,000 industry professionals

- Improve your learning with Skill Plans built especially for you

- Get a free eBook or video every month

- Fully searchable for easy access to vital information

- Copy and paste, print, and bookmark content

Did you know that Packt offers eBook versions of every book published, with PDF and ePub files available? You can upgrade to the eBook version at `packt.com` and as a print book customer, you are entitled to a discount on the eBook copy. Get in touch with us at `customercare@packtpub.com` for more details.

At `www.packt.com`, you can also read a collection of free technical articles, sign up for a range of free newsletters, and receive exclusive discounts and offers on Packt books and eBooks.

Other Books You May Enjoy

If you enjoyed this book, you may be interested in these other books by Packt:

PHP 8 Programming Tips, Tricks and Best Practices

Doug Bierer

ISBN: 978-1-80107-187-1

- Gain a comprehensive understanding of the new PHP 8 object-oriented features
- Discover new PHP 8 procedural programming enhancements
- Understand improvements in error handling in PHP 8
- Identify potential backward compatibility issues
- Avoid traps due to changes in PHP extensions
- Find out which features have been deprecated and/or removed in PHP 8
- Become well-versed with programming best practices enforced by PHP 8

Drupal 9 Module Development - Third Edition

Daniel Sipos

ISBN: 978-1-80020-462-1

- Develop custom Drupal 9 modules for your applications
- Master different Drupal 9 subsystems and APIs
- Model, store, manipulate, and process data for effective data management
- Display data and content in a clean and secure way using the theme system
- Test your business logic to prevent regression
- Stay ahead of the curve and write PHP code by implementing best practices

Packt is searching for authors like you

If you're interested in becoming an author for Packt, please visit `authors.packtpub.com` and apply today. We have worked with thousands of developers and tech professionals, just like you, to help them share their insight with the global tech community. You can make a general application, apply for a specific hot topic that we are recruiting an author for, or submit your own idea.

Share Your Thoughts

Dear Reader,

I really hope you enjoyed reading *The Art of Modern PHP 8*, I certainly had fun writing it!

I wondered if you could spare a little time to leave a review on Amazon sharing your thoughts on *The Art of Modern PHP 8*. Of course I hope you leave a glowing review, but really any and all reviews would be greatly appreciated.

Go to the link below or scan the QR code to leave your review:

https://packt.link/r/1800566158

Your review will help me to understand what's worked well in this book, and what could be improved upon for future editions, so it really is appreciated.

Cheers,

Joseph Edmonds

Index

Lightning Source UK Ltd.
Milton Keynes UK
UKHW031444271021
392931UK00006B/311